HARMONIZING GLOBAL EDUCATION

Distance education (DE) offers ways to reach the many people around the world who lack access to education and training by other means. International DE methods, however, are fragmented, and distance educators have often abandoned new technologies before giving them a chance to develop. As a result, many current DE tools and techniques are incompatible with the needs and cultures of different global regions. With the goal of designing efficient, relevant DE for worldwide audiences, *Harmonizing Global Education* invites scholars and practitioners to consider the historic development of technology-based education and communication studies, going back further in the literature than is often assumed necessary.

The book examines a wide range of historical ideas capable of shaping modern DE, including the Luddite Revolt among British textiles workers in 1811–12, the evolution of cubist art and musical aesthetics, and the visionary advances of early 20th-century Soviet multimedia specialists. The author urges an awareness of previous generations of communications studies, and shows how audience research relating to traditional media can be relevant in the design of current internet-based and social media approaches. Today's open universities have grown from these earlier historical efforts, and the future success of open and distance education depends on learning from the successes and the failures of the past.

Jon Baggaley is Professor of Educational Technology at the Centre for Distance Education, Athabasca University, Canada.

HARMONIZING GLOBAL EDUCATION

From Genghis Khan to Facebook

Jon Baggaley

 Routledge
Taylor & Francis Group

NEW YORK AND LONDON

First published 2012
by Routledge
711 Third Avenue, New York, NY 10017

Simultaneously published in the UK
by Routledge
2 Park Square, Milton Park, Abingdon, Oxon OX14 4RN

Routledge is an imprint of the Taylor & Francis Group, an informa business

© 2012 Taylor & Francis

Library of Congress Cataloging in Publication Data
Baggaley, Jon.
Harmonizing global education: from Genghis Khan to Facebook/Jon Baggaley.
    p. cm.
  Includes bibliographical references and index.
  1. Distance education. 2. Distance education—Developing countries.
  3. Internet in education. 4. Education and globalization I. Title.
  LC5800.B35 2011
  371.35—dc23   2011023777

ISBN13: 978-0-415-89265-0 (hbk)
ISBN 13: 978-0-415-89268-1 (pbk)
ISBN13: 978-0-203-81763-6 (ebk)

Typeset in Bembo by RefineCatch Limited, Bungay, Suffolk, UK
Printed in the USA by Walsworth Publishing Company, Marceline, MO

For Sheila, who devotes herself to exposing good

CONTENTS

TABLES

FIGURES

PREFACE

This book appears in Routledge's *Open and Flexible Learning* series, although it deals directly with neither open nor flexible learning, nor with their usual literature. So thanks to the publisher for taking it! Instead, the book focuses on literature not usually associated with these fields, but which offers a foundation for today's open and distance-based approaches to global education. The goals of open, flexible and distance education are not modern, although the academic practice of stressing only the latest writings can make us believe otherwise. We respond to this forgetful emphasis by forming the impression that ideas older than a decade or so are probably out-of-date; and our students follow our lead in this. Unfortunately, anxiety to embrace all that is new allows sound old ideas to be forgotten, good practices to decay, and the wheel to be reinvented under new headings. We tend to take note when an idea is declared to be one 'whose time has come', but we less commonly acknowledge the origins of ideas whose time has come back.

The book attempts to rectify this by taking a retrospective look at old and new educational media and the principles applied in communicating their messages. Some forgotten pioneers are discussed, and factors that caused their ideas to be eclipsed. Earlier versions of trends such as 'mobile learning' are examined, and the lessons they yielded that have yet to be rediscovered in the modern context. The risks as well as the benefits of communications media are examined, and the popular mentality that can prevent them from being addressed. The principles of educational media design are compared with those of communication ideas underlying the visual arts and music. Research approaches focusing on threats to academic quality—including plagiarism, media inaccessibility, and online security—are suggested, and some tall tales told about giant communication schemes of the past which failed for lack of quality control.

One of the saddest of historical stories is that of the Luddites. In the British textiles industry of 1811–12, disillusioned workers mobilized to oppose automated practices that they believed would destroy their artistry. I have had sympathy for these workers since a schoolboy, despite the fact that my great-great-great-grandfather was a factory boss in the Nottingham area where the Luddite revolt broke out. The bicentenary of this event seems to be passing relatively unnoticed in 2011, despite its contemporary lessons. Other events are marked by centenaries this year. In fact, 1910–11 saw a remarkable number of turning-points in world art and culture, as Virginia Woolf noted in describing December 1910, give or take a few months, as when "human character changed". That comment has intrigued me for years, and the current centenary period has prompted me to write about it. In the process, I have discovered other characters whom I had never previously considered.

For example, I first heard of my no-relation namesake William Bagley about 25 years ago, when I came across one of his yellowing 1911 books in a university library. It was strange in the 1980s to find that Bagley had analyzed specific educational issues which I was writing about as a young academic at the time, thinking my own ideas to be original. I now realize that his conclusions pre-empted a great many of today's educational principles, having been eclipsed for decades by opposing ideas 'whose time had come'. Taking slices through history in this way allows unrecognized thinkers to see the light of day.

Fine teachers have influenced this book. The finest has been my wife and 45-year best friend Sheila James, to whom the book is gratefully dedicated. Her love and understanding of history, the arts, their symbols, and thankfully me, have sustained my efforts over the years as well as our many joint projects in music, theater, and education. My children Helen, Edward, and Frances have always made my efforts feel worthwhile; and while writing the book I have thought constantly of my grandchildren Oliver, Darcy and Devon (I hope one day you will visit the places in the book). My mother Nellie gave me her music and my academic life, and my father Louis gave me his love of humor and the theater. Neville Welton, Peter McKellar, and Phillip Lord kindled my research interests. My friends Steve Duck and Harry Jamieson have shaped my ideas since the years we spent at neighboring desks at Sheffield and Liverpool Universities in the 1970s. I have worked in universities from Newfoundland to Quebec to Western Canada since then, finding more teachers among my colleagues and students. My collaborators in four continents have changed my ideas fundamentally, particularly those with whom I have worked across Asia during the last six years. I acknowledge their lessons and memory in the following list. I hope I have not accidentally omitted any special names, although I am afraid this is inevitable.

Tony Bates, Tian Belawati, Mark Bell, Max Blythe, Aaron-Henry Brauer, Philip Brooks, Roger Bullivant, Chen Li, Chen Qing, Chhuon Chanthan, Gary Coldevin, Robert Cook, Gail Crawford, John Daniel, Stewart Deas, Gajaraj Dhanarajan, Doung Vuth, William Empson, Pat Fahy, Louise Glegg, Iain Grant, Barb Hall,

Margaret Haughey, Patti Janega, Pauline Jones, Insung Jung, Paul Kawachi, Harry Kay, Jim Klaas, Claus Knudsen, Patti Janega, Colin Latchem, Caleb Lawrence, Percival Leeds, Felix Librero, George Linstead, Fred Lockwood, Brian Ludwig, Naveed Malik, Keith Mielke, Sanjaya Mishra, David Mitchell, Som Naidu, Maria Ng Lee Hoon, Rand Nickerson, Gwen Noble, John Noblet, David Nostbakken, V.K. Samaranayake, Clare Sargeant, Paulette Schatz, Wilbur Schramm, William Shallow, Basil Smallman, Kirk Smith, Bob Spencer, Chris Spencer, Arthur Sullivan (both of them!), Vlodymyr Tarasenko, Hal Thwaites, Clay Vollan, Peter Warr, Xiao Ying, Xu Yang, Herbert Zett, Zhang Shanshi.

For their dedication in preparing the book for publication, I thank Som Naidu (series editor); Alex Masulis and Katie Raissian at Routledge Taylor & Francis; the production and proofreading team of Mhairi Bennett, Heather Cushing, Caryn Maclean, Donna White, and Annette Wiseman; and Emma Usherwood for the cover design.

In conclusion, my thoughts go to the people whose minds traveled down similar tracks during the last century without achieving the universal recognition they deserve: Dziga Vertov on the railway lines of the early Soviet Union; Vladimir Tatlin who constructed innovative multimedia for global communication; and Alexander Scriabin whose music in 1911 contained more innovation than most people ever achieve. This book is respectfully sub-dedicated to their memories and accomplishments.

Jon Baggaley
Vancouver Island
July 2011

PUBLISHING AND FUNDING CREDITS

- Table 1.2 (*Five generations of ODL technology*) reprinted with original author's consent under a Creative Commons Attribution 3.0 license.
- Section 2.3 (*The Luddite Revolt*) contains material extracted under publisher's licence from: Baggaley, J. (2010). The Luddite Revolt continues. *Distance Education 31*(3), pp. 337–343.
- Figure 2.5 (*The Luddite Manifesto*) reprinted with publisher's permission.
- Table 3.1 (*TV production variable research categories*) reprinted with original author's consent under a Creative Commons Attribution 3.0 license.
- Figure 3.2 (*The Meumann-style ergograph*) reprinted with web site editor's consent under a Creative Commons Attribution 3.0 license.
- Table 3.2 (*Types of contribution to online text conferences*) reprinted with original author's consent under a Creative Commons Attribution 3.0 license.
- Section 3.3 (*Cubism online*): the web log analysis reported in this section was made possible by a research grant to the author from the Social Sciences & Humanities Research Council of Canada.
- Section 4.2 (*The asynchronous years*) contains material previously published as: Baggaley, J. (2009). Synchronous conferencing. In S. Mishra (ed.) *STRIDE Handbook on eLearning*. New Delhi: Indira Gandhi National Open University (author's copyright).
- Section 4.4 (*Practical evaluation guidelines*) contains material extracted with the publisher's permission from: Baggaley, J. (2010). Conducting and Reporting Distance Education Evaluations. In T. Belawati & J. Baggaley (eds.) *Policy and Practice in Asian Distance Education*. New Delhi: Sage India/Ottawa: International Development Research Centre.
- Figure 5.1 (*The world travels of a web hit*). Pacific world map courtesy of www.theodora.com/maps, used with permission.
- Figure 5.2 (*The political 'blogospheres' of the 2004 US Presidential election*) reprinted with the original authors' consent under a Creative Commons Attribution 3.0 license.
- Section 5.4 (*A giant structure*) contains material extracted under publisher's license from: Baggaley, J. (2011). A giant structure. *Distance Education 32*(1), pp. 133–140.

- Section 6.3 (*Global counterpoint*) contains material previously published as: Baggaley, J. (2009). Levels of Media Interactivity. In S. Mishra (ed.) *STRIDE Handbook on eLearning*. New Delhi: Indira Gandhi National Open University (author's copyright).
- Figure 6.1b (*TV-style speaker shot*) and Table 6.2 (*Webcam displays of interaction at a distance*) contain photographs used with owners' permission.
- Cover images provided by GettyImages.

1

THE NEW SILK ROAD

The Gold of Timbuktu

Global forms of education have a high priority in the early 21st century. The economic recession has encouraged educational institutions to develop strategic alliances aimed at increasing international exchanges, collaborative research funding, and student revenues. Potential advantages of inter-institutional collaboration include course sharing, joint development of new programs, and the sale and licensing of course materials. With the arrival of the internet, the ease with which such projects can be conducted has greatly increased during the last decade. In half a day, an educator may exchange e-mails with half-a-dozen countries—a very different academic world from that of 20 years ago. In the early 1990s, educators wrote letters that could take a month to arrive at a foreign destination. A conference took up to a year to organize based on 'snail-mail' correspondence, instead of the few months it can take to convene an international event nowadays. The fax machine helped to speed communications but, as with the postal service, international faxing could be costly for educators. When the internet and the early forms of e-mail arrived in the mid-1990s, instant communication became cost-free.

The goals formally defined for global educators cover the most complex issues of the age: international development and human rights, peace and conflict resolution, education on citizenship and intercultural issues, and sustainability. The Maastricht Global Education Declaration (2002) stated that:

> (g)lobal education is education that opens people's eyes and minds to the realities of the globalised world and awakens them to bring about a world of greater justice, equity and Human Rights for all.[1]

An overview of developments since the Maastricht conference has revealed the intensity with which these ideals are felt in the world, and of international initiatives that strive to achieve them.[2] Subsequent meetings in Palermo, Brussels, and Helsinki, and action groups in Australia, Canada, Europe, and the USA have amassed theoretical and practical guidelines for global education efforts by teachers and policy-makers.[3-6] O'Loughlin & Wegimont (2007) have concluded that global education is an issue that has "come in from the cold" and is now central to the development agenda, "a position that many advocates working in the 1990s might only have dreamt of" (p. 8). At the same time, these writers stress that the implementation of global education goals still needs "more adequate resources and stronger political and policy support (and) recognition of the need for more adequate evaluation and quality enhancement." How often the same accurate, sincere recommendations have been made in the literature of education, and how difficult they are to implement in local teaching practices, let alone in collaborative ventures spanning many miles and diverse cultures. The 21st century's new communications technologies can play a vital role in achieving global goals; and yet in fields such as open and distance education the best way to use them is still debated. Either the international communication attempts of history have yielded no useful lessons, or global education initiatives today have failed to learn from them.

The evidence of global communication goes back longer than mere centuries. Designs in Celtic art dated at 1000 BC are also found in Mongolian art of that period; and shamanistic beliefs, practices, and art forms are common to Mongolia and the native cultures of North America today. Ancient Chinese Taoism shares concepts with Hindu and Judaic traditions; and one of the oldest artistic symbols, the yin-yang (Figure 1.1), is found in all these ancient cultures. Over many years, the sharing of ideas generated universal cultural traditions through links that are only now becoming recognized. In history, as today, the globalization process was due to political and cultural goals. The Mongol nation's influence on the world is explained by the pan-Asian conquests of Genghis Khan that began 800 years ago. In 1209–10, Chinggis (as he is known to modern Mongolians) invaded China, and by his death in 1227 his troops had conquered the continent, raping and pillaging, from the Pacific to Eastern Europe (Figure 1.2). Chinggis' personal supervision of the quest has been persuasively demonstrated by the particular DNA pattern common to the people of those regions.[7] He used techniques to

FIGURE 1.1 The yin-yang symbol.

FIGURE 1.2   A Mongol commander's mobile home.

Source: Batpurev, 2006.

conquer the minds of his subjects that modern leaders employ, acting unpredictably to keep the people guessing, and tempering ruthlessness with unexpected kindness, especially in rewarding loyalty. Chinggis' practice of sending envoys with stories of his barbarous nature to the communities he was about to invade resembles the 'advance organizer' technique recommended in modern instructional design.[8] He also invented a postal service and an early form of 'mobile learning', using fast horsemen (arrow riders) to carry messages throughout the Mongol Empire.[9]

The trails used by Chinggis for marauding had already been blazed by others for commercial purposes. In 200 BC, China began trading with the west and developed routes since collectively known as the Silk Road. This network of trading routes stretched from Eastern China to Constantinople and Rome, and from Mongolia to Northern India and the Euphrates. Commercial interests motivated the smuggling of silk-worms, the exchange of silk goods, and sharing of the designs they bore. Communication of knowledge and culture in the British Empire can be similarly attributed to diverse interests from political to sporting. In covering the annual test matches (cricket tournaments) between Commonwealth countries, the media send journalists to report back not only on the games but on the nations in which they are played. As a result, the Commonwealth countries that host these games know more about each other than those which do not; and Canada, which does not play cricket, loses out in these annual exchanges and is more of a cultural mystery to its Commonwealth cousins than, for example, Australia or India. The connection between intercontinental travel and the communication of ideas was made by Roger Bacon in 1267: "There is no doubt that corporeal roads signify spiritual roads."[10]

Canada has a distinctive place in the history of global education ideas, however, thanks to the challenges posed by its wide open spaces. Harold Innis was fascinated by the interconnecting routes of lakes and rivers in his native Ontario and by the effects of communication routes and systems on trade and culture.[11] Extending his analysis to communication techniques, he proposed two types of media: 'space-binding' media such as radio and television which allow the dissemination of ideas over great distances but may not survive over lengthy periods of time, and 'time-binding' media including clay and stone tablets which are durable and allow ideas to be preserved over many years. It is as well to be mindful of the media's ephemeral nature in the internet age, given the sure prospect that digital images will decay more quickly than the written word and the clay tablet.

In July 1911, one of Innis' contemporaries, Marshall McLuhan was born in western Canada, and grew up in the farming provinces of Alberta and Manitoba. McLuhan too was shaped by his early environment. In the sprawling prairies, no roads, paths, fences or other landmarks may be visible from one horizon to the other, and as a boy McLuhan grew used to creating mental signposts that guided him through the prairie wheat and in his subsequent thinking.[12] His analyses of the communication media in the 1960s yielded distinctive terms that still influence communications thinking today. His "global village" term suggested that the media will create a worldwide homogenous community linked by uniform mediated information.[13] His motto "the medium is the message"[14] suggested that media presentation techniques are as influential as the information they convey; and he distinguished between two types of channel: 'hot' media such as print which engage a single sense and thereby a more intense form of attention; and 'cool' media such as television (not cool in today's slang sense) containing diffuse sensory information that requires a greater effort of interpretation. Based on the views he expressed in 1740, Lord Chesterfield would agree with McLuhan. Focusing on one stimulus at a time is the most intelligent way to learn, Chesterfield concluded:

> (The) steady and undissipated attention to one object, is a sure mark of a superior genius; as hurry, bustle, and agitation, are the never-failing symptoms of a weak and frivolous mind.[15]

The multimedia content of the internet would render it the coolest and least engaging of today's media in McLuhan's terminology. In Innis' terms, it would be defined as a 'space-binding' medium which allows ideas to be communicated over great distances but which may not survive over a long period of time. Yet the medium does have a distinctive feature that sets it apart from other stimulus-rich media such as television—its unprecedented levels of interactivity. This feature provides a particular incentive for today's communications designers, as in education, to develop solid working techniques that will help the internet to play a useful and abiding social role. McLuhan also used an esoteric term that will become a focus later in this book.[16] 'Synaesthesia' is the phenomenon whereby the sensations of one sense (e.g., music) are associated with those of another (e.g., color). The modern media have heightened the public's synaesthetic sense, McLuhan suggested, through a daily bombardment of multisensory information. This is an unorthodox use of the synaesthesia term. In psychology and the arts it refers to idiosyncratic associations between multimedia sensations: for example, the sound of the oboe and the taste of a pineapple. Individuals who experience such associations are often unable to explain them, though may have them for life; and bombardment with random multimedia images may impede natural synaesthesias rather than, as McLuhan suggested, heightening them. Many of his notions were debatable in this way although, as Jonathan Miller has suggested, this may explain his social influence:

> Perhaps McLuhan has accomplished the greatest paradox of all, creating the possibility of truth by shocking us all with a gigantic system of lies.[17]

The centenary of McLuhan's birth, and of other ideas discussed in this book, occurs in the year this book is being written. In fact, the book resonates with anniversaries—100 years, 200 years and, in the case of Chinggis Khan's notorious period of conquest, 800 years. This grand set of coincidences provides a timely excuse to discuss events not usually associated but which have striking connections. A recent opportunity of this kind occurred in 1984, a year etched in modern culture since 1948 when George Orwell wrote about it.[18] So many of Orwell's predictions have come true in the contemporary internet-based world: the instant access to information, the ease with which individuals can be monitored online, even the web browser was described in *Nineteen Eighty-Four* with chilling accuracy:

> Winston dialed 'back numbers' on the telescreen and called for the appropriate issues of *The Times*, which slide out of the pneumatic tube after only a few minutes' delay. (p. 34)

(Orwell would be interested to learn that today the same search on *Google* takes 0.23 seconds.) In 1965, the current author's Sheffield University tutor, Professor William Empson, told him about the early 1940s period when he worked with Orwell in the overseas radio service of the British Broadcasting Corporation (BBC). Orwell's diaries[19] recall that Empson was hostile to the BBC's broadcast training course, which he saw as an attempt to disguise his messages with artificial media technique: the "Liars' School", Empson called it. Five years after working in BBC booths next to one another, Orwell (real name Eric Blair) published

Nineteen Eighty-Four. In it he described the techniques of 'newspeak' and 'doublethink' practiced by the national "Ministry of Truth", whose purpose was to control the populace through propaganda. It is possible that Empson's stubborn views gave Orwell the idea for this famous fiction.

Empson has been described as one of the three greatest literary critics of the last 300 years, "not least because they are the funniest."[20] His broadcasting experience made him aware that the medium can be the message 20 years before McLuhan suggested it. Empson may have been responsible for that famous idea too. His first book, *Seven Types of Ambiguity* (1930), influenced the New Criticism school of Anglo-American literary analysis for the next 30 years.[21] In it, he described the techniques writers use to stimulate ideas in roundabout ways. The first, he indicated, is metaphor—the juxtaposition of dissimilar ideas to suggest a connection. Another technique is the use of bland, isolated statements which force the reader to provide the meaning, as in McLuhan's later concept of cool media. McLuhan, a teacher of English literature at the University of Toronto from 1946 to 1979, hosted Empson in 1973, and described his colleagues, leading Canadian scholars, as "awed by Empson, like rustics."[22]

Sir William Empson died in 1984.

Of course, all media information needs to be scrutinized for untruths, deliberate or otherwise. The newspaper article that announced the publication of Orwell's diaries in 2008, described him as being born in 1950—the year he actually died.[23]

[I too was awed by Professor Empson as I sat in his Sheffield University study for my 1965–66 tutorials. He also told us of his time as one of the 1930s 'Bloomsbury Group' of writers including W.H. Auden and Virginia Woolf.[24] One of his stories was of walking through Bloomsbury with T.S. Eliot. As they talked, Eliot stepped into the road and was knocked down by a car, "mid-sentence" as Empson put it. When Empson visited Eliot in hospital later that day, they "resumed the sentence."]

These philosophers and conquerors have shown that global messages are determined by the routes and vehicles that carry them, and that globalization attempts with numerous ulterior motives can have educational and cultural benefits. By the time one receives it, however, information has been shaped by numerous biasing factors, and no single cultural standard may be available by which to assess this process. The quest for global educational partnerships tends to assume that courses, programs, and other products can easily be coordinated across diverse cultures, but this may not be the case. The hopes and fate of such efforts are illustrated by the legend of the gold of Timbuktu, the notoriously remote city in the West African country of Mali.

In the 12th century, Timbuktu was a rich salt trading-post. Salt had been a major currency from ancient Chinese times onwards. Roman soldiers received their 'salary' in it, and the traders of Timbuktu bartered it for gold and ivory. The city's University, Sankore Masjid, was the centre of a rich Islamic global education movement, with 25,000 students in a city of 100,000 people, and a library housing an estimated 700,000 manuscripts.[25] In 1324, Emperor Kanka Moussa of Mali travelled from Timbuktu to Cairo, dispensing large amounts of gold along the way. Timbuktu gained a fabled reputation, and became an appealing target for gold seekers. In 1590 the city was sacked and its gold stolen by Sultan Ahmed el-Mansour of Morocco, and sank into poverty. The Sultan was known thereafter as 'The Golden One'. Timbuktu protected its reputation by closing its doors against the outside world. In 1824, the French Geographic Society offered a 10,000-franc prize to the first westerner to reach the city and return to Paris to report it. Muslims were not eligible to take part. All reported efforts ended in the teams' death from illness or at the hands of Tuareg tribesmen, until the explorer René-Auguste Caillie arrived in Timbuktu, disguised as a local Muslim, and made it back home in 1828 to report that the city had no gold. The story is graphically told by Josh Bernstein in his TV series *Into the Unknown*.[26] Its scholarship, say the Timbuktu interviewees in Bernstein's documentary, is the once golden city's true legacy.

The landscape of global education attempts is similarly littered with the bones of projects killed by commercial rivalry and lack of funding. The gold of Timbuktu is a fitting metaphor for these quests. When valuable educational assets such as courseware are shared, are they also likely to be stolen like the gold of Timbuktu? It is certainly all too easy to pillage educational materials once they have been published digitally on the internet. To prevent such an outcome, the first challenge of global education partners is to develop mutual reliance and trust. On this basis, the quest can begin.

Open and Mega-Universities

> Globalization is the flow of technology, economy, knowledge, people, values, ideas . . . across borders. Globalization affects each country in a different way due to a country's individual history, traditions, cultures and priorities. Internationalization of higher education is one of the ways a country responds to the impact of globalization.[27]

Collaborative agreements between educational partners typically stem from a chance meeting at an international meeting. The collaborative quest may begin with a written commitment to faculty or student exchanges for the purpose of defining shared teaching and research interests. In truth, the major motivation for partnership may be no more than an interest in foreign travel, and unless the parties have a genuine concern to add new work to their existing load, the agreement may be short-lived. It can also be blighted if it has been initiated in a 'top-down' manner by administrators who fail to enthuse the academics needed to conduct the project; and the reverse 'bottom-up' problem is equally problematic. Problems can also arise in the wording of the inter-institutional agreement. A formal commitment is useful to prevent one partner from making an intensive contribution, only to find that the other has lost interest. When the partners belong to different cultures, however, legalistic wordings in the agreement can be confusing or intimidating. The legalese in which western institutions tend to couch their contracts is foreign in many nations, and can be regarded as high-handed and lacking in trust despite its intentions to safeguard the agreement. The wording of even the simplest, non-binding contract needs to be carefully discussed by both sides to prevent it causing affront and doing more harm than good.

In economic down-times, the most attractive collaborations are those which increase revenues—as, for example, by the development of new teaching programs, and the sale and licensing of course materials. The educational institutions with the greatest potential for lucrative collaboration are those with large student enrollments. Those with 100,000 students or more have been labeled 'mega-universities'.[28] Of the world's ten largest mega-universities, nine are in Asia, and eight were founded in the last 40 years.[29] Each of them has at least half a million students. The Open Universities of India and Pakistan claim the highest enrollments, with an estimated 1.8 million students each. The Open University of China (OUC), known until 2009 as the China Central Radio and TV University, claims a higher number (approximately 2.8 million) though is not included in the *Wikipedia* list. A possible reason is that the OUC is an amalgam of 44 provincial radio and TV universities.[30] The exclusion appears inconsistent, however, considering that the University System of Ohio (USO, currently #10 in the *Wikipedia* ranking) is also an amalgam of state institutions.[31] Table 1.1 presents, with modifications by the current writer to improve its reliability, *Wikipedia's* listing of the world's 10 largest student enrollments, as of July 2011. The OUC has been inserted at #1 in the list. A further flaw in the *Wikipedia* listing is its inclusion of separate entries for Bangladesh National University (BNU) with 800,000 students, and Bangladesh Open University (BOU) with 600,000, giving the impression that these are independent institutions. As BOU exists within BNU and shares the same mailing address, I have merged them in the Table into a single item.

This exercise provides the first lesson in this book about the quality of online information in the early 21st century. Without sources such as *Wikipedia*, this book would not have been possible. Unlike the sources of past generations, however—books, journal articles, the press—the reliability and even the identities of online authors may be unknown, and their updates have to be assessed with care. The mega-university statistics on the *Wikipedia* web site change from month to month, anonymously updated by (presumably) responsible individuals at the universities in question. Some of these figures have the face-value appearance of precision, while others are rounded estimates. The site states that its figures are "the sum of undergraduate and graduate students in active enrollment," but no indication is provided as to whether the estimates are based on full-time or part-time enrollment, or on multiple course enrollments by individual students. If the data reproduced in Table 1.1 were submitted to a respectable academic journal,

TABLE 1.1 The world's largest mega-universities.

Rank	Institution	Location	Founded	Student enrollment
1	Open University of China	Campuses across China	1979	2,766,500
2	Allama Iqbal Open University	Islamabad, Pakistan	1974	1,806,214
3	Indira Gandhi National Open U	New Delhi, India	1985	1,800,000
4	Islamic Azad University	Tehran, Iran	1982	1,500,000
5	Anadolu Open University	Eskişehir, Turkey	1958	1,041,180
6	Bangladesh National U (incl. OU)	Gazipur, Bangladesh	1992	800,000
7	Universitas Terbuka	Jakarta, Indonesia	1984	646,467
8	Ramkhamhaeng University	Bangkok, Thailand	1971	525,000
9	University of Pune	Pune, India	1948	496,531
10	University System of Ohio	Campuses in Ohio, USA	2007	478,000

Source: *Wikipedia*, July 2011, with modifications.

the editor and reviewers would require evidence that a consistent data collection methodology was used. Today's online information often carries no such assurances, however, and the statistics in the Table should be taken as rough indicators rather than hard facts.

The approximate number of student enrollments claimed in these statistics is 12 million. This is a conservative estimate, for other institutions not included in these statistics have equivalent student enrollments though are not accredited as universities. The China Agricultural Broadcasting and Television School (CABTVS), for example, has another 3 million students. The major open universities of UK and Japan (with at least 250,000 and 100,000 enrollments respectively) have not seen fit to enter their statistics onto the *Wikipedia* site. Numerous other institutions, such as the writer's former employer, Canada's Open University at Athabasca in Alberta (approximately 50,000 enrollments), are not large enough to be classified as mega-universities, but collectively serve hundreds of thousands of students nonetheless. The largest mega-universities achieve their massive student numbers through open and distance learning (ODL) practices, which allow them to enroll students in remote rural regions as well as urban students who live near or on campus. As Figure 1.3 demonstrates, nine of the ten largest mega-universities are close to the ancient Asian silk routes, used in part by Marco Polo in his circumnavigation of Asia from 1260 to 1295. The map provides modern evidence for Innis' observation that both empire and culture are formed along the world's communications arteries.

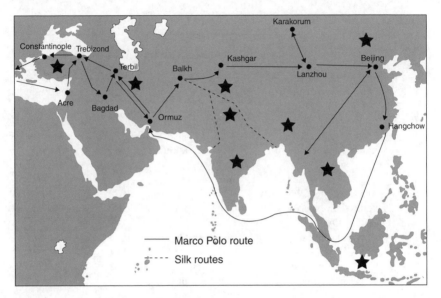

FIGURE 1.3 Ancient Asian trading routes.

Key: The asterisks indicate the largest Asian mega-universities.
Source: Adapted from Wikipedia Commons, 2010a.[32]

The ODL institutions share the belief that education should be made as accessible as possible on the following bases. For the benefit of students who are in full-time employment and cannot study during the day, *time constraints* should be removed by flexible scheduling. For students who live too far from a campus to attend face-to-face classes, *geographical constraints* should be removed by enabling them to receive their courses at a distance via communication media. For students whose education has not been completed for reasons other than academic ability, *entrance requirements* should be lifted, and students who cannot afford regular fees should receive special financial consideration.[33] In practice, these are idealistic goals to which ODL institutions aspire with varying success. Financial assistance to students is increasingly difficult to provide, and scholarships and bursaries to a few selected students all too frequently amount to tokenism. The bottom line, however, is the fact that ODL institutions provide education and vocational training to millions of students who would never have access to it otherwise.

To supply their distant students with course materials, ODL institutions typically house facilities for the production and distribution of print, audio, video, and web-based materials. In this respect they are a hybrid between traditional colleges and publishing houses, operating an integrated process of course creation, evaluation, and delivery. This model was adopted in 1970–71 by two of the oldest

ODL universities of the modern era, the Open University of the United Kingdom, and Athabasca University in Canada.[34] The idea of open public access to the media had been promoted in the UK by Harold Wilson's Labour Government:

> Broadcasting is too important to be left to the broadcasters, and somehow we must find some new way of using radio and television to allow us to talk to each other. (Anthony Wedgwood Benn, UK Minister of Technology, 1968)[35]

In Britain, the idea finally became reality in January 1971, with the creation of the OU as the 'University of the Air' in collaboration with the BBC. Simultaneously, universities and colleges across North America and Europe were creating in-house studios for the production of TV and radio-based courseware. In Canada, the practice became a mainstay of non-formal community education. Film and video had been used as catalysts for social change by the National Film Board since 1965 in Newfoundland, and had flourished in the 1967–80 *Challenge for Change* community development program. Following a visit by BBC producer Edward Goldwyn to Newfoundland, the Canadian approach was influential in the development of the BBC-TV series *Open Door,* an early experiment in broadcast programming directed and presented by members of the public.[36] Athabasca University was established by the Government of Alberta in June 1970 in the same spirit of openness, with a major priority for using the media to educate the province's large rural population; and the media-based model was subsequently adopted by ODL institutions throughout the world.[37] A notable example of the integrated multimedia approach to education today is provided by mega-university #7 in Table 1.1, the Open University of Indonesia (Universitas Terbuka, UT) (see Chapter 4).

In 2010, the ODL leader who coined the term 'mega-university', Sir John Daniel, has added the term 'mega-school' to the vocabulary, referring to the spread of ODL practices at all levels of formal education from the elementary school upwards, and to the rapid development of open schools in the developing world.[38] From 2004–10, for example, student enrollments at the National Institute of Open Schooling (NIOS) in India have risen from 289,905 to 481,513 per annum. In 2010, NIOS operates 3,910 study centers throughout India and in Nepal and the United Arab Emirates.[39] Daniel stresses that the trend towards ODL should continue at all levels of education so that escalating student numbers can be handled in the coming century. For western universities and colleges struggling to increase their revenues during a worldwide recession, it is attractive to imagine that Asian institutions may wish to share some of their vast student numbers via course sharing and joint programs; and, for Asian educators, access to courses in English has the appeal of increasing exposure to western literature and to unfamiliar pedagogical approaches.

Traditional and New Media

The media-based education tradition extends back far earlier than the modern ODL era. In the current global context, it is useful to recall the factors that stimulated the non-formal community development movement of the 1960s. The notion of open access education and media programming gained ground at that time owing to the increasing ease of use and portability of the equipment. Teachers with no experience of cameras and microphones could record simple presentations on audio or video cassettes for delivery to remotely situated students. In conjunction with broadcasting corporations such as the BBC in Britain, and the Knowledge Network, Access Alberta, and the Ontario Educational Communications Authority in Canada, increasingly skilled presentations were produced matching the broadcast quality to which students were accustomed. In the developing world, the principle that the broadcast media should be accessible to the masses is still upheld, and Asian mega-universities remain focused on making education and training affordable for poor and remote members in order to build their nations' economy. ODL institutions in the western-style world have departed from that philosophy, however. Today's ODL programs in the west are targeted at the affluent professional market on fee scales comparable with those of conventional education. Tuition fees for international students can be higher than fees for local students; and major readjustments are required to make western courses affordable in other nations. Recently, for example, an ODL team discussing the marketability of a Canadian university program in China realized that if the regular international student fees were charged, they would exceed the entire annual salary of a top Chinese University professor.

The use of media in non-formal education dates back to the 1920s. The BBC, founded in 1922, defined its mission as to "educate, inform, and entertain", so expressed by its first Director-General, Lord Reith. The BBC's official motto, *Nation Shall Speak Peace Unto Nation,* supplemented these goals; and in 1926 the BBC's first Director of Education, J.C. Stobart, proposed the development of a "wireless university" (wireless meaning radio), which could bring higher education via the media to the masses.[40] Simultaneously, in the USA, the Federal Communications Commission (FCC) allocated the low end of the FM radio waveband (88.1 to 91.9 mhz) to educational broadcasting, generating a tradition of formal and non-formal community radio. The Association of College and University Broadcasting Stations (ACUBS) was created in 1925, and went through a series of renamings over the next half-century until becoming National Public Radio (NPR) in 1970. NPR's TV equivalent originated as the Educational TV and Radio Center (ETRC) in 1952, and evolved into the National Educational Television network (NET) in 1963. In 1970, it was superseded by the Public Broadcasting System (PBS). NPR and PBS remain committed to social and cultural programming today. One of the most remarkable non-formal educational TV programs, both for its careful pedagogical design and its longevity, is *Sesame*

Street. The show was launched in 1969 by the Children's TV Workshop (CTW) in New York, and is still providing non-formal entertainment and education to preschool children in its 40th year.[41]

The modern era of educational media began in 1970 in more ways than one. Traditional universities and colleges were installing their own TV studios and 'audio-visual aids' services,[42] and the new ODL Universities were basing their student services on media-based delivery, in some cases to the exclusion of the central campus model. The evolution of ODL delivery from this point onwards has been described by Taylor in terms of five successive models, each existing side by side with the previous ones.[43]

1 The correspondence model was the initial focus of ODL in the 1970s. Communication between teachers and students based on this model is primarily *asynchronous* (e.g., print-based communication by mail, not receiving an instant reply). The model seeks to overcome barriers of time, place and pace, though at the expense of two-way interaction between the teacher and student. *Synchronous* (real-time) communication via the telephone can be added, though can be costly when used for teacher-student interaction across distances. Programmed instruction principles derived from the work of Skinner were applied in course design at this early evolutionary stage,[44–45] so that the materials themselves could guide students through varying study sequences according to their individual rates of progress.

2 The multimedia model evolved in the 1970s and 1980s, combining the most ubiquitous and illustrative media of the day (print, radio, TV, and the computer). Hybrid versions of these media evolved, though direct interaction with the teacher is still restricted to the mail and telephone.

3 The telelearning model combines multimedia, the phone, and online conferencing methods to create synchronous audio- and video-based interaction. This model, which has burgeoned since the 1990s, enables live interaction between teachers and remote students, though often at the expense of the initial ODL ideals of overcoming barriers of time and pace.

4 The flexible learning model uses the internet and World Wide Web for teacher-student and student–student interaction via text- and audio/video-based methods. Communication can be both synchronous and asynchronous. The most basic method is e-mail, developed in the 1960s though not widely used in education until the 1990s. By the late 1990s, e-mail-type communications had been re-packaged in asynchronous text-based conferencing applications, permitting many users to discuss the messages simultaneously. A decade later, internet techniques have developed, providing DE teachers and students with highly cost-effective online conferencing methods for overcoming the obstacles of time, place and pace of learning via real-time as well as asynchronous options.

5   The intelligent flexible learning model relates to the use of automated response systems to reduce the institutional costs of computer- and internet-based education. Technologies for this option have been available since the 1940s, though have been little used in education (as will be discussed in Chapter 6).

Taylor's analysis provides a useful comparison of educational media in terms of their ability to satisfy ODL's pedagogical needs. Table 1.2 indicates that the successive generations of ODL technology are distinguished by two factors: level of interactivity, and control over time, place and pace. Owing to the rapid development of internet-based education, Taylor has recently divided the 5th generation of his scheme into three levels,[46] involving combinations of online, multimedia, and face-to-face (f2f) communication—a partial return to classroom-based approaches that acknowledges the need for f2f tuition to be an element of the delivery system, if only occasionally.[47]

In regions including North America and Europe, where teachers and students have easy access to each new technology as it comes along, successive generations of ODL technology have tended to displace previous methods. The traditional media have been abandoned in the manner of the 'throw-away society', and otherwise valuable equipment discarded as institutions assume that the new media will do the task better. This process was described by Carpenter at the dawn of ODL in 1972:

> The pressures and goals for industrial growth and foreign markets, and . . . the frustrations of fully applying proved but less glamorous technologies in education often leads to 'leap frogging' over the proved and practical to high-risk adventures with the largest technological system.[48]

And the leap-frogging process has continued. In the 1980s, for example, the programmed learning methods of the 1970s were overlooked as teachers and designers adopted the new computer-assisted methods and developed their own (not necessarily new) techniques for using them. Similarly, in the 1990s, the educational radio and TV studios established at many North American and European universities during the 1970s were closed as internet-based education began to be popular. In Schramm's terms, the new media become the "glamor boys of the field", "big media" introduced "ostensibly for educational advantages (although) the real reasons have been prestige or social control."[49] Schramm's "little media" are the marginalized predecessors of the internet, such as radio and programmed text, which cost less though may actually teach better. Print has survived longer than all other media in this process. Despite its non-interactive one-way nature, students do not welcome the idea of their print-based course materials being totally replaced by less accessible online methods. Even the print form of educational delivery will become obsolete, however, if 'virtual university' plans to put all course materials online are fulfilled.

TABLE 1.2 Five generations of ODL technology.

Models of Distance Education and Associated Delivery Technologies	Characteristics of Delivery Technologies					
	Flexibility			Highly refined materials	Advanced interactive delivery	Institutional variable costs approaching zero
	Time	Place	Pace			
1ˢᵗ Generation: Correspondence						
• Print	Yes	Yes	Yes	Yes	No	No
2ⁿᵈ Generation: Multimedia						
• Print	Yes	Yes	Yes	Yes	No	No
• Audiotape	Yes	Yes	Yes	Yes	No	No
• Videotape	Yes	Yes	Yes	Yes	No	No
• Computer-based and interactive multimedia (IMM)	Yes	Yes	Yes	Yes	Yes	No
• Interactive video (disk and tape)	Yes	Yes	Yes	Yes	Yes	No
3ʳᵈ Generation: Telelearning						
• Audio-teleconferencing	No	No	No	No	No	No
• Videoconferencing	No	No	No	No	No	No
• Audiographic communication	No	No	No	Yes	Yes	No
• Broadcast TV/radio and audio-teleconferencing	No	No	No	Yes	Yes	No
4ᵗʰ Generation: Flexible Learning						
• Interactive multimedia (IMM) online	Yes	Yes	Yes	Yes	Yes	Yes
• Internet-based access to WWW resources	Yes	Yes	Yes	Yes	Yes	Yes
• Computer-mediated communication	Yes	Yes	Yes	Yes	Yes	No
5ᵗʰ Generation: Intelligent Flexible Learning						
• Interactive multimedia (IMM) online	Yes	Yes	Yes	Yes	Yes	Yes
• Internet-based access to WWW resources	Yes	Yes	Yes	Yes	Yes	Yes
• Computer mediated communication, using automated response systems	Yes	Yes	Yes	Yes	Yes	Yes
• Campus portal access to institutional processes and resources	Yes	Yes	Yes	Yes	Yes	Yes

Source: Taylor, 2001.

In the developing countries, the current 'big medium' of the west, the internet, has yet to become widely available. The 'digital divide' between those with and without technological access is as serious a problem in education as in society generally;[50] and the use of the internet in 'e-learning' has increased the global digital divide between internet 'haves' and 'have nots'.[51] "Nowhere is (the rich-poor) divide as clear as the one we have witnessed in education provisions and access at all levels and across all sectors" (Dhanarajan & Wong, 2007). Current statistics indicate that in 2008 the internet was accessible to 16% of students in Pakistan, and to 24% in Cambodia and Sri Lanka.[52] The extent to which students are able or willing to use online sources is even lower, as in the 5% statistic reported by the Open University of Indonesia. More fitting to the developing world context, a 4-generation evolution of technological usage has been offered by dela Pena-Bandalaria, referring to educational media approaches in the Philippines. This analysis is very different from Taylor's account and more closely related to the traditional practices of non-formal western education.[53]

- Generation/1: use of radio for formal and non-formal education, pioneered in 1952 by the Farmers' School-on-the-Air (FSA) model.
- Generation/2: combinations of print materials, radio, and face-to-face tuition offered by traditional universities: e.g., since 1995 by the University of the Philippines Open University (UPOU).
- Generation/3: use of audio-visual and online materials combined with f2f tuition, and with an increased emphasis on flexible learning ('anytime-anywhere') methods.
- Generation/4: the development in the 2000s of online and mobile learning (e-learning and m-learning), via text messages sent online and by cellphone (short message service, SMS).

The use of the cellphone for SMS communication was launched commercially in 1993 by Telia in Sweden. By the mid-2000s, the Philippines had become known as the texting capital of the world, a status it has retained.[54] In 2008, Filipino subscribers sent 142 billion text messages, more than in all the European countries combined.[55] Educational uses of the cellphone have been pioneered at UPOU for delivering course materials and a wide range of administrative and student services announcements.[56] Since 2004, it has been suggested that a new generation of online technologies has emerged, known as Web 2.0, stressing interaction between users and online material via 'social media' (e.g., social networking applications, wikis, and blogs).[57] Online interactivity of this type has been possible since the mid-1990s (as in Taylor's 4th and 5th generations); but, owing to enhanced streamlining and marketing, social media usage has seen a prodigious rise since the mid-2000s, notably in the case of *Facebook.com* (Figure 1.4). Educational applications of the social media and examinations of their pedagogical value are underway.[58–59] In the foreseeable future, *Facebook* and other

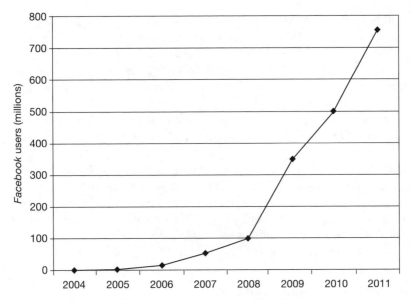

FIGURE 1.4   *Facebook* users (2004–11).

Source: Facebook.com (2011a).

social media will continue to evolve as the companies that provide them introduce new, competing features. Web 2.0 analysts are already competing to define Webs 3.0, 4.0 and 5.0.

In countries where access to new media is lacking, however, the traditional media (e.g., in Table 1.2, generations 1–3) continue to play a central role. Radio, TV, and audio/video conferencing remain central to the education systems of many Asian countries—notably India and China—with CDs, video CDs, DVDs, and other multimedia used for the delivery of course material. These nations are resisting the 'developed' world's example of abandoning the traditional media in favor of new ones, and are finding ways to combine the older media for educational purposes that the newer media cannot as yet fulfill on their own. In affluent and less geographically dispersed Asian countries (e.g., Japan and South Korea), which have nation-wide internet penetration, a convergence of traditional and new media is developing. South Korea, for example, currently has 18 online universities with TV studios and instructional design facilities. Twelve of these 'cyber-universities' are in Seoul alone. In western-style institutions meanwhile, the closure of production facilities in the 1990s has produced a new generation of teachers and media staff with little or no experience of traditional media techniques. Since 2000, enthusiasts in the European DIVERSE network[60] have attempted to revive the traditional video technologies of education. Initially, their conferences and publications stressed the need for a return to traditional TV and video-conferencing media; but their attention has since moved to the convergence of these media with the internet—a welcome development from the point of view of rekindling video production skills, though of little immediate value to students in developing nations who have yet to gain adequate online access.

So the global digital divide is reversing, with the western world becoming the poor relation. It is reasonable of western educators to suppose that, as internet access becomes increasingly universal, concentrating on developing new online techniques is the most cost-effective educational solution. The unnecessarily complicated, cost-ineffective approaches of ETV production are frequently noted in this context, even by those who defend that medium's educational potential.[61-62] As a result, however, different regions of the world now use incompatible educational technologies, and this is a major obstacle to global collaboration in education, especially in relation to international course-sharing. As long as western educators continue to stress online methods to the exclusion of the traditional media, developing-world institutions may find that it makes more sense to collaborate with partners in their own region.

The Mobile Learning Tradition

The meaning of 'mobile learning' was not always as it is today, relating to uses of the cellphone and other hand-held devices. In many ways it used to be richer. Innis' observation that culture spreads via the world's roads and rivers may seem old-fashioned in the electronic age, but earlier mobile traditions offer many lessons for current m-learning designers. The old trading routes carried goods of infinite variety and quality to the extremes of Asia, which the traders of many nations bartered with one another. McLuhan coined the term 'super-medium' for a vehicle which could carry all types of content in this way. In his day, television was the 'super-medium', being the only technology that could carry the auditory and visual images of all other media.[63] It also did this, moreover, on all continents. Today, the internet carries TV images, and has been described as the new super-medium for global education;[64] but as the internet is not equally accessible on all continents, its adoption by western institutions as a replacement for educational television has created a road-block in the effort to build an educational medium with international reach. If an efficient methodology can be developed for m-learning using the mobile phone, this situation may change. Unlike the internet, the cellphone is widely used in all parts of the world, and if adequate content is produced for it in the years ahead, it may succeed in bridging the 'digital divide'. The types of application with potential for m-learning are already popular in the international domestic market. Just as e-mail-type messaging evolved into asynchronous text-conferencing to automate the process of sharing messages with many people at once, so the process has been further streamlined by SMS (texting) methods such as *Twitter*. In May 2010, *Twitter.com* had 106 million subscriber accounts,[65] and a year later the number has doubled.[66] As in the case of *Facebook*, this represents a prodigious increase since *Twitter's* launch in June

2006. The m-learning potential of such techniques is being widely discussed in the current educational literature.[67-68]

But mobile learning has a far longer history than its current proponents may imagine. Seventy years ago, academics and film-makers in Canada identified a major national problem—its status as the 2nd largest national landmass in the world. To bridge the immense distances from north to south, and from Atlantic to Pacific, they placed a high priority on developing media-supported education, training and social development projects. The *Challenge for Change* program (see the previous section) was created by the English division of the National Film Board of Canada (NFB) to disseminate film and video information emphasizing rural development issues. The project used a distinctive community development technique whereby local people were filmed in discussion with one another, and the recordings played back to stimulate further discussion within the group, in other communities, and with provincial officials. Twenty-seven of the 140 *Challenge* productions were recorded on remote Fogo Island in the rural province of Newfoundland, and the approach became known as the 'Fogo Process'. This initiative did not originate the process, however, for the same techniques had been used in the 1950s by producers in the NFB's French-Canadian division, notably by Michel Brault and Fernand Dansereau.[69] Even these detailed initiatives were not the origin of the tradition, for both of the NFB factions had emulated the *agit-prop* methods developed in France in the 1940s and 1950s. These in turn had copied techniques initiated by Soviet film-makers in the 1920s and 1930s.

In the year after the Russian Revolution, Lenin dispatched the most promising young film-makers of the day to convey education, training, and propaganda films by road, rail, and river transport throughout Russia and its satellites.[70-71] The team leader was a 26-year-old Polish film editor, Denis Kaufman, known today by the more Russian-sounding pseudonym that he gave himself, Dziga Vertov ('spinning top').[72] For the project, Vertov requested the addition of a specialized film production carriage to the project's railway train, so that he could make his films on the move; and until the mid-1930s an *agit-poezda* (film-train), fully equipped with film lab and cinema carriages, was a central feature of Russian *agit-prop*. Vertov devised a procedure for processing, editing, and playing back his films in the towns and villages where he had just recorded them. He inserted shots of the local surroundings to make the material immediate and meaningful for his viewers, and shots of their reactions to the raw film in order to encourage viewers in similar communities to identify with it. Vertov also re-edited the pilot versions of his films on the basis of his audience's comments, as in modern marketing focus groups; and he packaged the whole in a program of lectures and events that added face-to-face interaction to the process. These practices have since been defined in the educational literature as *formative evaluation* and *collaborative learning*. Vertov's approach thus holds lessons for the designers of educational media content today.

Vertov was a free thinker, however, and the frank criticism in his films of poverty and working conditions did not commend him to the Soviet leadership.

His film-train projects were discontinued in 1922, and his documentary film-making career was curtailed in the early 1930s. In 1932, the Stalinist regime revived the film-train method under the supervision of film-maker Alexander Medvedkin, who described the powerful effects of the process on the communities who took part:

> It was as if the dam had suddenly burst: everyone was talking with unaccustomed force; we had given the people's anger an outlet. (Nowadays we tread softly, afraid of upsetting the comrades—we were not afraid in those days!).[73]

In Medvedkin's hands, however, just as with Vertov, the mobile railroad approach was bringing more power to the people than the regime found acceptable, and in the mid-1930s his film-train project too was discontinued. Medvedkin's daughter recalled the time: "There were drawbacks, negative signs which really were concealed from the people and from everybody so the train goes hushed up."[74] Vertov's method spread to other lands nonetheless. The Canadian NFB projects from the 1940s onwards applied his techniques under the guidance of French film-maker Jean Rouch and Scottish documentary maker John Grierson. Grierson had assisted in the creation of the NFB in 1938, inviting Vertov's brother, Boris Kaufman, to join him in Montreal as an advisor. While the NFB's francophone division and European film scholars openly acknowledged the source of their ideas, the English contingent did not. Archival research by James has chronicled the political reasons that Vertov's methods were applied without accreditation in this way, and points to Grierson as the architect of a deliberate plagiarism.

Vertov died in obscurity in 1954, in James' words "heart-broken and bewildered by 25 years of rejection and suppression, yet having seen his work copied and praised in the hands of others, himself uncredited." Today, he is well remembered for his influence on documentary film-making in general, and in particular for pioneering the techniques of *Kino-Pravda* (*cinéma vérité*, the pursuit of film truth). Vertov's distinctive pedagogical contribution, however, has become eclipsed by others whom he influenced. For example, one of his junior assistants in the film-train project was Serge Eisenstein, a painter who decorated the film-train exteriors with colorful artwork and, following Vertov's tutelage, became famous as the director of films including *Battleship Potemkin* and *Ivan the Terrible*. Vertov had created a powerful new version of an earlier form of mobile community education, already popular in Russia and the USA in the 19th century. Concerts and other events were transported by road and river in Russia for many years, produced by leading impresarios; and the Chautauqua movement in New York State had hosted international cultural visits on the banks of Lake Chautauqua since 1874, featuring lectures and performances by artists including the Russian army choir. In 1910, the conductor and publisher Serge Koussevitsky engaged the pianist-composer Alexander Scriabin to play on a steamer on the river Volga, with stops in concert-halls along the route—precisely the approach for education used ten years later by Dziga Vertov. This mobile arts and culture tradition reaches back to the Middle Ages, with peripatetic minstrels and the Miracle Plays as its inspiration.[75] Similarly, modern formative evaluation practices are commonly traced back to the adaptation of WWI training films for public usage.[76] But Vertov, for his in-depth sensitivity to the social and psychological processes underlying media practice, may fairly be described as the unsung father of the modern m-learning tradition. James recognized this in proposing the 'Vertov Process' as the fairest and most accurate label for it.

[There is a video at *YouTube.com* of the kindly young Vertov, shepherding his students onto the educational train.[77] Thanks to Marek Budzynski for making it available. James recalls Maximos Planudes' praise for the long-overlooked work of Ptolemy: "This work is such a One | As, rescued from oblivion after years | By one whose heart loves beauty, was received | With all due speed into the light of day."[78]]

Today's m-learning designer can learn from the long tradition of community development by applying its principles in the development of pedagogical practices. James identifies three principles underlying Vertov's community media work: namely, the importance of functioning as a catalyst for:

1 discussion of participants' problems;
2 bridge-building between opposing groups (e.g., workers and managers); and
3 development of mutual understanding between local and national groups.

These goals, and their emphasis on the media's role to stimulate human interaction, are well established in international development work, under the headings of *participatory development*,[79] *capacity building*,[80] and *action research*.[81–82] A remarkable example of the mobile tradition is currently in operation in India, home of the largest network of railway lines in the world. The Vigyan Rail[83] and Science Express[84] projects have demonstrated that road and rail routes can take modern educational technologies into the most remote rural regions where the internet may remain inaccessible for years to come. By taking media content into local communities in colorfully designed packages, these projects seek to reduce its impersonal, non-interactive nature. Ironically, the early era of internet-based education has maintained the impersonal media approach by creating a non-interactive 'cafeteria style' of education akin to reaching down a pre-prepared meal from the kitchen shelf. The approach is lamented by critics such as Ed Hirsch Junior:

> Cafeteria-style education, combined with the unwillingness of our schools to place demands on students, has resulted in a steady diminishment of commonly shared information between generations and between young people themselves.[85]

In its early years, m-learning via the cellphone and other mobile technologies are also stressing the packaging of materials in one-way, cafeteria-style formats, even to the point of neglecting the interactive function for which these gadgets were invented. M-learning is currently being designed less to make information more mobile for the benefit of students in remote regions, than to make it more convenient for students to study while on the move—whether at home, on the bus to work, in the workplace, or on the beach. The social media promise to add much-needed interactivity to technology-assisted education; and m-learning has the potential to create a unified global delivery system for educational materials. Although the internet has not yet evolved into a new Silk Road of high-quality global education, the new networking and mobile tools, owing to their interactivity and flexibility, may effectively do so. In designing m-learning techniques for global education, it should be recalled that the community media tradition has stressed mobile teaching as well as learning, and that practices from Vertov onwards have emphasized teacher-learner interaction as well as the simple provision of one-way media content.

Dipping back and forth in history in this way illustrates that the same ideas have been constantly reinvented in educational practice, fading from view and reappearing when the time is once again right for them. At particular times the same idea can emerge simultaneously in different minds and disciplines, influenced both consciously and unconsciously by the discussions of the day. Orwell and McLuhan were doubtless influenced by the critic Empson regardless of the fact that they knew him personally, for his ideas had entered the culture years earlier; and in a 1944 essay McLuhan praised Empson for focusing attention, albeit in different words, on the process that McLuhan himself popularized 20 years later— the interpretation of the medium and the message.[86] Similarly, the Canadians who came together to develop the 'Fogo Process' in the 1960s may not have realized that the idea was not their own, for its origins in Vertov's work had been obscured by Grierson 25 years earlier—just as the original owners of the gold of Timbuktu were eclipsed when the Sultan of Morocco made off with it four centuries ago. As new ideas arrive, old ones can meet a surprisingly abrupt end. The Mongol Empire covered the whole of Asia and seemed set to include Europe, when suddenly the Khan's uncle died, leaving a power vacuum. The Mongol invaders pulled out of the west and returned home leaving, in Jackson's words, "nobody to piss against a wall" (p. 60).[87]

[The current writer has twice been arrested in his travels, once in Mongolia. After an evening of German beer, I had a 30-minute walk to the Ulaanbaatar hotel and found a shadowy wall to relieve myself. Hurrying up the road a minute later, I was surrounded by six guards who hustled me towards large iron gates. I connected on my cellphone with my highly-placed host, who told the guards I was just a stupid foreign academic who had no idea the wall belonged to the Chinese Embassy. He recommended that I should give them a modest fee, and with $20 to share they hurried away before I might change my mind.

[On another occasion, while on a project, my wife and I were frog-marched from a train on the Russia–Ukraine border at dawn, and placed under guard for six hours in a basement in the woods. Our visas had been mis-stamped and were invalid. When at last I was allowed to call my government host in Kiev, we were escorted to the train and entered Ukraine without visas. It seemed possible that with no entry visas we would be unable to get exit visas; but when it came time to leave, our host whispered to a foreign office official who leapt to attention and stamped our passports. This and the Mongolian adventure illustrate the value of good connectivity!]

As with the dynasties of history, the educational TV tradition in western universities and colleges appeared permanent and yet came to a similarly precipitate end in the 1990s. Good ideas can emerge at the wrong times, ahead of themselves and perhaps politically inappropriate, lacking support from the converging ideas of others. That is the situation in which their authors may suffer the unkindest cut. James noted a metaphor, recorded in Vertov's 1945 diary, by which he consoled himself for the fact that his pioneering media ideas had become associated with others' names rather than his own:

> Appreciate those who invent, not those who acquire . . . Let those who sow reap the fruits of their labours. Encourage the art of the bold gardeners, not that of the fruit pickers.[88]

Summary

Road, rail and river routes have enabled the global exchange of education and culture for millennia, predating the electronic media as communication tools. In the 20th century, the capacity for educational and cultural exchange was increased by the development of the modern mega-universities, mainly in Asia, and of open and distance education principles for their use. The communications media have underpinned this effort in formal and non-formal educational programs; and pedagogical principles for mobile education have predated the current 'mobile learning' trend by a hundred years. The high standards represented by ancient currencies, whether they be salt or silk, remain elusive, however, as old ideas are replaced by new ones, not necessarily for the better.

2

WAX AND WANE

Fin de siècle

With mutual trust and a common delivery platform, would-be educational partners can move to the development stage. The idea of global education is ambitious, however, and the time may not be ripe for it. On the other hand, the timing may be perfect, with all the necessary conditions 'harmonized'. Just such a convergence of conditions was described as occurring a century ago by Virginia Woolf.

> (O)n or about December 1910, human character changed. I am not saying that one went out, as one might into a garden, and there saw that a rose had flowered, or that a hen had laid an egg. The change was not sudden and definite like that. But a change there was, nevertheless.[1]

It is tempting to take Woolf's comment literally, and to search for a meaningful 'harmonic convergence' of events in 1910, just as the ancients believed that Halley's comet appeared at times of historic significance. (Incidentally, the comet did appear in 1910!) Her remark has a more specialized interpretation, however, illustrating how new ideas can emerge in different minds and disciplines simultaneously, and the consternation that occurs as they collide with the old ideas. Woolf believed that an unfortunate change had taken place in English literature since the turn of the 20th century, caused by a climate of social reform that generated stark fictional portrayals based on new moral and political views.[2] The literary modernist approach that Woolf espoused attempted to depict the complexity of human nature in greater depth. She made her comment about 1910 in an essay critical of the realist writer Arnold Bennett, who had published the first of his trilogy of *Clayhanger* novels in that year; so her comment can be interpreted as a jibe at the idea that human character was now redefined, thanks to Bennett, as being simpler than others had assumed. As the rival literary camps argued about their competing ideas, their field was plunged into confusion. "Lights swing about; we hear the bottom of the sea; it is all dark, terrible, and uncharted", Woolf lamented.[3]

A similar *fin de siècle* malaise occurred in the educational field at the end of the 20th century. In both theory and practice, the previous 50 years had defined the field well. The 1950s to 1980s saw extensive theorizing about pedagogy and instructional design. Bloom's taxonomy of learning 'domains' (1956) identified three learning types: *cognitive* (mental skills and knowledge); *affective* (emotional development and attitude); and *psychomotor* (physical skills).[4] Vygotsky (1962) described the learning benefits derived from social collaboration.[5] Bandura updated these views in 'social learning theory' (1963);[6] Piaget (1967) analyzed the stages of intellectual development in children;[7] and Bruner stressed the value of 'discovery learning' (1967), whereby the teacher helps students to discover principles for themselves.[8–9] These ideas have since influenced 'constructivist' views of the way in which learning evolves from collaboration between learners, and of the 'learner-constructed' methods that facilitate it. Meanwhile, detailed connections between learning theory and practice were defined by Gagné (1965) in terms of nine 'instructional events'.[10]

1   gaining the learner's attention;
2   informing the learner of the objective;
3   stimulating recall of previously acquired knowledge and skill;
4   presenting the stimulus material;
5   providing learning guidance;
6   eliciting learning performance;
7   providing feedback;
8   assessing learning performance; and
9   enhancing retention and transfer of learning.

The systematic blue-print for educational media practice that was emerging encouraged the 1970s development of in-house TV production studios in universities and colleges; and the educational media researchers of that time gave detailed attention to instructional design principles,[11–13] and to the evaluation of media materials.[14–16] Theoretical support for the effort was provided by conversation theory (Pask, 1976), which defined the learner as engaged in a massive set of interactions with the teacher, educational materials, prior experiences, and the world beyond.[17] While some learning occurs in a systematic step-by-step sequence (*serialist*), Pask indicated that it can also occur when a general framework is found and specific ideas are fitted into it (*holist*). In the 1980s, techniques for the development of computer-assisted instruction (CAI) were proposed.[18–19] Skinner's behaviorist concepts of reinforcement and conditioning remained influential throughout this period.[20] His adaptive principles of programmed learning have been built into educational materials delivered by print, interactive video, computer and internet hybrids, so that learners can use them in customized sequences and at their own rates.[21] Ausubel too focused on the sequences and structure of learning materials, with emphasis on the use of 'advance organizers' to guide the learning process.[22] A particularly practical contribution was made by Scriven,[23] in stressing the importance of 'formative evaluation' conducted during the development process while there is still time to make essential revisions, as opposed to summative evaluation which takes place after the process and may be too late to be of immediate practical use. The use of formative evaluation in developing and modifying effective production techniques for pre-school children is a prime reason for the long-term success of the Children's TV Workshop's *Sesame Street.*[24]

In the 1980s, however, the terms 'programmed learning' and 'programmed instruction' fell out of favor as new terms evolved for their in-depth discussion. Merrill and others developed the concept of "learner control" in discussing how the design of educational materials can enable students to use them in sequences catering to their individual needs.[25] Merrill's component display theory (1983) and component design theory (1994) added principles of course and class design to the analysis of educational content, and shifted the emphasis from the design of instructional formats to 'instructional transactions', Meanwhile, 'best practices' in education were summarized by Chickering & Gamson (1987). Reigeluth's elaboration theory (1983)[26] provided a reminder of the need to present information in sequences from simple to more complex; and the 1999 update of his theory[27] has had a modern influence on 'learner-constructed' approaches similar to that of the programmed learning principles in the 1960s, and conversation theory in the 1970s. Further justifications for learner-constructed learning were presented by Jonassen (1991); and 'constructivist'[28] and 'connectivist'[29] notions have continued to emerge during the decade from 2000 onwards.

In the mid-1990s, however, a loss of momentum was observed in the instructional design and evaluation fields. In North America and Europe, educational institutions were closing the in-house media studios they had established 20 years earlier, believing that the educational functions of TV and radio were about to be assumed more cost-effectively by the internet. Researchers turned their attention to internet and web-based instruction, exploring the potential of online methods in the same way as 1970s educators had experimented with television. It was the kind of watershed period known to economists as 'Schumpeter's Gale':

(a) process of industrial mutation that incessantly revolutionises the economic structure from within, incessantly destroying the old one, incessantly creating a new one ... (It) must be seen in its role in the perennial gale of creative destruction.[30]

The low level of attention to instructional media principles at that time is indicated by a review by Latchem and colleagues of the conference proceedings of the Asian Association of Open Universities (AAOU) from 1995–98. The analysis showed that the techniques and planning of instruction were little discussed by researchers and planners in that region, despite the massive ODL 'mega-universities' established there.[31] Latchem conducted a similar review of the 374 articles published in the *British Journal of Educational Technology* from 2000–04, and showed that their main focus was on emerging hardware and software opportunities rather than on evaluation and planning issues associated with their use.[32] In the 2000s, the star of instructional design is rising again, with updated analyses of instructional design models for turn-of-the-century technologies provided by Liu *et al.* (2001), Scott *et al.* (2003), Smith & Ragan (2005), Laurillard (2002, 2009), and Carr-Chelmann.[33–34] A recent survey of course development at Asian open universities, however, indicates that the training of their instructional designers is still based on western textbooks written in the 1970s to 1980s, and is largely insensitive to current media, and to local economic and cultural needs.[35] Carr-Chelmann has been particularly critical about the implications of these issues for global education;[36] and the concerns that she has collated are confirmed by current data about the inaccessibility of online education for Asian students.[37]

This *fin de siècle* account of educational media research, theory and evaluation is supported by a content analysis conducted for the purpose of this book. An unusually detailed source for evidence is provided by *Educational Technology Abstracts* (ETA), a publication that completed its 25th year in 2010. ETA collates the abstracts of the articles published annually in a worldwide set of journals dealing with technology issues in numerous disciplinary areas. From the 224 journals abstracted in 1985, ETA's coverage has since swelled to approximately a thousand. The last issue in each annual volume provides a cumulative list of the hundreds of keywords used by journal authors in summarizing their topics. The current analysis compares the year-by-year usage of the following keywords:

- *distance* (as in distance education, distance learning, distance delivery);
- *e-learning* (as in e-learning methods, e-learning resources);
- *evaluation* (course evaluation, formative evaluation, summative evaluation);
- *instructional design*;
- *instructional effectiveness*;
- *interaction* (as in interactive media, interactive video, interactivity);
- *internet* (as in internet courses, internet-based learning);
- *online* (as in online course, online education);
- *quality* (quality assurance, quality control);
- *TV* (as in television, educational television, TV production);
- *video* (as in video-based education, video equipment);
- *web* (as in web-based education, World-Wide Web).

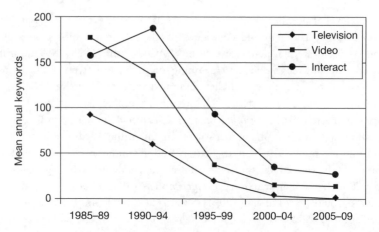

FIGURE 2.1 Declining research use of ETV and video keywords.

Source: Author.

The mean annual frequencies of these keywords' usage are charted for each five-year period from 1985 to 2009. The analysis begins at the point at which the educational TV and video tradition was still at its height (Figure 2.1). The graph confirms that by the mid-1990s writings about ETV had started to decline to their current zero level. The medium gained a new lease of life in the early 1990s owing to the perceived potential of the new interactive videodisc technology. Since then, the 'video' tradition has also declined to near zero in the educational literature, and terms involving 'interaction' have fallen from favor as numerous alternative terms (social media, social networking, Web 2.0, constructivism, etc.) have come to the fore in the context of web-based education.

Figure 2.2 shows a corresponding loss of interest in evaluation studies since the mid-1990s. In fact, the very term 'evaluation' became unpopular at that time, owing to the threat commonly perceived by educators in the evaluation practices used by educational institutions. Terms such as 'instructional design' and 'instructional effectiveness' also waned at the time, and the use of both of these terms as a publication keyword has dropped to a minimal level in the 2000s. No terms have yet emerged to take the place of these keywords; and no terms relating to 'quality' gained currency in the educational media literature throughout the whole 25-year period.

Figure 2.3 indicates the reason for this shift in research focus. During the 2000–05 period that witnessed the waning of interest in TV, video, instructional design and evaluation studies, interest in internet, web-based and online research themes burgeoned. It is not encouraging to see that new online media are being promoted in the absence of evaluation and instructional design studies, although this process is essentially no different from the enthusiastic exploratory period that accompanied the emergence of educational TV in the 1960s. At the time of

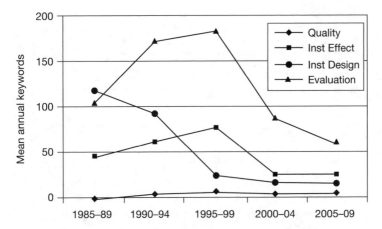

FIGURE 2.2 Declining research use of instructional design and evaluation keywords.

Source: Author.

writing (2011), a critical process is evolving which may place the enthusiasm for new online techniques (social media, learner-constructed approaches, virtual worlds, etc.) into perspective.[38–40]

Distance education has never been a major focus in the educational technology literature, despite a steady rise in its usage from the mid-1980s to early 2000s. Since 2005, the use of 'distance education' and 'distance learning' as publishing keywords has dropped sharply, though this may be due to the emergence of specialized journals for this sub-field of education, not yet covered by the ETA abstracting service (Figure 2.4).

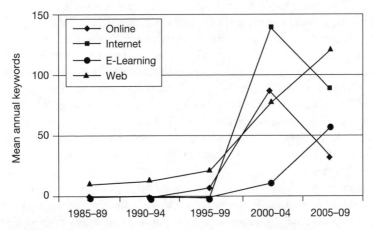

FIGURE 2.3 Increasing research use of internet-related keywords.

Source: Author.

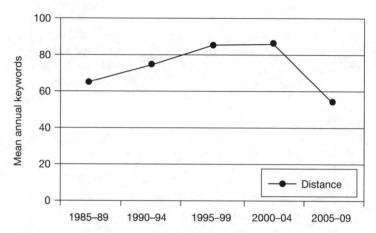

FIGURE 2.4 Research use of distance education keywords.

Source: Author.

According to this analysis, the educational technology field since the 1960s has waxed and waned through two phases. The TV and video phase spanned the 1970s to 1990s, the result of major investments by educational institutions in media production facilities. It began with an exploratory period leading to intensive activity in instructional design and evaluation, which built until the internet's arrival in the mid-1990s. At this point, westernized educational institutions closed their traditional media studios, arguing that they had not proved cost-effective; and research and related publishing activities came to an abrupt halt. The second phase, relating to online education, has begun in the new century with a similar exploratory process. At the time of writing (2011), the online media are on the up-curve of a new cycle of innovation, graduating, it is to be hoped, from the exploratory period into an evaluation phase.

It may not be coincidental that a similar watershed was perceived in the academic world of 1910. Numerous similar factors may have contributed to the rise and fall of academic approaches during the two turn-of-the-century periods. Perhaps the ideas involved had all been expressed before and needed to be reinvented in new forms. Maybe both eras became weighed down by the increasingly obscure language that academics use when they try to imply new thinking, often expressing incredibly simple and obvious notions in brazenly complex ways. Maybe the educational media field itself became confounded by rivalries between its experts just as the English literature field was unsettled by the arguments of the realists and modernists a century ago. Many of today's media evaluation models overlap greatly with one another, and none of them is ideal for all situations. Republishing them in new jargon is a common way of suggesting that they now have new relevance. Or perhaps the origins of some of the ideas simply became lost since 1910, as new academics and their students reported, as though new, the ideas of people long deceased. The developmental psychologist Lev Vygotsky is a case in point. Common references to him as 'Vygotsky (1962)', '1981' or '2000' fail to recognize that English translations of his work may live on but that their author died in 1934. Similarly, references to Vygotsky as the originator of the social learning concept fail to give credit to identical ideas by Dewey (1897) and Rousseau (1762).

Knowledge is Power

> Old men and comets have been reverenced for the same reason; their long beards, and pretences to foretell events.[41]

Observing events over a period provides the gift of anticipation—the ability to predict the stages through which trends will logically pass. The above trend analysis of research keywords, for example, suggests that the westernized educational world is out-of-step with developing-world nations at the turn of the 21st century. In India and China, for example, a more gradual cycle of change is occurring, as educational institutions preserve the educational TV and radio traditions until such time as the newer online media have become more widely accessible to their students. The prospects for global education partnerships will be jeopardized unless these separate rates of change can be harmonized, based on an awareness of the events and forces that lead to their rise and fall. While the rise of educational approaches tends to be gradual—new ideas evolving and being absorbed—their decay can be sudden, due to independent factors rather than to the ideas' actual obsolescence. Shifts of this type are more common in nature than stability, as mathematician René Thom observed in catastrophe theory.[42] Relatively small excuses for change lead to sudden, dramatic landslides, in the natural world and the physical and social sciences alike;[43] and "all that is solid melts into air."[44]

The world of information provides numerous examples of this process, and suggests that the most powerful approaches to the spreading of information may actually be the most likely to flounder. For example, the concept of 'spreading' information was promoted in 1622, with the publication of Pope Gregory XV's papal bull *Inscrutabili Divinae*, and with the creation of a Church administration responsible for *propaganda fidei*, the spreading of the faith. In 1982 the Vatican renamed the process the 'evangelization of peoples' to overcome the negative perception of the word 'propaganda'. Even the term 'spreading' has gained ambiguous connotations over the years (in 'muck-spreading', 'spreading alarm and despondency', etc.), depending on whether or not one agrees with the ideas being spread. Many educational media terms carry negative and even hostile associations in this way ('target audience', 'bullet theory of communication', 'hypodermic theory', etc), having derived from the shallow assumption that the recipients of a message will submit to it passively and obediently. But "knowledge is power" (Bacon, 1597), and the more aggressive the process of knowledge dissemination, the more likely it is to generate powerful responses in both positive and negative directions.

Propaganda and 'active stirring' were the primary purposes of Lenin's *agit-prop* railway project. As indicated above, its designer, Dziga Vertov was removed from *agit-prop* work because his style of 'prop' was just too 'agit' and free-thinking for the Stalinist regime's taste. Vertov had used the film-train to highlight not only the political promise of the new Soviet system, but also the problems it needed to address—working conditions, hygiene and safety issues, alcoholism, boot-legging, drug-addition, gambling, nutrition, tuberculosis, and an issue sadly familiar to educators of all eras, cheating. Vertov's frank messages would probably have drawn little political attention, however, if it had not been for the powerful media he used to convey them; for he used a multimedia mixture of every popular medium at his disposal, complete with interactive methodology and remedial techniques. He filmed interviews in factories, schools, hospitals, taverns, doss-houses, and the streets, and encouraged his subjects to speak freely and act naturally.[45] His brightly-painted *agit-prop* train carried lecturers, actors, and musicians with shared educational themes and, in addition to mobile film production facilities, a print shop for the production of support materials. Stalin was not the only one to shut down this approach (see Chapter 1). When the National Film Board of Canada's francophone producers emulated it in the 1950s to promote Québec nationalism, the anglophone management shut them down too, slashing their funds and taking the process over for English-Canadian purposes.[46]

> The boisterous birth of a 'national' Québecois cinema occurred inside a Canadian government apparatus, which never intended it and always renounced it. The NFB . . . tried everything to inhibit the consolidation of the cinema: through project refusals; administrative snags; censorship, involving both cuts and outright bans.[47]

The use of media in community development has been associated since the 1950s period with the term 'extension'. Brunner & Hsin Pao Yang (1949) described the major purpose of rural extension work as being to give local people control over their community's goals, and to help them to achieve their objectives on their own terms.[48] At universities such as Memorial University of Newfoundland, where the English-Canadian version of the Vertov process was developed, the process became the responsibility of 'extension media' departments, whose film and video producers address rural issues locally and internationally. But the term 'extension' has the same ambiguous connotations as 'propaganda', as the Brazilian scholar Paolo Freire indicated in a scathing indictment of the term in his 1969 essay *Extension or Communication*.[49]

Freire believed passionately in the power of the media to help the poor. Using, in Schramm's terms, the "little medium" of print, he developed an approach to non-formal education which was as free-thinking as that of the early Soviet film-makers. From 1946, Freire's literacy program used an interactive process whereby the local people were encouraged to interact with visiting teachers and to challenge them with questions. The teacher and student were seen as co-equal in this process, according to the principles of 'liberation technology', a tradition evoked today in connection with the potential of the cellphone and social media as political action tools.[50] Following the Brazilian military coup in 1964, Freire's work led to his imprisonment and subsequent 15-year exile. He responded in 1969 with an essay on the manner in which the extension process is co-opted by authoritarian regimes, by taking ideas to other parts of the world to 'normalize' them. Normalization in this context is inevitably defined, Freire pointed out, according to the criteria of the normalizer. He described it as a process of cultural invasion whereby "the invader thinks, at most, about the invaded, never with them. The invader dictates; the invaded patiently accept what is dictated." Introducing educational content into other cultures, he argued, is all too often a process of propaganda, myth spinning and "slogan making." In 1970 Freire consolidated these criticisms in his classic text *Pedagogy of the Oppressed*,[51] describing traditional pedagogy as a "banking model" whereby students are filled with facts unquestioningly in the manner of a piggy-bank. Two hundred years earlier, Rousseau's *Emile* had made the same criticisms of traditional educational approaches in pre-Revolutionary France, and copies of the book were ceremonially burned.[52] During the French Revolution, however, *Emile* became the model for the nation's new educational system.

I first realized the double-edged nature of many of the terms used in western writings, in dealing with the concerns of a Cuban student in the 1980s. He was attending my Montreal graduate course on formative evaluation, designed to proclaim the pedagogical value of the process. Clearly the student was unhappy, and after one lecture I asked him why. "You are assuming in your formative evaluations that there is no question that your messages are worthwhile, and that you need feel no guilt in using any strategy to make them effective," he told me. "In my country, we view this as an autocratic and deceitful approach that allows the people no right to have their own opinions." A few months later I visited the Dominican Republic to advise on the formative evaluation and adaptation of a western health campaign for Dominican street kids. My government host received me with an angry lecture about the cultural imperialism of western educators. I realized that it would take some time, if ever, for him to see that the campaign had an open-minded concern for children of all cultures. He did gather this, and we became firm friends. I have not looked at 'formative evaluation' in the same naïve way since, and have been lastingly suspicious of the cross-cultural suspicions raised by western jargon. Other terms share this problem. Community and student 'outreach', for example, suggests an expansive and caring attitude, as in an image of outstretched arms. But so does 'extension', and Freire's objections to that term are well taken. Perhaps the most unashamedly obvious *double-entendre* lies in the notion of quality 'control'. Even quality 'assurance' may be perceived as tactless and patronizing in cultures where the people perceive no assurance that any public information will be designed with their needs at heart.

Even altruistic global education programs can be perceived as harboring in-built prejudices about the need for 'backward' parts of the world to be educated according to visiting educators' criteria. McMichael indicates that this was a common problem with international development programs in the 19th and early 20th century.[53] Subsequently, the emphasis placed on globalization programs since the increasing global management of the economy in the 1980s, has involved new practices that Freire, for one, might criticize as being at least as insensitive as those of the 'colonizing' era: for example, the recommendation of inaccessible and cost-ineffective western-style educational technologies in developing countries, based on little or no awareness of local conditions. Today, the 'learner-constructed' approach of western open and distance learning is being enthusiastically adopted in developing nations. Asian educators refer frequently to the 'paradigm shift' from teacher-centered to learner-centered methods, and are eagerly adopting western practices of making learning materials available for students to download from the internet, even at the cost of dismissing the teacher from the process.[54–55] For the vast majority of students who, in 2011, still lack internet access, however, this approach fulfills exactly Freire's analysis whereby "the invader thinks, at most, about the invaded, never with them." In nations with a recent history of author-itarian abuse, it is easy to understand educators' excitement about the shift towards learner control in education, unimagined in their lifetimes. It is not necessarily the teacher who is the enemy in the knowledge dissemination process, however, but the lack of assurance that the learners are capable of conveying high-quality information to each other. Learner-constructed learning can always benefit from a just teacher's prompting; and temptations to shift the paradigm from teacher involvement to the opposite extreme should be tempered by recalling the view of Vertov and Freire, that capable extension involves solid teacher–student interaction.

As Virginia Woolf showed in pointing attention to the year 1910, it is useful to assess academic ideas in terms of the mood of the times in which they were expressed. The often repetitive nature of educational theories, and their tendency to state what some might regard as obvious, may have served a useful purpose at the time. Current perspectives in online education can seem particularly obvious outside the context in which they were proposed. The principle underlying the current 'connectivist' viewpoint, for example, is that students fare better when they are not isolated from the influence of others—a suggestion that many educators might regard as not worth stating. Considering, however, that this concept has re-emerged in the modern context of online education, where face-to-face communication between the student, teacher, and other students is rare or non-existent, it is possible to perceive connectivism as providing a useful reminder that efficient interpersonal interaction is an educational essential and should not be marginalized. Theoretical as well as practical issues may be valid in response to the prevailing moods and ideas of the day.

Just as constructivist principles may be a welcome approach for the previously oppressed, so the concept of "extension media" has been seized upon by parties for whom it too plays a useful role—the media themselves. McLuhan's description of the media as "extensions of man" portrayed 1960s western society as empowered by the media's ability to express thoughts and feelings on its behalf.[56] McLuhan praised the persuasive techniques of media advertising in terms previously reserved for high art—an approach criticized by Jonathan Miller for playing to the gallery of media practitioners.[57] McLuhan's perspective was eagerly embraced and promoted by the media, Miller (1971) argued, as a defense against less complementary criticisms of their social role:

> It is easy to imagine their pleasure on discovering a university professor who recognises, in their joint undertaking, not merely a creative element, but a creative element which represents one of the 'most hopeful developments in thought and feeling'. (p. 74)

Freire, with his strong views on propaganda, would have agreed with Miller in this. Emphasis on the media's capacity to extend man overlooks the need for man to extend the media by using them fairly and efficiently.

The presentation of politically unpopular messages via powerful media is the most obvious combination of factors likely to cause the rise and fall of educational principles and practices. The Soviet *agit-prop* tradition of Vertov arose and was crushed between the early 1920s and mid-1930s. Its community development principles took root again following WWII, as did the testing and training principles that had developed in response to wartime needs. In the 1940s and 1950s, the French anthropologist Jean Rouch applied Vertov's methods in making films about the lives and dreams of communities in West Africa. These too were banned by their governments for their democratizing effects.[58] In francophone Québec, the same tradition survived for approximately 15 years from the 1950s to 1960s, until being terminated by anglophone rivals, who then applied the tradition for their own purposes in the 1960s and 1970s. Political factors only partly explain the 15–20-year cycles underlying these trends, however. Educational TV rose in the early 1970s and flourished for approximately 20 years until being replaced by computer-assisted video methods in the 1980s; and the rise of internet-based education began 15 years later. A similar 20-year periodicity was revealed by an analysis of the repeated rise and fall of central agencies attempting to steer health education in 20th-century England (Blythe, 1987). The analysis examined the composition and leadership of the UK's national health education authority from 1927 to 1968. The Central Council for Health Education (CCHE) lasted from 1927–68 but underwent mid-term reorganization. Its successor, the Health Education Council (HEC) survived from 1968–87, at which point the Health Education Authority (HEA) took its place from 1987–2006.[59] The reasons for these reorganizations included problems of constitution, funding, leadership, and sustainability strategy. The CCHE and HEC were tackling politically sensitive issues without an adequate power-base for the purpose. In the case of all of these centralized bodies, failure to base their work within national frameworks for health and educational services caused them to be regarded as inefficient and ineffective within 10–15 years of existence, and terminated within 20 years. This cyclic rise and fall occurred in a manner Blythe terms "reinventing the misshapen wheel." The current automated era, he points out, has replaced England's 80-year tradition of active health education and promotion expertise by an online database.[60]

In part at least, the waxing and waning of educational methods is due to the fact that it takes a given number of years for individuals to become skilled in using them. In the pre-internet world of educational media research, it seemed to take approximately four years for one's idea to take root: the first year to play with the new medium and to formulate and test how to use it; the second to write up and publish the idea; the third for the work to be read by others; and the fourth for it to be quoted. If a sufficient critical mass of users is available, as in the 1970s development of educational television, an approach may take a decade to take root, and another to flower. Once the main principles underlying a trend have been developed, however, members of the mass can grow restive and be tempted away to apply them in the development of upcoming media, as in the rise of computer-based video research over approximately 15 years in the 1980s and 1990s (Figure 2.1). Today, a decade into the first internet-based phase of educational technology, sufficient familiarity with its potential appears to have been gained for evaluation activities to begin. It remains to see if these will be intensive, and will lead to improved techniques, or whether the adoption of the internet will merely lead to passive, depersonalized forms of education as suggested in Blythe's analysis of UK health education.

The Luddite Revolt

The basic principle behind Reigeluth's elaboration theory—the need to structure information from the simple to the complex—is one of those ideas that on first hearing seems only too obvious. Explaining elaboration theory in this simplified way does not do it justice, however; and more elaboration is needed! For simplicity is relative—to the needs of different students, for example; and even simple laws may need to be re-explained on the basis of concepts more familiar to particular audiences. To deal with the individual differences between students, Reigeluth identified a range of instructional sequences—conceptual, theoretical and 'simplifying conditions'—and a holistic framework for the teacher to use in selecting the most appropriate approach for a given situation. In this respect, elaboration theory embraced the linear and holistic notions of Pask's conversation theory (1976). Simplicity is also relative to the approaches that work best for individual teachers. At an early stage of its 1970s work on *Sesame Street,* the

Children's TV Workshop found that production techniques which work well in commercial broadcasting can be too complicated for their pre-school audience, and need to be simplified. The conflict this instructional design finding created between educators and TV producers was a serious obstacle to the development of efficient educational productions, each group believing that they knew better than the other how to do the job. The same type of disagreement occurred in one of the most tragic "gales of destruction" in social history, an event currently being recalled in its bicentennial year.[61]

In 1811–12, spinners and weavers in the British textiles industry opposed the introduction of automated methods that they believed would ruin their livelihoods. They believed that their work depended on the sophisticated artistry handed down to them by their forefathers. The factory owners, however, required them to move to a simpler mass production strategy that would reduce prices and increase profit. To express their position, the workers grouped themselves in the name of a popular figure of local legend, Ned Ludd, who was reputed to have smashed some spinning equipment in a row with his father. On 1 January 1812, the Luddites published a formal manifesto of their objections to the new management policy (Figure 2.5), threatening to evoke a royal charter agreed under an earlier sovereign, Charles II, and to smash their looms, if their objections were not heeded. The charter justified them, the Luddites argued, in decommissioning their equipment if it did not allow them to do their jobs according to agreed quality principles.

With sly (though in the event unwise) British humor, the Luddites signed their manifesto "Ned Ludd's Office, Sherwood Forest", hangout of Nottingham's other fabled renegade, Robin Hood. With the Industrial Revolution gathering speed, the government of King George III was in no mood for jesting, however, and was more concerned to side with the new industrialists. To send a decisive message to any workers who might oppose their orders, the authorities depicted the Luddites as hooligans, and placed a bounty on them (the capitals are theirs):

> Whereas EVIL-MINDED PERSONS have assembled together in a riotous manner, and DESTROYED a NUMBER of FRAMES, in different Parts of the Country . . . any person who will impeach his Accomplices shall, upon CONVICTION, receive (a 50-guinea) Reward, and every Effort made to procure his Pardon.[62]

To quell the angry workers, an army of 12,000 British troops was dispatched to the Midlands and North of England—twice as many as were sent to Europe to defeat Napoleon. Seventeen Luddite leaders were hanged, and hundreds exported to Australia.[63] The term 'Luddite' became synonymous with ignorant hostility to new technology, distorted into a label of "contempt and abuse that has lasted all the way to (the) 21st century."[64]

375. The declaration of the framework knitters, 1 Jan. 1812

(Public Record Office, Home Office, 42/119.)

The Luddite riots of 1811-1812 began in Nottinghamshire, where the hosiery workers objected, not to the use of new machinery but to certain trade practices by the employers. The Yorkshire riots (Nos. 376 and 377), on the other hand, were directed chiefly against the introduction of cloth-dressing machinery.

BY THE FRAMEWORK KNITTERS.

A Declaration.

Whereas by the charter granted by our late sovereign Lord Charles II by the Grace of God King of Great Britain France and Ireland, the framework knitters are empowered to break and destroy all frames and engines that fabricate articles in a fraudulent and deceitful manner and to destroy all framework knitters' goods whatsoever that are so made and whereas a number of deceitful unprincipled and intriguing persons did attain an Act to be passed in the 28th year of our present sovereign Lord George III whereby it was enacted that persons entering by force into any house shop or place to break or destroy frames should be adjudged guilty of felony and as we are fully convinced that such Act was obtained in the most fraudulent interested and electioneering manner and that the honourable the Parliament of Great Britain was deceived as to the motives and intentions of the persons who obtained such Act we therefore the framework knitters do hereby declare the aforesaid Act to be null and void to all intents and purposes whatsoever as by the passing of this Act villainous and imposing persons are enabled to make fraudulent and deceitful manufactures to the discredit and utter ruin of our trade. And whereas we declare that the aforementioned Charter is as much in force as though no such Act had been passed. . . . And we do hereby declare to all hosiers lace manufacturers and proprietors of frames that we will break and destroy all manner of frames whatsoever that make the following spurious articles and all frames whatsoever that do not pay the regular prices heretofore agreed to [by] the masters and workmen–All print net frames making single press and frames not working by the rack and rent and not paying the price regulated in 1810: warp frames working single yarn or two coarse hole–not working by the rack, not paying the rent and prices regulated in 1809–whereas all plain silk frames not making work according to the gage–frames not marking the work according to quality, whereas all frames of whatsoever description the workmen of whom are not paid in the current coin of the realm will invariably be destroyed. . . .

Given under my hand this first day of January 1812.

God protect the Trade.

Ned Lud's Office
Sherwood Forest.

FIGURE 2.5 The Luddite Manifesto.

Source: Aspinall & Smith, 1996.

The Luddite Manifesto (1812) certainly does not appear to have been produced by a band of hooligans, however, nor by the kind of hooligan group that would secure the services of a lawyer. In respectably obtuse legalese, it declared the workers' goal as to prevent practices that would lead "to the discredit and utter ruin of our trade." It demonstrated that their objections were to the ways in which the management was requiring them to use the technology, rather than arising from hostility to the technology itself. In fact, the workers and their forefathers had already been using the same machinery for two centuries when the Luddites objected to its planned usage.[65] Their Manifesto identified the usage practices clearly: "print net frames making single press and frames not working by the rack ... warp frames working single yarn or two coarse hole—not working by the rack ... (and) all plain silk frames not making work according to the gage." To ensure that quality would be preserved, they called for quality control measures. Automated methods that were not quality-assured ("frames not marking the work according to quality") should be discontinued, the workers proposed, and the products priced according to quality criteria.[66] They demanded adherence to "the regular prices heretofore agreed to (by) the masters and the workmen" and for their wages to be paid "in the current coin of the realm"—reasonable positions for workers to take.

Sadly, these Luddite demands were untimely, and led to catastrophe. In classical Greek drama, a 'catastrophe' is not necessarily a negative event but a resolution of factors that were previously in conflict. For the Luddites and their families, however, this was catastrophe in every sense of the word—their movement smashed, its leaders executed, and their craftsmanship precipitately replaced by cheaper, automated processes. To the workers, the new techniques destroyed the artistry handed down to them over many generations. Just as the Luddites differed with their bosses about the techniques of textiles production, so educational TV practitioners in the 1970s to 1990s debated the relative merits of complex broadcast styles versus time-honored teaching principles. Today's online educational software tends to be similarly imperfect in its facilities and navigation procedures, leading to differences between teachers in the ways it is used in course delivery.[67] The principles of Reigeluth or Pask may mean nothing to these practitioners, because their professorial appointments as historians, chemists, or literature specialists do not require them to have read the educational literature. Even in distance education universities, faculty members are typically appointed as subject-matter experts rather than as having any particular interest and skill in teaching or media usage. In the absence of institutional guidance as to how to use the technologies, it tends to be regarded as a point of academic freedom for faculty members to design their courses in their own individual way; and when institutions try to impose a centralized instructional 'look and feel' on their courses, teaching staff express frustration as the poor Luddites did, albeit less dramatically.

Evaluation and quality assurance studies can certainly help to resolve debates about educational practice. As the Luddites found, however, calling for evaluation studies is to no avail in an institution if no-one in a decision-making position feels obliged to pay attention to their conclusions. Today's journals of online education regularly report cost-effectiveness comparisons between software products; and since 2002 an average of two papers per issue on this topic have been published by one such journal alone, the *International Review of Research in Open & Distance Learning*. A theme of this literature in the first decade of this century has been the pros and cons of online learning management systems (LMS), and the relative inflexibility yet costliness of commercial LMS products. For a while, specific commercial LMS platforms have been the default in online education, their annual licenses renewed by institutions with or without the benefit of evaluative evidence. A study by Morningstar *et al.* (2004) illustrated the common tendency for institutional administrators to invest in even the most expensive educational technologies available without presenting evaluative evidence justifying the decision.

At that time, the vendor of a popular LMS, *WebCT*, was about to launch a more expensive version to which many educational institutions were planning to upgrade. Morningstar and colleagues demonstrated the cost-ineffectiveness of transferring to this new system, and pointed out that the 1st-year costs of implementing it at a large academic institution would be over USD 600,000, compared with the minimal operational costs of more flexible freeware alternatives. Two years later, the writer's DE institution was about to renew its license for the same commercial product nonetheless. In response, faculty advocates of open-source software (OSS) mounted a campaign based on evidence that the University should move instead to the OSS product, *Moodle*. The faculty members behind this campaign were, according to the more enlightened view of the word, true Luddites. They argued that the costs of teaching should be reduced by abandoning cost-ineffective systems; and they stressed that the move to OSS would give the teachers greater flexibility in adapting their courseware to student needs. In the spirit of the Luddite Manifesto, they also presented detailed comparisons of licensing and infrastructure costs; and the University administration accepted their cost-effectiveness case. Similar concerns are raised by online students when asked to bear the extra cost of printing online course materials. Such evaluations produce solid justification for quality control in online education, and those who argue for the evidence to be heeded are Luddites in the original, unsmeared sense of the word.

The process of implementing such evidence, however, is complicated by the pell-mell emergence of new ways for teachers to embellish their online course materials with quizzes, blogs, wikis, tweets, e-portfolio methods, etc.[68–69] Developing good pedagogical uses of all of these techniques at once is a difficult challenge, even for the most committed of teachers and technology enthusiasts. *Moodle*, the OSS learning management system enthusiastically embraced as the latest best thing four years ago, is already becoming increasingly inaccessible in the hands of designers who do not appreciate the need to maintain its accessibility over low-bandwidth connections;[70] and an evaluation by Elias has indicated that *Moodle*-based distance education courses typically use only 25% of the instructional accessibility features available to them.[71] One can anticipate the institutional explanation for this—lack of resource staff to keep the LMS platform up-to-date. It is also possible, however, that no-one has seen the need to instruct the resource staff to give platform updates a high priority.

Could a Luddite Revolt occur again? It has been suggested that times have changed since the Luddites' day:

> Let's be grateful that we live in a more open society where we can debate labor and technology problems via peaceful and democratic means, and remember General Ludd's Army as the product of a time when others couldn't do the same.[72]

If it would be impossible for new workplace practices to be implemented today with the disregard for the workers that industry and government demonstrated in 1811, a Luddite revolt will never happen again. Today's priorities and those of the early 19th century are similar, however. The governing priority of that era was to bring society into the Industrial Revolution. Now it is to create the internet-based industrial revolution. If this process is managed cohesively, without marginalizing the populace that lacks internet access, it will indeed be arguable that society has become more peaceful and democratic over two centuries. If educational institutions shift their attention away from media that students find accessible, however, the attitudes that destroyed the Luddites will not have changed. The late David Noble, a confirmed critic of automated distance education, insisted that these attitudes definitely have not changed. His writings depict the Luddites as heroes standing for tradition and artistry against blind automation;[73] and are particularly frank on the subject of technology-based education, describing it as

> shadow cyber-education . . . a dismal new era of higher education has dawned. In future years we will look upon the wired remains of our once great democratic higher education system and wonder how we let it happen. That is, unless we decide now not to let it happen.[74]

The media critic Neil Postman also portrayed the Luddites as heroes, who "seemed to be the only group in England that could foresee the catastrophic effects of the factory system."[75] Postman was well aware that this attitude could cause him to be described as a modern Luddite, and he regarded that as no disgrace. Noble and Postman both stressed the need to justify the adoption of technologies in terms of technique, just as the Luddites recommended.

Media Adoption

The complexity of media adoption is illustrated by the wide range of educational 'stakeholders' who bring conflicting motives and priorities to technology selection. The interests of these parties need to be 'harmonized', as well as the technical conditions in which they operate.

1   Personnel who perceive their role as being to encourage technology innovation. Individuals and committees encouraging the adoption of new technologies should be required to provide reasonable evidence that new media are actually needed and represent improvement.

2   Hardware and software vendors. One can hardly expect a salesman to give impartial accounts of new technologies, but the academics and administrators who purchase the systems should be required to conduct product comparisons justifying their selections.

[In my first week of University employment 40 years ago, I asked for a demonstration of a large blue box designed to convert Super-8 film into TV images. Unfortunately, the University had paid £3,000 for the gadget before discovering that no educational film was being produced for it.]

3   Institutional administrators have a similar responsibility to ensure that the features, licensing fees and running costs of educational hardware and software are compared with those of alternative products when commercial licenses are selected and renewed.

4   Instructional designers. The copy editors and multimedia specialists involved in course design have the same awkward relationship with the academic content specialist as ETV producers did in the 1970s–1990s. Both parties need to work at resolving the differences between their design criteria.

5   Educational researchers and evaluators. In the 1970s and 1980s, the methodology of media research and evaluation was a major focus in the educational literature, and should be revisited in relation to the new online media.

6   Funding agencies. Agencies that favor funding research into the educational potential of new media rather than traditional ones have a responsibility to consider the accessibility and sustainability issues relating to their decisions.

7   Government policy-makers. Ultimately, technology implementation can depend on government priorities. Policy-makers have a responsibility to ensure that traditional media are preserved in order to provide education and training until new media are ready to take over the task.

Among these parties, a particular burden of responsibility rests upon the researchers and designers. The other interest groups (e.g., administrators, policy-makers, funding agencies) are not necessarily equipped to conduct reliable research into the benefits of different technologies in specific situations, and they depend on research findings by evaluation specialists in making media adoption decisions. The study of media effects has a lengthy tradition in communication studies, initially identified with the mass audience and evolving to an appreciation of the different effects of information upon individuals.[76] This subtler level of understanding was acknowledged, in the statement by Lasswell (1948) that the communication process is a complex interaction between five variables: *who says what, in which channel, to whom, with what effect?*[77] Earlier still, in a study of 4,800 people's reactions to health education films produced for US troops in WWI, Lashley and Watson had drawn conclusions not only about the types of information needed by the public, but about the ways in which they need to be presented in order to avoid undesirable effects. They concluded that gratuitous dramatization and attention-getting techniques are ineffective in health education, because they "hold attention more through their action than through their relation to [the facts]"; and they criticized the use of colloquial terms as tending to diminish the credibility of health-related messages.[78]

In educational contexts, the credibility of the message relates directly to the *who?* in Lasswell's definition. In assessing whether or not to accept information, the first question one is likely to ask relates to the credibility of the person or agency responsible for it; and 'source credibility' became a prime focus of communication research following the work of Hovland and team. As with Lashley and Watson's work, Hovland's studies derived from wartime questions about how to design effective propaganda messages.[79–80] The *what?* in Lasswell's definition (the nature of message content) was also addressed in Hovland's research, in terms of the sequencing and structural aspects of information subsequently emphasized by educational theorists. Concluding that a two-sided message is likely to be more credible than a one-sided one, Hovland challenged the simple-minded assumption of propagandists that a one-sided strategy is more effective. The effects of two-sided messages, he noted, also depend on the critical ability of the recipient (the *to whom?* in Lasswell's terms), and on the sequence in which the contrasting arguments are presented. He noted that the viewpoint favored by the message designer should strategically be presented last.

So communication effects are dependent on at least three factors: the message sender, the recipient, and the message design. The fourth factor, *in which channel?*, relates to the properties of the communication media. In the 1960s, McLuhan argued that individual media have fixed properties unaffected by other variables: thus, print in McLuhan's terms is a 'hot' medium, and television a 'cool' one—a view that obscures the media's subtler effects. McLuhan's popular account of the media as "extensions of man" also drew attention away from the methods by which people can shape media products—i.e., man becoming an extension of the media. Early studies of the media's educational impact shared McLuhan's view of media, posing questions such as whether, for example, television was a more effective teaching tool than print, or whether either medium added to or subtracted from face-to-face education. In 1967, Chu & Schramm amassed the evidence of 300 publications indicating that television could be a useful educational tool, but only if it was used carefully in relation to specific goals and types of student.[81] Their conclusions stressed the:

1   need to integrate media presentation into face-to-face instruction;
2   use of straightforward production techniques rather than 'fanciness';
3   need to evaluate presentation effects on different kinds of student;

4   need to avoid techniques that might cause students to resist information; and
     the
5   importance of carefully considering the medium's viability in developing
     regions.

By the 1970s, media researchers had agreed with Chu and Schramm that a
subtler focus was needed.[82–84] McLuhan's simplified view was redressed in a 1974
analysis by Williams, which showed that broadcast TV effects are due to interactions
between messages, cultural formats, and the audience's subtle reactions to both;[85]
and researchers developed more complex questions about whether, for example,
medium X is more effective than medium Y for particular instructional techniques. Chu and Schramm's emphasis on the reactions of different types of student
was explicitly recognized in the late 1970s, when multi-way interactions involving
the differing responses of students were discussed as "aptitude-treatment
interactions",[86] and as the "interaction of media, cognition and learning."[87]

Thus, in the 1960s and 1970s the questions underlying educational media
research slowly caught up with those posed in other areas of communication
studies 40 years earlier, when the complex interaction effects of media were
explored in depth by Lashley and Watson, and in community-based practice by
Vertov. The academic literature relating to the new online educational media has
not yet evolved to either of these earlier levels. A 2009 theme edition of the
Learning Media & Technology journal, for example, contained seven articles about
the uses of social networking media in education. All referred to the potential of
the new media rather than to their actual usage to date by educators, and none
dealt with media effects as complex as the multi-way interactions studied in the
earlier educational TV literature. A predominant purpose of the 2009 articles was
to provide an exploratory description of the types of function that social media
such as *Facebook* might play in education. For their data, several of the authors
reported the uses to which students are putting these new tools—seeking guidance
from the students, in effect, as to approaches that might prove educationally useful.
The current state-of-the-art reflected by the articles was discreetly summarized
by the journal edition's editors:

> We hope that these papers provide ample food-for-thought, not least
> in highlighting some glaring gaps in the literature (and in) moving edu-
> cation research and commentary beyond speculation and supposition and
> towards sustained empirical consideration of contemporary educational
> technology use.[88]

At one level, the current exploratory level of questioning may seem to be an
indictment of educational media analysts' unfamiliarity with their new tools
and lack of awareness of the communication and cultural studies literature that
contains guidelines for current practice. Educational technology has grown into

an unwieldy field crossing many academic borders; and the thousand journals covered by *Educational Technology Abstracts* (used in the earlier analysis of research trends) are divided into numerous camps—communication studies, educational media, non-formal education, computer-assisted learning, North American-centric, European-centric, campus-based, distance education, etc. Citations of one academic cadre by others are inevitably limited. At another level, however, the current level of analysis is typical of the early onset of a new research cycle. It is impossible for researchers to ask detailed research questions about a medium before they have become familiar with its technical possibilities; and phenomenological analyses of the current new media are an appropriate place to start.

In order to increase their familiarity with the new mobile media, western educators can learn much from their developing world counterparts. To a traveler in Asia, the high level of familiarity with mobile phones in that region, compared with that of many North Americans, has been clear for a decade.

> The 'developed' and 'developing' worlds (of DE) are drawing nearer to one another with remarkable speed, and (western) scholars who take sabbatical leave in parts of the developing world are shocked to find that the facilities there are often superior to those of their own universities back home.[89]

Their facility with cellphones makes developing-world students a natural market for mobile courseware from western institutions, if western educators were to turn their attention to creating it. The impetus to develop educational uses of mobile media, however, is proving greater in Asian countries than in the west. As an institution in the "texting capital of the world",[90] the University of the Philippines Open University is currently several years ahead of western institutions in using the cellphone to provide course materials and information.[91-92] This regional difference is demonstrated by national cellphone usage statistics (Table 2.1), and appears due to one factor alone: the cost of cellphone usage. In North America, it costs as much as 15 to 30 cents to send a text message,[93] compared with an affordable peso (= 2 US cents) in the Philippines.[94] Even western

TABLE 2.1 Daily text messages per person (USA, Canada, and the Philippines).

	Population (millions)	Estimated daily SMS calls per person per day	Source
USA	304	11	Haveinternetwilltravel.com (Jan 2009)
Canada	33	1.4	Canada.com (July 2008)
The Philippines	96	20	Haveinternetwilltravel.com (Jan 2009)
		28	wayodd.com (July 2008)

Source: Author.

TABLE 2.2 Population usage of graphics-based cellphones (3G).

	Population (millions)	3G penetration	Source
Canada	33	25.3%	Betanews.com (June 2008)
USA	304	28.4%	Broadbandreports.com (Feb 2008)
Australia	21	60–70%	Reuters India (Feb 2008)
Indonesia	237	15% (highest in SE Asia)	International Telecommunication Union: www.itu.int (June 2008)
India	1.15 billion	0.018% (2010 prediction) 0.026% (2012 prediction)	Voice&Data.com (Feb 2007) Siliconindia.com (Nov 2008)

Source: Author.

researchers can find the cost of exploring the educational possibilities of cellphones by playing with them relatively prohibitive.

Cellphone users in North America exhibit lower usage rates than those of the developing world despite having more sophisticated cellphones (Table 2.2). The majority of subscribers in low-income developing nations uses 1st-generation text-based phones (1G), whereas users in Canada and the USA have moved to the graphics-based displays of higher-generation hardware. As the Table indicates, less than 0.03% of the Indian population is expected to have 3G cellphone access by 2012; and innovative 1G methods need to be developed if m-learning materials are to be created that will be globally shareable. Unfortunately, the research and development needed for this initiative is not a current focus. This incompatibility issue may recur with each new educational medium that comes along, hindering efforts to coordinate its global usage.

In addition to technological incompatibility, Latchem *et al.* have indicated a series of reasons that open and distance learning (ODL) initiatives in low-income nations tend to fail.[95] These include:

1   incorrect diagnosis of needs and circumstances;
2   inadequate needs analysis;
3   lack of informed champions;
4   lack of follow-through to strategic planning;
5   lack of evaluation and accountability;
6   inadequate costing, poor provision, and lack of collaboration;
7   shortcomings in introducing new technology; and
8   shortcomings in staff development.

These factors overlap markedly with the summary of reasons given by Blythe[96] for the instability of health education in 20th-century England (discussed earlier):

1 inappropriate strategies and application;
2 divisiveness within the health education movement;
3 unrealistic expectations;
4 low public, political and professional support; and
5 low and uncertain funding.

At the worst extremes of mismanagement, projects flounder, Blythe indicates, and traditions wane when "fundamental inhibitors act in what seems to be a vicious cycle to bring down (periodically and almost predictably) attempts at central leadership." Psychological reasons for such failures were summarized in a classic paper by Hyman and Sheatsley on "why information campaigns fail":[97]

1 there exists a hard core of chronic "know-nothings";
2 interested people acquire the most information;
3 people seek information congenial to prior attitudes;
4 people interpret the same information differently; and
5 information does not necessarily change attitudes.

Harmonizing these many factors in media education is difficult but not impossible, as is evident in the long-term educational and commercial success of at least one major initiative. The pre-school children's TV series *Sesame Street*,[98] currently celebrating 40 years of stable development since 1970, has broken the mould in numerous ways—in its observance of pedagogical theory, its appropriate use of fun, wit, and color, and its routine use of formative evaluation.[99–100] Commercial TV producers are not usually trained in an environment that gives them evaluation skills; but at an early stage in its history the producer of *Sesame Street*, the Children's TV Workshop (CTW), made it a condition of employment that its producers would be required to work with evaluators, and vice versa. Leading academic experts were gathered to guide this process. The CTW's advisory board was chaired by Harvard professor and child psychologist, Gerald Lesser;[101] and the vice-president of research was Keith Mielke, attracted to the position from a professorship of mass communication research at Indiana University. Combining academic rigor with artistic awareness, Mielke brought the CTW's producers and researchers together with kindergarten audiences in the evaluation of program rough-cuts at formative stages of *Sesame Street*'s development. From an early tendency to over-complexity, the show developed a simple, straightforward approach carefully tailored to the children's attention level and need to focus on one message at a time, together with a witty tendency to pitch its humorous content just slightly above their heads so as to keep them intrigued.

Perhaps the CTW's task was somehow easier than that of other educational media producers in history. After all, pre-school children don't argue about the political implications of the medium's message; and their parents and teachers have happily been entertained alongside their children as the witty Muppets of Jim Henson have delivered *Sesame Street*'s lessons about literacy, numeracy and social values.[102] The show could have run into problems in its attempts to deliver its material to different cultures, at home in the USA and globally; but it has avoided this for 40 years by conducting culturally-sensitive evaluation studies in many of the 20 countries in which it is broadcast.[103] The demise of educational TV in western universities and colleges in the 1990s might even have been avoided if their producers had applied the CTW's formative evaluation results and kept their production techniques simple and cost-effective. The *Sesame Street* research continues today in the show's 40th anniversary year. It represents a much-needed model in the global education field where sustained success is more the exception than the rule; and it exemplifies an analytical process worthy of wide-ranging application.

Summary

Theoretical and practical approaches are replaced in education at regular intervals. As communication approaches become successful, they tend to be opposed by those who disagree with the messages conveyed; and conflicting definitions of quality can lead to catastrophic events as in the case of the Luddite Revolt in the early 19th century. Clashes between the priorities of different interest groups obstruct the smooth evolution of communication technique; and theoretical positions and styles of research questioning emerge and re-emerge in response to prevailing circumstances. In global education, ideas can evolve in one geographical region while they are failing in others. New trendsetters can increase their momentum by heeding the principles developed in other regions and times.

3
WHY IS THE SKY BLUE?

Cubist Analysis

> To-day we have naming of parts. Yesterday,
> We had daily cleaning. And to-morrow morning,
> We shall have what to do after firing. But to-day,
> To-day we have naming of parts. Japonica
> Glistens like coral in all of the neighboring gardens,
> And to-day we have naming of parts.[1]

Reed's monologue mimics the tone of the military trainer as he strips a rifle into its components, and as his mind wanders wistfully elsewhere. The activity reflects the efforts of communication researchers to analyze media images and techniques in seeking to explain their effects. In 1910, a striking example of this approach was created by Pablo Picasso and Georges Braque in developing the new art movement, 'analytical cubism'.[2] Their work fragmented the 3-dimensional image into cubes, squares, rectangles, and curvilinear shapes, enabling objects to be represented 2-dimensionally from multiple viewpoints and angles. The inspection of an object by moving around it in time was now converted into an inspection of its separate elements simultaneously. The premise is illustrated by Picasso's *Girl with a Mandolin* (1910), whose head is tilted to show her right profile while her body is seen from the front.[3] The colors of the image are muted to avoid suggesting visual depth, and perspective is further minimized by the fusion of foreground and background elements on a single 2-dimensional plane. By artfully separating time and space in this way, Picasso and Braque demonstrated that in perceptual contexts neither of these dimensions can be interpreted in the absence of the other.

Simultaneously, Albert Einstein was drawing very similar conclusions in his evolving theory of relativity. In the special theory of relativity (1905), Einstein demonstrated that the physics of space and time cannot be explained in isolation from one another, and need to be examined simultaneously via the concept of *space-time*.[4] As in analytical cubism, he created the means to inspect the two dimensions in a single activity. In 1910, Einstein demonstrated how light is diffused in the atmosphere to answer the question "Why is the sky blue?" The analysis of cyclic wavelengths, he indicated, leads to a synthesis that explains the sky's hues in different conditions. The parallel between Einstein's and Picasso's ideas has been analyzed in good detail over the years,[5–6] and was also clear to the observers of the day. Apollinaire indicated (1913) that, by charting the simultaneous contrasts between objects in space and time, Picasso had created the same fourth dimension in art that Einstein had identified in physics.[7] Arthur I. Miller has argued that the simultaneous development of these principles in cubism and physics derived from a growing realization throughout the arts and sciences that reality cannot be understood by the senses alone. So Virginia Woolf's comment, discussed above— that 1910 or thereabouts was the moment at which "human character changed"— may refer to more than her views about the representation of reality in literature.

In 1911, Picasso completed the analysis of art form to his satisfaction and, in the period since labelled *synthetic cubism*, began to combine its elements in new ways. During the following decade, similar analyses and syntheses were being conducted in Soviet cinema. The pioneering influence of Dziga Vertov was matched by that of one of his fellow film directors, Lev Kuleshov. As a teenager studying film editing, Kuleshov observed that actors were perceived differently on the basis of the shots with which their images were juxtaposed. The 'Kuleshov effect' established montage techniques as a central feature of pre-WWII Soviet cinema, influencing film makers and theorists including Eisenstein[8] and Pudovkin.[9] In the 1950s and 1960s, aesthetic factors affecting the perception and interpretation of visual images were analyzed theoretically by Arnheim,[10] and in relation to TV images by Zettl.[11] Meanwhile, researchers analyzed the educational TV image into component parts with varying effects on learning, as summarized by Baggaley[12] and Coldevin[13] (Table 3.1). In the current chapter, the potential of analytic research of this type is indicated for the field of online education.

The analysis of media presentation techniques is a research field deriving from educational and social psychology, in which learning has been shown to be affected by perceptual, attitudinal, verbal, and nonverbal factors. The areas of media research in which such analysis is useful were discussed by McGuire.[14] Media effectiveness is a myth, McGuire suggested, created by researchers' motivation to conclude that, for example, media advertising is more powerful than the evidence may show. In fairness to researchers, McGuire pointed out that genuine media effects may be masked by 'clutter': communication variables with conflicting simultaneous effects that an analysis may not detect owing to the "mutual cancellation of conflicting messages." Broadcasters and academics have considered that possibility in hundreds of effects analyses relating to media production techniques since the 1960s. At the Swedish Broadcasting Corporation, for example, Findahl & Höijer varied the presentation of TV news formats (e.g., with versus

TABLE 3.1 TV production variable research categories.

Shepherd (1967)[15]	Zettl (1968)[16]		Anderson (1972)[17]		Schramm (1972)[18]
Camera factors	**Lighting**	External (studio)	**Visualization**	Graphics	Picture
Lighting		Internal (camera)		Sets	Sound
Setting	**Space**	Aspect ratio		Lighting	Picture-sound relationships
Graphics designs		Staging axis	**Camera and transitional factors**	Movements	Simplicity/complexity of treatment
Audio factors	**Time & Motion**	Pacing		Composition	Teacher
Performer variables		Tempo		Animation	Teaching strategies
Open/closing format		Rhythm		Special effects	
		Sound		Colour	

Source: Coldevin, 1976.

without newscaster; different types of background image), and observed that viewers' retention of information varied as a result.[19]

Numerous studies of this type illustrated subtle and often conflicting effects of image variation. Millerson, for example, suggested that learning is likely to be more efficient when information is presented on the right rather than the left side of the TV screen, owing to left-brain/right-brain asymmetry.[20] When Metallinos & Tiemens varied the placement of information on different sides of the TV screen, however, they found the opposite effect.[21] Similarly, Naftulin and colleagues recorded an actor portraying a fictitious lecturer, named 'Doctor Fox', in a charismatic presentation of meaningless information that 'seduced' audiences into giving his lecture high ratings.[22] The 'Doctor Fox effect' prompted a series of studies comparing effects of expressiveness and content variation (high vs. low levels of each) on audience ratings and achievement measures and in relation to variables including student personality and grading standards. A meta-analysis of these studies indicated that viewers' ratings and achievement levels could not be reliably related to specific variables, and were "the net result of dozens, perhaps hundreds, of causal processes."[23] Some of these processes may have related to performance style and content, while others may have been caused by TV techniques used in the studies. Wurtzel & Dominick conducted a study that indicated this 'clutter' interaction, comparing audience reactions to a TV play using contrasting acting styles (low-key vs. theatrical) and camera shots (medium vs. close-up).[24] The close-up shot elicited more positive audience reactions when the low-key presentation style was used, while the longer shot was more appealing for mediating the expansive theatrical style. These studies illustrate the major difficulty of isolating individual presentation elements to the exclusion of extraneous factors.

In 1976, Bates performed a useful service to educational media researchers by bringing together international specialists for an extended conference at the UK Open University.[25] The papers presented covered practical issues of media production as well as the evaluation and decision-making processes by which they are applied. A memorable moment in the conference helped to inspire the theme of the current book: the tendency for ideas to repeat, apparently *ad infinitum*, with cyclic regularity. In his closing address, UNESCO's Director-General of Methods, Materials & Techniques, Henri Dieuzeide concluded that media researchers and producers should work together more closely on overcoming the obstacles to collaborative research between different cultures. He then noted that the same conclusion had been drawn at an European Union conference a decade earlier, since when little advance had been made.[26] Thanks to the cyclic waxing and waning of educational media themes, these conclusions apply as much in the early years of the 21st-century as they did in the 1960s and 1970s.

Many media researchers of that time remained in the field to make extensive contributions to the theory and practice of media presentation over three or more decades. Wurtzel's textbook on TV production was reissued four times in the 1980s and 1990s;[27] and Millerson's book remains influential 40 years on, currently in its 14th edition. Bates has continued to focus on the selection of appropriate educational media, and has placed consistent emphasis on the importance of evaluation in the design of open and distance education.[28-30] Baggaley & Duck have examined the theoretical and practical bases for the effects of TV formats on learning;[31] and Baggaley presented the results of 30 Kuleshov-type experiments in which camera techniques, edited sequence, types of reaction shot, studio formats, performance style, and soundtrack were varied in TV news contexts.[32] Baggaley's studies used attitude measures based on the 7-point 'semantic differential' scale of Osgood and colleagues.[33] Factor analyses of the attitude ratings[34] indicated that viewers assess televised information on the basis of distinctive professional and personal attributes (Figure 3.1): the presenter(s)' apparent *mastery* of the content, *integrity*, *empathy* and *poise*. The analyses indicated that viewers apply these criteria selectively in specific situations. Personal mastery of the subject-matter is not viewed as essential in a TV newscaster, for example, although poise is regarded as important; mastery and integrity are high priorities for presenters claiming to be subject-matter experts; and warmth of presentation (empathy) is helpful in general communication contexts, depending on the nature of the message being conveyed. Certain attitude scales (e.g., expert/inexpert, fair/unfair) correlate highly with more than one factor, while others are unique to specific factors.

These studies indicate that message recipients feel an urgent need to assess the credibility of information and those who present it, and will grasp at even tenuous visual and aural clues to believability in the absence of the concrete evidence they

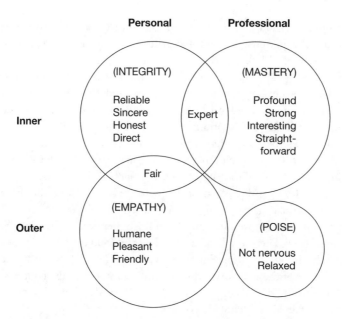

FIGURE 3.1   Four types of attitude to content presentation.

Source: Baggaley, 1980.

would receive in face-to-face communication. The factor analyses demonstrate the sophisticated basis of viewers' assessments on criteria corresponding closely to four attitude factors identified by Osgood in his original uses of the semantic differential technique:

1   a "morally evaluative" factor (*Integrity*);
2   an "aesthetically evaluative" factor (*Empathy*);
3   a factor described by Osgood as relating to 'strength' (*Mastery*); and
4   an "emotionally evaluative" factor relating to relaxedness (*Poise*).

After the 1980s, the analytical phase of educational TV research slowed down apace with the general waning of interest in the medium at that time. A 20-year phase beginning in the 1960s had run its course, and a new era evolved during which interactive video and online formats attracted interest. Lessons learned from the earlier phase were applied in overseas development contexts: for example, by Alfian & Chu in an analysis of television's impact in Indonesia,[35] and by Baggaley, Duby & Lewy in the design and evaluation of educational broadcasting techniques in South Africa.[36] A meta-analysis of TV aesthetics was conducted by Metallinos, examining the medium's compositional variables in relation to perceptual, cognitive, and neurological principles.[37] The US literature began to question whether the media have any identifiable effects at all, as in McGuire's discussion of media 'clutter'; and Clark suggested that the media add no value to the educational experience beyond that generated by its users.[38] A much-quoted discussion between Clark and Kozma[39] ended in general agreement that the inherent features of specific media can assist the learning of particular types of student. The debate did nothing to advance understanding of the media's educational impact to a new level, however, and may even have contributed to the loss of momentum felt in educational media research at that time.

By contrast, Herbert Zettl has advanced and enlivened the understanding of media effects for a remarkable 50 years since his first study of TV production design in 1961. Zettl's *Television Production Handbook* is currently in its 11th edition.[40] It updates his discussion of the "screen forces" that guide the eye and brain through visual images, as the cubists analyzed the perception of form in space and time; and it examines the 2- and 3-dimensional fields in which the images are situated. The variable of time and motion, and five elements of musical sound (pitch, timbre, duration, loudness, and attack-decay) are examined. The aesthetic impact of these factors is discussed in traditional media contexts as well as in relation to the digital media of the 21st century. Zettl's work represents the field's most sustained and scholarly content.

The current *fin de siècle* period of educational media research has run for 20 years from the 1990s to the present day, and the educational potential of new online media is now under study.[41] Verleur has marked this new era with a call for renewed attention to the lessons of 1970s and 1980s TV research, and has drawn gracious attention to the relatively unusual empirical approach of Baggaley & Duck.[42] In a series of studies from 2006–10, Verleur has shown that variables such as camera height, focal length, and presenter characteristics have the same kinds of effect on credibility, problem solving and learning activities online as in previous educational TV contexts, and that the designers of web-based education need to revisit the classic ETV literature for guidance in producing efficient presentations.[43–44] Verleur and her colleagues are examining the persuasive effects of new technologies such as 3D graphics and the design of cartoon personae ('avatars') in 3D environments,[45–46] and are placing much-needed emphasis on the need to deal with the effects of the offensive online comments known as 'flaming'.[47] They are emulating the researchers of the 1970s in their studies of online delivery, just as the latter re-examined questions raised by Pudovkin and Kuleshov about film design in the 1920s. Thus, the recycling of analytical approaches remains constant to this day, necessitated by the need to check whether old findings still apply in the context of new media.

Cubist Synthesis

The difficulty of isolating its elements is a major problem of analytic studies of communication technique. In research cultures dominated by the standard *hypothetico-deductive* approach,[48] the practice is to form a general hypothesis and to isolate specific variables by testing it. To determine the significance of these variables effects, complex multivariate statistical methods are often employed. These methods may generate meaningful results in the academic laboratory context, but can be quite beyond the scope of, for example, audience researchers in the hectic broadcasting industry. In real-life situations with a constantly shifting clutter of interrelated variables, hypothetico-deductive conclusions may also be too specific and with limited generalizability. The alternative is the *inductive* approach, by which specific observations are amassed for the purpose of drawing general conclusions. Once the deductive approach has succeeded in identifying the component parts of a phenomenon and has laid them on the table for inspection, an inductive approach is the next logical step to understanding how they relate to each other in real life.

The development of educational TV research in the 1970s and 1980s followed this route from deductive to inductive in a manner directly comparable with the shift from analytical to synthetic cubism (1910–12). Once they had isolated sufficient visual elements to demonstrate that spatial form needs to be analyzed in isolation from 3-dimensional perspective, Picasso and Braque began to combine abstract shapes and colors with real-world imagery, creating collages that allow the viewer to explore 2- and 3-dimensional forms simultaneously. This restored the concept of time to the process, and recognized that in the real world it takes time for the viewer to explore 3-dimensional objects by moving around them. In *Still Life with Chair Caning* (1912), Picasso combined 2D geometric shapes with 3D representations of cane for a deeper understanding of numerous elements simultaneously.[49] The approaches of 'synthetic cubism' allowed artists to represent different elemental combinations in this way, rather than limiting them to studies of individual variables in isolation, just as in subsequent media research.

Thus, communication effects in numerous media are defined by the unpredictable combinations of technique over time. Researchers have addressed this complication with the help of techniques for time-based recording and analysis of audience reactions. A classic use of time-based measurement was reported by Carl Jung (1910) in a lecture at Clark University, Massachusetts. Jung had used a complex piece of laboratory equipment to measure the speed of psychoanalytic patients' responses to his word association test. His writings tend to give the impression that Jung designed this equipment himself,[50] but the same type of hardware was popular with numerous experimental psychologists at that time, and was known as the 'Meumann-style ergograph' (Figure 3.2) after one of its users Ernst Meumann.[51] [Currently, the origins of this invention are clouded even further by a *Wikipedia* item, which suggests that the term 'ergograph' was coined much later for time-based studies by University of Edinburgh geographers.[52] This fails to point out that the Edinburgh usage of the term referred to a way of graphing data rather than to the data collection equipment itself.]

This polygraph-type method led Jung to identify differences in response time with particular psychoanalytic conditions. Figure 3.3 examines a pattern of

FIGURE 3.2 The Meumann-style ergograph.

Source: Zimmermann, 1903.[53]

reaction times measured in seconds (vertical axis) relating to a series of words (horizontal axis). Jung identified this particular profile as typical of patients with symptoms of hysteria. The tall grey bars on the diagram indicate words to which hysteria sufferers did not respond at all. Jung was frank in recognizing that numerous other factors may affect verbal implications and inferences. Unconsciously, he even betrayed this in his own wordings, selected according to the political incorrectness of his day: e.g., the diagnosis in his Clark University lecture that a particular type of response "is chiefly found in stupid persons . . . But it can also be found in persons who are not really stupid, but who do not wish to be taken as stupid."

Thus, 1910 marked the development of time-based approaches in perceptual and psychological research by Carl Jung and the synthetic cubists simultaneously. From the 1930s onwards, time-based research methods were adopted in the broadcasting industry, as recorded by Millard.[54] At that time, Paul Lazarsfeld, later to become Chair of Sociology at Columbia University, developed a way of recording his moment-by-moment reactions to music on the separate pages of a calendar turned to the beat of a metronome. He developed this 'continuous response measurement' (CRM) method in conjunction with Frank Stanton, later President of Columbia Broadcasting System (CBS), who had devised a polygraph-type instrument to record the moment-by-moment responses of radio listeners.[55] The Lazarsfeld–Stanton Program Analyzer was harnessed in CBS' audience

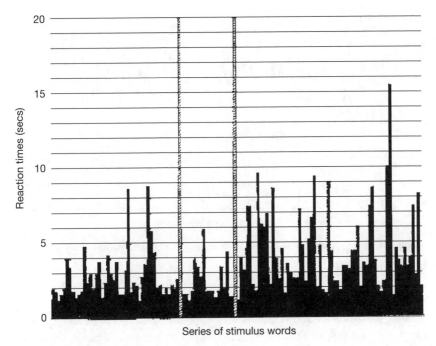

FIGURE 3.3   Word association speeds (seconds) observed in hysteria patients.

Source: Jung, 1910.

research in 1940, and was used in the company's radio and TV research for the next 50 years. Known as 'Big Annie', the hardware had a simple 2-button mechanism allowing audience members to express a binary response (e.g., like or dislike) to media presentations by depressing one button or the other over time. The frequencies of the two responses from minute to minute were compared with the recorded presentations to determine the events that coincided with response changes. Figure 3.4 plots the frequencies of push-button responses by 59 CBS radio listeners to a current affairs program

Versions of the Program Analyzer evolved rapidly in the advertising industry. In the 1950s, McCann-Erickson Inc. compared the reliability of two- and three-button time-based responses, and improved the methodology by the use of forced-choice scales. Since then, numerous analyzers using buttons, dials, and levers have been developed, whose total number is impossible to gauge owing to the protection of many of them as trade secrets in broadcasting, advertising, and political research. In the late 1970s, however, this state of secrecy changed through a collaboration between the Children's TV Workshop and the Ontario Educational Communications Authority (TV Ontario). In both of these studios, formative evaluation was central to the educational production processes. Seeking precise second-by-second measures of viewers' response, the studios' heads of audience

Number of responses

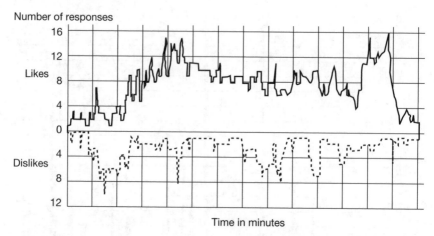

FIGURE 3.4   Continuous response measurement by the Lazarsfeld–Stanton analyzer.

Source: Peterman, 1940.

research, Keith Mielke and Rand Nickerson, collaborated on the development of a keypad-based CRM system using the first portable microcomputer, the Apple II. The Program Evaluation Analysis Computer (PEAC system) was introduced to academic researchers at the Association for Educational Communications & Technology conference in 1979, and removed the CRM approach from behind the closed doors of commercial research. In emigrating to Canada in the same year, the current writer began to use the PEAC system to extend his previous research into TV production techniques.

During the 1980s, Baggaley used the PEAC system in dozens of studies of news and current affairs productions, with a particular interest in the analysis of the TV political debates accompanying national election campaigns.[56] A particular feature of these studies was the rapid (though not simultaneous) analysis and feedback of CRM results in national media reports, in the manner of a 'blow-by-blow' boxing commentary. Examining audience reactions to real-life combinations of elements in this way enables researchers and media producers to identify the effects of presentation variables over time just as synthetic cubist principles allowed artists to inspect space-time combinations. Once the elements of presentation technique have been isolated and recombined, a new level of analysis becomes possible. Patterns of response can be compared with the moment-by-moment presentation of events, and response profiles established for different audience sub-groups, as in Jung's study (Figure 3.3)—an approach that overcomes the clutter problem described by McGuire as "the mutual cancellation of conflicting messages." CRM data collection tasks have also been shown responsible for invalid and unreliable results, however, and the profiles they generate need careful justification.[57–58]

In the late 1980s and 1990s, the writer developed his own CRM system featuring instantaneous collection, analysis and graphical feedback of second-by-second responses. The CRM displays were instantly superimposed on a video recording of the media presentation in animated graphs comparing the responses of different demographic and psychographic groups. This permitted producers and TV viewers to identify statistically significant shifts in the responses of audience sub-groups within seconds of the on-screen event that had stimulated them. The shifts were statistically compared with pre- and post-test measures of prejudice, overall attitude shifts, and learning gain, and indicated the moments in a presentation at which a particular overall effect occurred. The system included touch-tone (DTMF) telephone facilities for CRM data collection. In studies for the US Centers for Disease Control (CDC), second-by-second reactions were collected from up to 250 persons simultaneously, viewing TV health education broadcasts in their homes across North America from Atlantic to Pacific. The real-time analysis was fed back instantaneously to the producers during the program's live transmission, generating ideas for revising the presentations for later use. An online interface was launched in a study of the Canadian federal election debates in 2000, and since adapted for the cellphone (Figures 3.5 and 3.6).[59]

The use of this CRM system in educational media design is illustrated by a comparison of responses given by three audience sub-groups to a public information video about HIV-AIDS (Figure 3.7). While two of the groups varied little in their positive responses to the video over time, individuals in the third group reacted to it negatively at particular moments. The characteristics of this group that set it apart it from the other audience members were their age (18–35 years) and high-risk sexual activity. The moments at which they responded negatively coincided with specific statements, images or presenters in the video, and confirmed the classic conclusions by Hyman & Sheatsley that "people seek

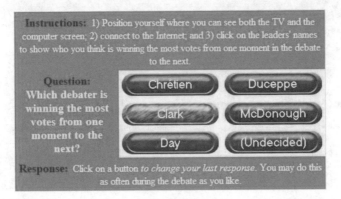

FIGURE 3.5 Web-based CRM interface.

Source: Baggaley, 1985.

FIGURE 3.6   Cellphone CRM interface.

Source: Baggaley, 1985.

information congenial to prior attitudes",[60] and by Krech *et al.* that people with attitudes opposed to the message conveyed will resist it to the point of being "driven still further away from the position advocated by the propagandist."[61] Resistance by audience sub-groups at specific moments of media presentation has

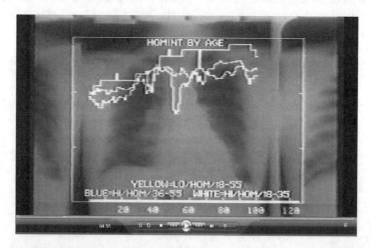

FIGURE 3.7   CRM responses of audience sub-groups to a video about HIV-AIDS.

Source: Author.

been a common finding of these studies, and is typically related to hostility to political or health campaign messages that recommend a change in attitude and behavior.[62]

The major benefit of such feedback for educators is to suggest, at the pilot stage of a production, the need for modifications that may have been quite unpredictable beforehand. Producers are never apt to accept an idea for changing their programs if they do not believe that it makes sense; but they readily recognize the good sense of subtle program revisions that they did not foresee. Figure 3.8a shows the average ratings of 128 urban and rural viewers to the pilot version of a film about the causes of skin cancer. The film's director used the positive and negative responses to the film to make some simple and ingenious revisions to its edited sequence. Figure 3.8b shows the average ratings of a follow-up sample of 194 viewers, drawn from the same urban and rural populations, after the modifications had been made. Comparison of the two graphs shows how the simple editing revisions reduced the negative CRM responses of high-risk viewers to the film—a result associated with significantly enhanced pre- to post-test attitude shifts and learning gain.

A particular benefit of these time-based methods is the anonymous and nonverbal nature of responses made possible by the data collection gadgetry. In studies of responses to sensitive topics such as HIV-AIDS, the fact that the audience members know that their responses are traceable to a hand-unit number rather than to themselves personally can encourage them to give frank and self-disclosing responses. For example, a study of responses to *Not a Love Story*, a National Film Board of Canada film about pornography, concluded that the film

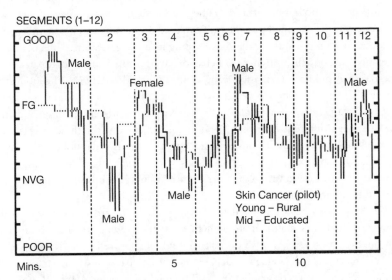

FIGURE 3.8a CRM responses to a health education video (pilot version).

Source: Baggaley, 1986.

SEGMENTS (1–13)

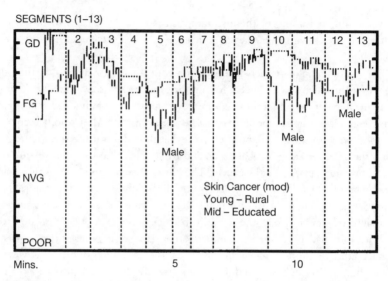

FIGURE 3.8b CRM responses to a health education video (modified version).

Source: Baggaley, 1986.

increased university students' hostility to the effects of pornography in society.[63] Students whose post-test responses revealed this also tended to react negatively at sexually explicit moments in the film, apparently offended by them. From other viewers, however, the same moments drew positive responses, and pre-post shifts towards pro-pornographic attitudes. These unpredicted effects suggest that even the most well-intentioned presentation can contain fleeting moments interpreted by some viewers as justifying them in resisting its messages. Similar effects, linking resistant attitudes and high-risk behavior, were noted in a comparison of international public information campaigns about HIV-AIDS.[64] The nonverbal aspect of the CRM response task has also helped to obtain data from low-literacy individuals, and in cross-cultural contexts where the researchers and their audience samples speak different languages.[65] The complex reasons for these effects were represented on three dimensions by Heider as "the variable manifold of mediating events",[66] and are expressed in terms of CRM data in Figure 3.9. (The 3D cubic representation of these variables in the Figure has no relationship with the use of the 'cubist' concept in art.)

CRM systems have remained in media research use from the 1990s to the present, though still maintain an element of secrecy owing to their commercial and political uses. They receive occasional public exposure in the live analyses of viewers' reactions to TV election debates. Political debates in Australia, for example, are frequently accompanied by a moment-by-moment graph of audience

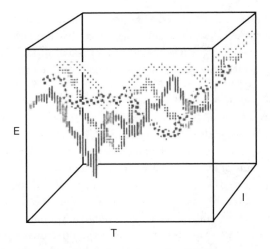

FIGURE 3.9   Interacting dimensions of audience response.

Key: E = Intensity of the effect (cognitive, affective, or behavioral)
    T = Fluctuations of effect across time
    I = Individual differences in responses by audience sub-groups
Source: Baggaley, 1986.

responses, known to the public as the "white worm." Current 'wormology' in that country, owing to its inadequate methodology, has been criticized for its lack of ability as a "barometer of electoral success."[67] Failure to use reliable audience sampling methods, and to isolate the responses of different audience sub-groups, remain common problems in CRM analyses, generating flat-line moment-by-moment graphs of the cluttered responses of audience sub-groups. An observer of the real-time CRM analysis accompanying the 2008 Obama-McCain TV debate on the CNN network jested that flat-line graphs "spell death for hospital patient" and made her watch the debate anxiously for signs of life![68] In introducing such studies, on-air presenters typically stress that they are "not scientific" but may yield some interesting indications nonetheless. Considering that numerous researchers have raised the standards of CRM methods to a high level over the years, it is unfortunate that such publicity can give this powerful technique an unscientific reputation. It is also irresponsible to use a technique unreliably in public, risking unjustified effects on important issues.

Cubism Online

Despite its precision and numerous applications, CRM has never become a mainstream method in educational research. This is due in part to the high costs of the hardware and software, to the relatively sophisticated technical ability required for their operation, and to the low-level reputation given to the technique by flawed public uses. The online information era has the potential to remove these hurdles. Web-site usage is automatically recorded in log files on the web server, yielding detailed second-by-second information about individual users' site activity. These data show the visitors' web-page 'hits', the dates and times at which these occurred, and the location of the computers from which the hits came. In educational research, this information can be used to analyze the precise patterns of course materials usage, the efficiency of web-site designs and course delivery methods, and levels of teacher-student interaction. Many online learning management systems provide log-file summaries for teachers and administrators, although more precise data are usually to be found in the raw log files. These rich sources of information are superior to the partial, often subjective data yielded by face-to-face interaction, and can generate insights into traditional teaching and learning processes. They enable researchers to ask multi-dimensional questions of the type posed by the cubist movement in art; and the greater use of such techniques in educational research is to be encouraged.

In the online log files, each web-page hit is recorded in a line of text-based code containing the following information. For example:

1   *IP Address*: the electronic address of the user making the server request. The address comprises four numbers ranging from 0 to 255, each separated by a dot (e.g., 146.23.12.200). At the time of the web request, the IP address is unique to the user making it, and is shared by no other internet-based user.

2   *Date and Time*: each web request generates a record of the time that the request was made, based on the local time on the server. This does not indicate the local time of the user, for the server does not usually identify the time-zone difference between the user and the time at the server's location.

3   *URL* (Uniform Resource Locator) of the web object: this indicates the unique internet address of the web page or object displayed within it (e.g., a graphic) that is being requested.

4   *URL* of the referring page: when the user accesses page X on a web site via a link on page Y, the latter is listed in the log record of page X as the 'referral page'. This information indicates the different routes by which users access the web site and its pages.

5   *User Time*: the amount of time taken by a user to complete a web request (e.g., individual web page). This information can be used to track the responsiveness of the web site and of its individual objects (pages, graphics, etc.).

6   *User Agent*: this information indicates the type and version of web browser used to access the web page. It allows a site designer to anticipate the strengths and weaknesses of the browsers in current use.

In addition to these basic facts about web-page hits, server log files record technical information used by marketing specialists to identify the usage patterns and preferences of different demographic groups, and by web administrators to anticipate problems of internet traffic congestion. Although educational and social-science researchers are becoming increasingly aware of these 'data-mining' and 'web-analytic' techniques,[69] they may have no access to their institutions' server log files for security reasons. The value of collaboration between server administrators and academics in designing convenient and secure procedures for accessing these data is illustrated by the following studies.

In 2000, the Centre for Distance Education (CDE) at Athabasca University in Canada began collating the server log files of its departmental web site. During the following four years, approximately 10 million log entries provided more than enough data for a lifetime of research. The following basic information was derived from an analysis for the 4-month period, 1 January to 30 April 2002.[70-71]

a. The 121-day period yielded 2,796,060 requests for individual web-site objects (i.e., pages, graphics, etc.). These were made by 23,206 unique computers or 'visitors', during a total of 79,257 individual user sessions. An hourly average of 8.06 individual visitors viewed a total of 4,173.48 megabytes of information over the period. These conclusions were based on the users' unique IP addresses.

b. During the same period, a total of 905,242 pages was viewed or re-viewed, as isolated displays or in the separate 'frames' of a composite display. A page is defined as a file containing an .htm or other internet extension (e.g., .html, .asp, .pdf, .jpg). A typical web-site display using frames consists of two or more sub-pages, each represented by an individual request in the server log files. Most log-file analysis packages list the pages in order of the frequency of their access by users.

c. The majority of the CDE site's requests came from Canada, the US, Britain, and Japan, in that order.

d. The most common session duration was 60+ seconds. Most users (73%) visited the site once only. The balance of users (primarily composed of the CDE's students) frequented the site 50–99 times during the 121-day period.

e. The day associated with the most page hits across the period was Monday, and the most common access time was 11:00–11:59 am. The total site traffic utilized approximately 4.26% of a 64 kbps internet connection.

f. The most frequent route by which users reached the site's pages was by typing its URL directly into their web browser. The most common search engine used to find the CDE site was *Google*. The search term most frequently used to arrive at the site was "Athabasca University."

g. The most popular web browser used was internet Explorer v6.0. The most common operating system was Windows 98.

h. Specific navigation paths between web-site pages were identified, indicating numerous ways in which the site could be made more efficient by simplifying its internal design. Figure 3.10 shows the number of times each page was visited from the point at which the visitors entered the site (left-hand of the Figure) and the routes they took between pages. This analysis indicated the need to highlight more direct routes to important areas of the site, and to draw attention to pages rarely found.

An extended analysis of the CDE's log-file data for 2000–03 revealed similar month-by-month usage patterns from one year to the next, and increasing annual usage (Figure 3.11).

The CDE log-file data also yielded detailed information about social interaction patterns, a prominent focus in traditional social-science research. Moreno (1951) devised the 'sociogram' as a way of depicting the patterns of interaction between members of social groups, and the 'isolates' who interact little with others, or not at all.[72] Figure 3.12 contains a sociogram of interaction patterns yielded by the CDE log files of a 13-week asynchronous text conference. The teacher-moderator (participant # 1) is shown at the centre of the discussion, engaged with questioning and comments by 8 of the 11 students. Participant #12 posted contributions generating replies from 4 people, and replied to 2 of them. Participant #4 was an

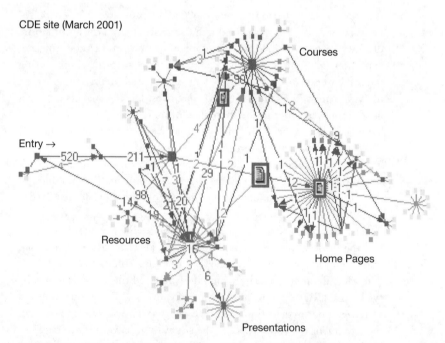

FIGURE 3.10 Web site navigation routes and page-hit frequencies.

Source: Baggaley & Ludwig, 2003.

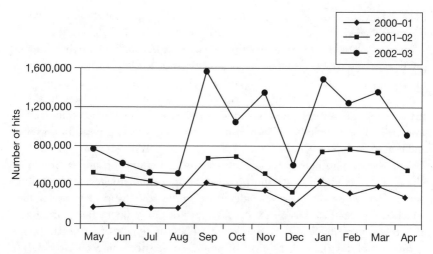

FIGURE 3.11   Quarterly visits to a departmental web site.

Source: Baggaley & Ludwig, 2003.

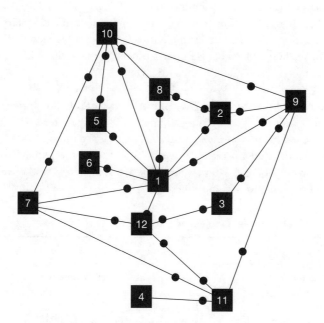

FIGURE 3.12   Sociogram of an online text-conference.

Key: A black dot adjacent to a participant indicates one or more replies
to that participant.
Source: Author.

isolate, replying to one person's posting(s), and making no contribution to which others replied.

In the 1960s, Flanders' Interaction Analysis (FIA) defined teacher-student interaction of this type into ten categories: 3 types of 'teacher talk' (direct), 4 types of 'teacher-talk' (indirect), and 3 types of 'student talk' including a category for 'student silence or confusion'.[73] A paper-and-pencil method was developed so that classroom observers could record the occurrence of each type of interaction over time. This notation task proved daunting over extended periods, however, and required a high level of practice. Video recordings were easier to analyze than real-time classroom behavior, but omitted untold amounts of information. As a result, FIA enjoyed a relatively short period of popularity in the research literature, despite its promise. Online text-conferences, on the other hand, generate log files which the researcher can use to identify types of group interaction during and after the event. Fahy *et al.* have developed a Flanders-style system, the Transcript Analysis Tool, for the classification of online conference content (Table 3.2).[74] These researchers indicated the relative rarity of questioning in the conferences they examined, and the absence of crucial information about online participants' intentions and motives which would enable other participants in face-to-face discussions to design their contributions more efficiently.

Server log files and conference transcripts provide complementary data in online interaction analysis. For example, the CDE log files recorded students' activities in reading and replying to each others' messages in a 13-week asynchronous conference attended by 18 participants:

- the teacher-moderator and 17 students made a total of 856 postings;
- the moderator made 196 postings (23% of the total); he read or re-read 546 postings; and his postings were read or re-read 1,376 times;
- the individual students made between 15 and 65 postings; they read or re-read between 214 and 540 postings, and each student was read or re-read by others between 130 and 458 times.

TABLE 3.2 Types of contribution to online text-conferences.

Primary Categories	Secondary Categories
T1 – Questioning	T1a – vertical (correct answer assumed)
	T1b – horizontal (correct answer not assumed)
T2 – Statements	T2a – direct
	T2b – answers or comments
T3 – Reflections	
T4 – Scaffolding	
T5 – References, authorities	T5a – references, quotations, paraphrases
	T5b – citations or attributions

Source: Fahy *et al.* (2001).

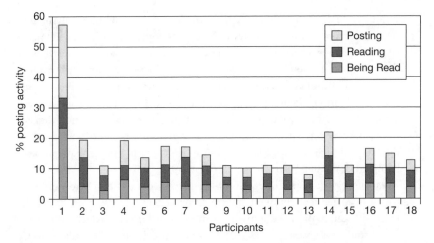

FIGURE 3.13   Activity by an online conference moderator (#1) and 17 students.

Source: Author.

Figure 3.13 shows that students tended to read the postings of the teacher-moderator (person #1 on the horizontal axis) more frequently than those of other students (#2–#18). Particular students contributed more than others. For example, #4 and #14 made more postings and were read more frequently than others. The data also reveal the extent to which individual students (e.g., #2 and #7) 'lurked' in the conferences, reading postings but making relatively few postings. Conversely, it was evident that student #9 made a moderate number of postings but read very few—a 'coping strategy' giving the impression that the student was active in the forum despite paying little attention to its content.

Such analyses provide valuable insights into the process of online education, and can be a useful formative evaluation activity during a course, allowing the teacher to identify students' problems with the course materials and discussion, and to address them at the group or individual level. The precision of online CRM data is simply not available in traditional classroom-based research. Server log files have been used in the analysis of online health promotion[75] in the same way as they were used in CRM studies of traditional media health campaigns. Researchers need to guard against the limitations of server log data, however, in order to avoid misleading conclusions. For example:

1   *Framed displays.* As noted above, a web page can include numerous actual web objects. A display using frames, for example, includes multiple sub-pages, each yielding its own separate web request. In the CDE web site, frames were used to create a consistent appearance between displays; and a visit to a single framed display could generate as many as four simultaneous page hits. Certain pages were common to many framed displays, and for that reason yielded

unusually high request totals capable of distorting conclusions about web traffic effects over time. An analysis of the most popular displays in a site needs to exclude such pages. When the pages common to framed displays were filtered out of the CDE analysis, only 1,256,893 meaningful requests remained (44% of the original total for the 4-month period). This revised total gave a more accurate reflection of the actual number of page requests during the usage period. The 'hypertext preprocessor' scripting language (.php) used in current web page creation overcomes the problems of framed displays, although reduces data reliability by generating pages that appear to be new but contain material presented on other pages.

2   *Auto-refreshing displays.* The results of log-file analysis can also be distorted by pages that the web browser automatically checks ('refreshes') at regular intervals against the page housed on the server. An early conclusion of the CDE study, for example, was that Monday was the most 'popular' day for users to access the site. It was realized, however, that one of the CDE's online courses was using an audio conferencing program on Monday evenings. The instructor had created a 'chat room' on an external server, containing a link to a banner display on the CDE site that refreshed itself every 15 seconds. The constant hits by every student's computer on this display exaggerated the number of page hits observed on Mondays in comparison with other days. When the hits on the banner display were filtered out of the analysis, Monday was still the most popular day for site visits, but the frequency of page hits was reduced by over 50%.

3   *Cached displays.* Many web users use default settings in their browsers which store each web page visited in their computers' 'cache' memory. Each time the user requests a page visited previously, the computer saves time by displaying its stored version rather than re-visiting it on the server; and the server log files fail to display this repeated hit. Failure to take account of cache hits makes many useful research questions impossible (regarding page popularity, user navigation patterns, etc.). In the CDE analysis, cache hits as well as direct page hits were investigated by: 1) configuring users' browsers to recover each page from the server every time it is visited; and 2) inserting a line of code in the web pages, preventing them from being stored in the cache memory of the users' computers. This information is useful in its own right as an index of repeat visits to a page in a single session. Ultimately, however, it is impossible to control the browser settings of the vast, unknown audience of public web sites such as the CDE site examined in the current study; and the addition of 'no-cache' code lines to pages can cause unacceptable delays in download time.

4   *Dynamic IP addresses.* The total of 'unique visitors' to a web site calculated by analysis packages is usually based on the site visitors' IP addresses. In reality, the number of actual site visitors (i.e., computers) is likely to be lower than that. Internet users either have a static, unchanging IP address or

a dynamic IP address which changes every time the user connects to the internet service provider. Static IP addresses provide a relatively accurate indication of a site's unique visitors (assuming that only one person ever uses each computer). A user with a dynamic IP, however, is associated with multiple addresses, which cause an exaggerated estimate of the number of site visitors recorded in the log files. This problem was anticipated in the CDE study by cross-matching students' IPs with their names as identified in the CDE site's text conferences. As the research was not designed for the purpose of giving formative feedback to the teacher of students during the course, a blind-coding approach was used whereby a graduate student who did not know the participants converted the students' names to a numerical ID, so that the teacher-researcher could not identify individual students that the analysis highlighted.

The predictive ability of online CRM data is enhanced when they are analyzed in conjunction with other sources of information (e.g., student and instructor characteristics, online material design variables, and academic outcome measures); and web-based CRM research can be facilitated by the development of data warehousing techniques for rapid and reliable analyses of this type. Educational institutions need to address the ethics of transcript and server log analysis, however, in order to develop ways to assist teachers and students to use the web efficiently without compromising their anonymity and confidentiality.

Online Constructivism

Providing debriefing feedback to those who give their time and effort to participate in research studies is a common courtesy that can also be socially and educationally beneficial. In educational and training contexts, knowledge of results can give constructive insights to individuals and groups about their attitudes and performance, and about within-group differences; and feedback to students following research and evaluation studies can be a powerful means of teaching and motivating them.[76] The instantaneous analysis methodology of CRM studies permits feedback where it may previously have been impossible. In the 1980s, the writer reported the results of his CRM analyses of TV election debates on national television within minutes of the live broadcasts, and follow-up analyses on TV and radio the next day. Viewers of election debates appear avid for clues as to who 'scored the most points' or won the debate overall; and the interpretations of media pundits on these topics are influential even when they are not based on firm audience research data.[77] The writer always declined broadcasters' requests to superimpose his animated moment-by-moment graphs on air during the debates, however, in order to prevent misleading and incomplete spur-of-the-moment conclusions.

Owing to their anonymous and nonverbal nature, the responses collected on hand-unit devices can also transcend global barriers of culture and language. In community development contexts, instant analysis methods can be used as a catalyst for discussion of development goals, problems, and solutions. It is significant that the current writer developed an interest in CRM methods in the Canadian province of Newfoundland during the 1980s, influenced by the island's media-based community development tradition. In the 1980s and 1990s, he used instantaneous CRM analyses to give feedback to audiences including fishermen in Newfoundland, Somali immigrant children in Toronto, pre-school children in Johannesburg, HIV-AIDS patients in Atlanta, and street kids in the Dominican Republic. These studies, usually sponsored by education or health ministries in order to evaluate a media education campaign, shed as much light on the audiences as on the media productions. The principal of the Toronto secondary school attended by Somali refugee children described the difficulty of knowing them well enough to design programs for their needs.[78] The strangeness of their new Canadian environment, and the natural reticence of their preadolescent age group usually prevented the children from expressing themselves, whereas the anonymity of the data collection system allowed them to indicate the unfriendliness and isolation that they experienced in their new lives with candor. In a similar study, the writer and a team of graduate students created a mobile feedback process to help the Government of Ukraine to recreate Vertov's 1920s educational train tradition. Traveling on a train formerly used for cultural exchanges by the Communist Youth Union (Comsomol), the team played educational videos about HIV-AIDS in schools and community centers across Ukraine, video-taped the discussions they generated, edited the video recordings on the train overnight, and played them back in other communities subsequently, as Vertov had done in the 1920s. With the added benefits of instantaneous CRM feedback, this modern version of the Vertov Process generated detailed community development insights as well as guidelines for teachers, campaign designers, media producers, and government policy-makers.

Feedback procedures generate ethical issues, however. When they are analyzed in conjunction with demographic data about political or sexual preferences, for example, viewers' continuous responses to a presentation can generate a personal profile of responses more revealing than they might ever suspect; and this profile can be compared with the responses of other participants who have not revealed their personal preferences. The writer's analysis of student reactions to the anti-pornography film *Not a Love Story*, discussed above, revealed reactions by individual viewers to explicit moments that seemed due to vicarious pleasure, and were associated statistically with increased pro-pornography attitudes in pre-test/post-test comparisons. As this result had not been predicted, no blind-coding procedure had been put in place to protect the individuals' identities, and it did not seem ethically appropriate to discuss the result in debriefing the participants, let alone to publish the results; so the study was abandoned. The predictive use of CRM data in this way is identical to that reported by Jung in 1910, whereby patients were diagnosed with hysteria based on their second-by-second responses to the word association test (Figure 3.3). The media researcher's focus in this situation is the reverse of the normal approach whereby audience responses are used to identify the properties of a stimulus. In diagnostic contexts, a media stimulus is used to focus on the psychology of its individual viewers; and a video or film becomes a 'moving inkblot test' with the diagnostic potential of the inkblot test developed by Hermann Rorschach for projective testing in 1911.[79]

Medical and social-science procedures require researchers and evaluators to follow strict ethical guidelines about data collection and debriefing. Individuals must be informed in advance of the purpose for which their data will be used so that they can give their 'informed consent' to receive a treatment or to take part in a survey or experiment, "based upon an appreciation and understanding of the facts, implications and future consequence."[80] If disclosing the purpose of a study to the participants in advance could compromise the integrity of the data, it may be justified to explain the study to them retroactively, for the purpose of gaining *post hoc* informed consent to use their data. Classical studies in the social sciences did not always follow such guidelines. In 1961, for example, an investigation of the psychology of obedience by Milgram placed people in situations where they were pressured into doing things that were morally wrong. Milgram's study has become notorious for giving its participants deceptive instructions and subjecting them to questionable procedures without warning or explanation.[81]

The ethics of data collection are further complicated in situations where individuals generate a personal profile without even knowing they are doing so. Currently, this is the situation underlying studies of web usage. Many internet users are still unaware of the extent to which their online activities are open for inspection. They may be shocked to realize that the computer screen is actually a two-way mirror as transparent as the 'telescreen' in Orwell's *Nineteen Eighty-Four*. Their responses to it reflect their private behavioral profile as well as the impact of information upon them. While the analysis of server log files to describe students' activity has useful educational potential, it is only strictly justified when the students have given informed consent for their log-file data to be used. Web users need to be informed in advance that their online navigation patterns and transcripts are automatically stored, timed, classified, and identified with them, and that this information may be used for research and evaluation purposes. Similar ethical issues arise in relation to feeding back the results of log-file analyses into online discussions—an idea sometimes suggested by enthusiastic teachers who have not considered the embarrassing nature of some findings for students who may be recognizable even behind a coded alias. The anonymity and confidentiality procedures attached to such studies need to be carefully designed to ensure that no individual's identity is revealed nor can be inferred. "The picture had fallen from the wall, uncovering the telescreen behind it" (Orwell, 1949).[82]

Researchers can also feel disturbed by the realization that an educational study has raised participants' expectations of improvement in their personal situations, but that these hopes cannot be implemented nor sustained. In 1993, the writer took CRM techniques into the farm fields of Mount Kenya, for a formative evaluation study designed to help improve a radio agriculture series.[83] Farmers gathered in their weekly 'learning circles' in a dozen villages, and listened to pilot versions of the audiotapes (Figure 3.14). The writer's electronic keypads, powered from the cigarette-lighter socket of his jeep, were placed in the farmers' hands to enable them to give second-by-second responses to the tapes on a red button (associated in their culture with 'positive') and a blue button associated with 'negative'. Any fears that the farmers would not comprehend this task were dispelled when they demanded a 5-point push-button scale with a 'don't know' midpoint, to do justice to the subtlety of their responses. The nonverbal, anonymous nature of the activity allowed the farmers to give continual responses indicating moments in the tapes of which they approved and disapproved. They also gave pre-and post-test responses about their demographics and the extent of their learning from the tapes. Asked about their responses in debriefing sessions, they gave sophisticated explanations which led the tapes to be revised

FIGURE 3.14 Kenyan farmers give push-button responses to agriculture audio-tapes.

Source: Author.

before they were broadcast. In the process, they commonly revealed that they were more expert than the agricultural specialists who had designed the programs.

In many respects, this was the writer's most satisfying project; but it was also a troubling one. Working through a trusted local teacher, the visiting researchers gave the farmers detailed immediate feedback of their responses. These, they were later told, revealed within-group differences in knowledge and attitudes of which the people had not been aware previously. The study had transported a powerful technique more commonly associated with advertising and political research out of the laboratory and, literally, into the field; and the participants were clearly impressed with the way the push-button technology had allowed them to criticize the audio tapes without offending the academics and bureaucrats who had produced them. While packing up his equipment at the end of one data collection session, however, the writer became aware of the stern gaze being fixed upon him by an elderly lady, and suspected in that instant that she feared that this was a one-off visit which would never be repeated. As the researcher flew out of Nairobi later that week to return to Montreal, he felt that he had raised hopes of community training and development among the Mount Kenyan farmers that could not be sustained.

In such research, it is possible to glimpse that communications research can evolve, in the manner than cubist art developed in the early 20th century, to levels beyond the analytical and synthetic. After the cubist forms of art had been defined via analysis and synthesis, 'constructivist' methods evolved. (This use of the term is unrelated to the 'learner-centered' type of constructivism of the educational literature.) The constructivist school of art was motivated by a desire to make aesthetic principles accessible to a wider public, by lifting them from the 2-dimensional canvas and expressing them in 3-dimensional construc-tions: sculpture, architecture, theater and technological design. The movement originated in the work of Vladimir Tatlin, a professional musician and son of a Ukrainian railway worker.[84] In 1913, the 28-year-old Tatlin began to apply cubist ideas in sculptural forms using wire, glass, metals and other materials. In 1920, he completed the design of a 400-foot tower headquarters for the communist organization, Comintern, in St. Petersburg (Petrograd). The design included offices, and conference facilities, a radio broadcasting centre, and a projector for broadcasting on a giant open-air screen and on the clouds (Figure 3.15). It also added a mischievous tweak to the cubist desire to represent movement. Instead of depicting an object from the different perspectives gained when an observer moves around it, segments of the tower revolved through 360 degrees on the observer's behalf. Had it ever been built, Tatlin's Tower would have been 75 meters taller than the Eiffel Tower, and would have combined art, science and mobile technology—a vision similar to the concept of Vertov's educational railway train. Considered unbuildable at the time, Tatlin's Tower has since been constructed on smaller scales as a monument to his grand vision.

FIGURE 3.15 Tatlin's Tower.

Source: Wikipedia Commons, 2010b.

The parallels between Tatlin and Vertov, constructivist art, and educational media research lie in the impulse to make art, science, and culture publicly accessible. The abstract thinking behind the cubism of Picasso and the relativity concepts of Einstein has never been fully accessible to the general public, requiring specialized knowledge in order to understand it. Picasso for one was not interested in explaining his rationales to anyone. When asked about the 'experimental' nature of his works, he replied that they were the results of experiments rather than experiments in their own right:

> Among the several sins that I have been accused of committing, none is more false than the one that I have, as the principal objective in my work, the spirit of research. When I paint, my object is to show what I have found and not what I am looking for.[85]

The graphs, tables, and jargon of academic researchers are similarly inaccessible to those who lack the training to decode them; and it can take a century of researchers to decode their mysteries. By communicating the results of analytical and synthetic studies in educational courses, broadcasts, and community feedback sessions, the researcher attempts to reach beyond the confines of the academic environment into the real world. The underlying motive of 'constructivist' research is to make answers to questions such as "Why is the sky blue?" more widely available, using even the clouds as a backdrop.

Summary

Educational approaches evolve through analysis and synthesis as in the cubist art movement of the early 20th century. Each new communications medium is analyzed into its component parts, for examination in terms of the effects each element yields in different situations. As their properties become more familiar, the variables can be re-synthesized, and their effects examined as they fluctuate over time. The data collection methods developed for this purpose in broadcasting, political and advertising research have reached a new level of precision in the study of the server log files that record individuals' web-site uses. Feeding research findings back to the participants who gave the data has the same social goals as the constructivist movement in art, though raises ethical issues.

4

BUILDING GLOBAL PRACTICES

Lost Foundations

The account so far has shown that, with each new medium that emerges, a wealth of guidelines is available for its development in a long but often repetitive literature. Before Gagné, Schramm, Vertov, and the dozen other educational theorists mentioned above, there was Bagley. From 1902 to 1940, William Chandler Bagley was a professor of education at universities in Montana, Illinois, and New York. His ideas have been eclipsed over the course of a hundred years, and he might never have come to the current writer's attention if their names had not been similar. In 1910, Bagley co-founded the *Journal of Educational Psychology*; and in 1911 he published three books (*Classroom Management*,[1] *Craftsmanship in Teaching*,[2] and *Educational Values*[3]), analyzing key aspects of educational practice including verbal and nonverbal strategy, teacher-student interaction, problem-based learning, and study skills, long before they became debated in today's educational literature. By 1911, Bagley's ideas had evolved through analysis and synthesis as in the cubist art of his time. He wrote of the need for flexible principles capable of generating applicable theory, and he criticized the deductive approach that attempts to work "backward from highly wrought theory to concrete practice . . . a survival of the deductive habit of mind which science has long since discarded as totally inadequate to the discovery of truth" (Bagley, 1911a, pp. v–vi). Educational principles, he argued, can be invalid if not derived inductively from observations "based upon successful school practice . . . A given practice may be effective in one school and ineffective in another" (p. vi) In his view, concepts such as 'intelligence' were similarly flawed, being defined on the basis of a limited range of activities in non-generalizable situations; and he argued ahead of his time that deductive uses of educational testing labelled students unfairly, devaluing the need to help weaker students improve their study skills.

Bagley's recommendation that teachers should draw upon flexible combinations of teaching methods in different situations, however, was opposed by influential psychologists of the day, including his Columbia University colleagues Edward Thorndike and William Kilpatrick, staunch advocates of learner-constructed methods. Whereas Bagley attempted to express the complexity of the educational process and the need for flexible pedagogical approaches catering to specific situations, these theorists offered the generalized viewpoints of 'connectionism'[4] and 'progressivism'.[5] In 1938, Bagley attempted to match their penchant for 'isms' by identifying educational 'essentialism', which emphasized the student's right to a teacher's guidance, and the need for all teachers to receive formal professional training.[6] In a century "obsessed with economic efficiency",[7] however, his early version of flexible learning was marginalized. Vertov developed his awareness of educational principles in a similarly inductive manner during his community development experience on the Soviet railroads.[8] Forty years later, Chu & Schramm followed suit in an analysis of over 200 studies about the effects of educational television, from which they concluded that to deduce a convenient set of principles from them for all educational situations would be impossible. These educational tacticians did derive consistent practical lessons from their studies, however. Chu & Schramm's conclusions about educational media presentation, for example, related to:

> some of the basic requirements of all teaching and learning, rather than about the production devices that we have at hand with television. The studies . . . call for simplicity of presentation, clear organization of the material, motivation of the learners, knowledge of results, practice . . . We might expect that the basic requirements of good teaching would not be greatly different if all the teaching is done in the classroom or part of it is done in the studio.[9]

Since the 1960s, scholars have persisted in the attempt to deduce generalizable 'best practices' for education and training. Uppermost in their schemes has been the importance of simplicity and clarity in educational presentations. These unsurprising attributes are featured in Gagné's nine instructional events, originally identified in the specific context of military training,[10] and in Chickering & Gamson's seven universal instructional design (UID) principles,[11] recently increased to nine by Scott et al.[12] Other pedagogical principles are overlooked in these schemes. Bagley would have attributed this to the deductive approach that he decried as "totally inadequate to the discovery of truth" owing to its attempt to identify fixed principles that may not be equally applicable in all contexts. The value of his inductive approach to pedagogical principles is illustrated by a comparison of the range of his ideas with those developed in the century since. Table 4.1 compares the wide range of teaching principles encouraged by Bagley, Vertov and Schramm with those of more deductive analyses conducted by Gagné and the UID researchers.

TABLE 4.1 Successive definitions of teaching and learning principles.

Principles of efficient communication	Bagley (1911) Classroom methods	Vertov (1920s) Agit prop methods	Chu & Schramm (1967) Educational television	Gagné (1965) Military training	Chickering & Gamson (1987)	Scott, McGuire & Shaw (2003) 'Universal Design for Instruction'
	Inductive approach			*Deductive approach*		
Materials and activities: accessible	Yes	Yes	Yes	1		1
Flexible	Yes	Yes	Yes	2, 4		2
Straightforward and consistent	Yes	Yes	Yes	2, 4		3
Explicit	Yes	Yes	Yes	2, 4		4
Teacher–student interaction	Yes	Yes	Yes	5	1	5
Minimize effort	Yes	Yes	Yes		5	6
Accommodate diverse approaches	Yes	Yes	Yes		7	7
Tolerance for error	Yes	Yes	Yes			8
Environmental size and space	Yes	Yes	Yes			9
Active, motivated learning	Yes	Yes	Yes	3, 6	3	
Feedback/knowledge of results	Yes	Yes	Yes	7, 8	4	
Enhance retention and transfer	Yes	Yes	Yes	9		
Collaboration between learners	Yes	Yes	Yes		2	
Accommodate cultural differences	Yes	Yes	Yes			
Communicate high expectations	Yes	Yes	Yes		6	

Key: The numbers in the table indicate the priorities placed upon each principle in different classification systems.
Source: Author.

Perhaps Bagley's flexible approach was too complicated for some of his peers, for whom simpler, generalized lists were easier to absorb and prescribe. On the other hand, the Table suggests that the interest in defining generalized principles during the last century appears to have reduced the recognition given to wide-ranging educational principles. The educational principles of a century ago have been winnowed down to a set of common denominators, and the solid practical foundations of a century ago gradually lost to sight. The latest definition of UID principles, for example (right-hand column in the Table), makes no reference to the value of giving students knowledge of results, nor to the benefits of collaborative study, whereas the previous UID set featured both of these principles. Neither of the UID classification schemes refers to the need to take students' cultural differences into account in designing instruction, despite the implication that their principles have 'universal' scope. Yet 40 years ago Schramm *et al.* examined the cross-cultural effects of educational television in detail, drawing culturally sensitive conclusions about the medium's usage in Algeria, Australia, Colombia, India, the Ivory Coast, Japan, Niger, Peru, Samoa, Thailand, and Togo.[13] Six of the teaching principles recognized by Bagley in 1911 are not covered at all by Gagné and the UID advocates. In their defense it might be suggested that it is not really important for practical guidelines to be exhaustive, since good teachers instinctively practice sound principles without needing to read a theoretical account of them. On the other hand, an analysis by Elias (2010) of learning management system configurations at an online university has found that only 26% of the 121 options available for fulfilling UID principles are currently in use there.[14] Apparently, some course designers and programmers still need to be reminded of wide-ranging, flexible pedagogical principles in order to prevent them from being overlooked.

If such principles had always been heeded by media designers over the years, time and money might have been saved. For example, a long-standing principle that educational TV segments should last no more than 20 minutes derives from a finding in early industrial psychology that vigilance in monotonous conveyor-belt tasks deteriorates after 20 minutes.[15] Applying that particular finding out of context in instructional design fails to recognize that not all educational segments are monotonous. In fact, educational media production has frequently suffered from the opposite problem, being eye-catching and eventful to the point of distraction. One of the reasons for ETV's marginalization in the 1990s was the counter-productive complexity and expensiveness of its production styles. Postman recognized the problem of 'edutainment' explicitly in *Amusing Ourselves to Death*,[16] and some studios learned to rectify them, as in the simplification of the *Sesame Street* approach mentioned previously. Following the show's success with pre-schoolers, the CTW attempted to repeat its entertaining techniques in series for older children (e.g., *3-2-1 Contact*, *The Electric Company* and *Feeling Good*), though none of these shows achieved *Sesame Street*'s long-lasting popularity. If used strategically, entertainment techniques can be useful in relieving monotony;

but audiences older than the pre-school age require such approaches to be clearly relevant to the tasks at hand. Since they would probably not attend to educational presentations at all if they were not motivated to learn from them, older students are apt to regard gratuitous entertainment segments as a wasteful and even patronizing use of their time.[17] Thus, design guidelines should not be taken out of the situation-specific contexts in which they derived and applied across the board.

The often ineffectual nature of a century of recommendations is less the fault of those who offer them than of those who fail to read the small print and apply the principles appropriately. Bagley's 1911 advice included numerous examples of how teaching and learning principles can succeed in one context and not in another. He denounced the use of rote-learning, though pointed out that in specific situations it can save the student time and effort. He encouraged the use of problem-solving activities, but only if their purpose is explained to the students so that they can transfer the benefits to other situations. He also encouraged attempts to inject fun into education in the form of light relief following 'irksome tasks', although he warned that:

> (i)f carried too far, the pupil is apt to gain the notion that all of the routine work of the school must be made interesting and attractive by the intro-duction of the play element. (1911a, p. 151)

The use of humor is particularly prone to miscalculation, notably in health campaigns. Unlike other types of educational material, presentations about health commonly aim to achieve more than merely convey facts, and actually attempt to change behavior so as to reduce the risks of, for example, lung cancer or HIV-AIDS. Yet individuals may have no wish to change their behavior, particularly if they are addicted to it. In that situation, they are apt to resist a humorous presentation as a propagandist attempt to disarm them—hence the moment-by-moment audience reactions summarized in Chapter 3. Resistance can also occur in response to the 'gloom and doom' tactics often used in health promotion campaigns, in view of the impression they give of melodramatic manipulation. Although shown by researchers to be counter-productive,[18] ill-judged fear tactics remain common in public health campaigns to this day, potentially doing more damage than good to their impact. Chu & Schramm acknowledged the counter-productive effects of such tactics explicitly, and urged that educational media designers "need to avoid techniques that might cause people to resist information." (Chapter 2) Schramm's practice of assessing educational practices in relation to specific contexts, rather than in terms of principles claiming to be generalizable, made it less easy for his recommendations to be misapplied—although of course it may be more difficult for readers to absorb and cite flexible guidelines than simply enumerated, finite principles.

Some educational theorists focus on just one principle at a time. The risk of misinterpretation is even greater in this situation, notably when jargon terms are invented that focus attention on one principle to the apparent exclusion of all others. Such terms commonly end with 'ism'! Thus, a 'behaviorist' viewpoint can be interpreted as indicating that the only option for considering psychological phenomena is as a form of conditioned behavior. Inductive leaps of imagination are not easy to explain via this simplistic philosophy. Skinner's behaviorist notions had a major influence on 20th-century education by explaining all psychological events as conditioned behavior. (He is said, perhaps apocryphally, to have encountered the mind-narrowing influence of his ideas during a media interview. Asked if he truly believed that there is no such thing as thought, and that everything is merely a conditioned reflex, he replied, "I think so.") Likewise, the 'constructivist' philosophy in education may be taken to imply that learner-constructed learning is the only valid educational practice, rather than being one among many. This narrow frame of reference, discounting a wide range of alternative approaches, is observed in the 'paradigm shift' currently being claimed in online education, which attempts to justify the downgrading of 'teacher-centered' methods in favor of learner-centered activities. If one believes with Schramm that the basic practices of good education are the same regardless of the medium used, and that teachers can be useful for guiding them, it is clear that a total abandonment of tradition in this way would be unwise.

It is refreshing therefore to find the term 'ism-ism' in the *Urban Dictionary*, indicating a condition "commonly seen in academia, where terms (ending with ism) are incessantly created and applied to every new situation. Ismists are too focused on labeling everything to appreciate anything."[19] Even the terms used to describe today's new online media are the same as those used in relation to the new media of yesterday. Schramm *et al.* described television and film as intervening "in the communication process in such as way as to extend a student's sight and hearing through space and time" (1967, p. 13); and Jacobson (1993) described online graphic environments in the same terms:

> A person's ability in the virtual world to transcend space and time, to be anywhere, anytime, as or with anyone, is the principal attraction of the virtual world. It is very seductive.[20]

Virtual world techniques have seduced educational technologists since the 1960s, but did not become widely accessible until the launch of *Second Life* (*SL*) in 2003. With increasing access to high-bandwidth internet, virtual-world applications are becoming widely accessible, in developed nations at least. *SL* users navigate around a 3-dimensional world in the personage of a cartoon 'avatar', visiting virtual shopping malls, clubs, places of worship, educational institutions, and other public and private establishments. The enthusiasm generated by *SL*'s brilliant 3D software recalls the excitement when color was added to television, and when universities established their in-house TV studios; and *SL* is in use at hundreds of universities for purposes ranging from the simulation of real-life tasks in medical training, to the stimulation of creative expression in the arts. The educational developers of these online worlds have access to pedagogical recommendations that have remained constant across generations of research.

It is clear, however, that they are not uniformly taking advantage of this stockpile of guidance, and that old mistakes are being repeated. Cheal reports that students who are concerned about the learning outcomes of their work express frustration at being asked to join in *SL* 'virtual world' activities that they regard as educationally unproductive. Many students "wanted a playful course," Cheal observes, "but by the end of the semester, they questioned the value of a learning environment they perceived as a place for play."[21] Hughes indicates that learner-constructed activities in social networking communities can be divisive, resulting in some students being ostracized, with de-motivating effects on their learning.[22] Carr indicates the need to develop inclusive activities in virtual environments, noting that when deaf people have attempted to join in *SL* activities with hearing users they have been insulted and marginalized.[23] Oliver gives a reminder that online environments provide the same opportunities for antisocial behavior as face-to-face environments, and that their activities need to be carefully monitored.[24] In the absence of teacher-guided learning, as Garber has noted, online communities frequently decline and close owing to lack of direction, facilitation, and control, and to the resulting dissatisfaction and loss of interest on the part of the users.[25 - 26] As Moore & Pflugfelder have noted:

> without a deeper understanding of how to scaffold, engage, and interact with our students in these new worlds, we run the risk of doing them a particular disservice, potentially leaving them bored and/or lost.[27]

It is to be hoped that the social media will not diminish their chances of fulfilling solid pedagogical goals by being associated, as Hughes has suggested, with "over-optimism and hyperbole." Postman described the same attitude in terms of the "cheery, gee-whiz tone" of those who advocate new technologies, and criticized educational institutions for all too readily restructuring themselves to accommodate innovation for the sake of it.[28] Berg also criticized the "polemical optimism . . . based on ignorance" that often accompanies innovation.[29] This is not to suggest that the impact of new media is necessarily negative.

> Whereas the new media . . . are not miracle drugs for educational systems, they are tools of great potential power . . . They offer an uncommon opportunity, if used efficiently and appropriately, to help education go further, do more, and do it better.[30]

The Asynchronous Years

So definitions of efficient teaching practice established a century ago, and earlier, do not differ markedly from those discussed today; and it should not be assumed that views are irrelevant or outdated just because they are 100 years old. Each of the risks discussed above in relation to virtual world activities could have been inferred from William Bagley's 1911 educational principles, and from studies of 'edutainment' techniques in the years since. Bagley spoke highly at that time of a particular approach designed to avoid a number of the counter-productive effects of educational media that are observed today. The Batavia school commission in western New York State had devised a compromise between the classroom approach and individual instruction. Classroom methods, while economical and conducive to the development of social skills can, if inefficiently organized, lose the individual student in "a machine" approach to education (Bagley, 1911a, p. 214), in which individual needs and differences are neglected. Such views remain unchanged in modern criticisms of mechanized forms of distance education: e.g., in Robertson's *No More Teachers, No More Books*,[31] and Noble's *Progress without People*.[32] The 'Batavia System' attempted to resolve these problems via a hybrid instructional approach which:

> aims to preserve the stimulus which comes from group-instruction, and, at the same time, to provide explicitly and systematically for whatever extra instruction the weaker members of the class may need to keep them abreast of the brighter members.[33]

Modern open and distance learning has developed a wide range of principles for fulfilling the Batavia system's group-based and individual instruction goals. As Taylor's analysis of educational technologies showed (Table 1.2), correspondence methods in the 1970s overcame educational restrictions of time, place, and pace, but sacrificed the benefits of live teacher–student interaction. Multimedia approaches in the 1970s and 1980s expanded these methods, though with the same advantages and disadvantages; and the teleconferencing approaches of the 1990s had the reverse effect, restoring interactivity to the process while sacrificing flexibility with regard to time, place and pace. Since the mid-1990s, a wide range of methods is being used for different situations in exactly the way recommended by William Bagley a century ago. Synchronous (real-time) conferencing is provided in text and audio-visual forms by telephony and internet-based methods, and asynchronous (delayed) versions are provided by primarily text-based methods including e-mail, blogging and cellphone texting. In practice, however, some distance educators continue to adhere to the methods they have used for 30 years—the one-to-one telephone conversation, for example; and they may have good reasons for preferring traditional approaches, notably in regions of the world where the newer media are still in their infancy. At the other extreme, 'fast adopters' move enthusiastically from one new medium to the next, regardless of their respective merits and demerits. Missing from the current picture is the emphasis placed a hundred years ago on the need for teachers to be formally trained in the use of appropriate approaches in different situations. In the absence of such training, McKee indicates, teachers and students alike experience a bewildering "deluge of pedagogies and technologies, depending on the favored course delivery methods of the day."[34]

This bombardment is clearly evident in the vast array of commercial products available in today's online education. From 2002–10, the *International Review of Research in Open & Distance Learning* reported reviews by the writer's distance education graduate students of 182 software products for online teaching and learning. The evaluative framework used in many of these studies was developed by the American Society for Training & Development (ASTD),[35] which recommends the evaluation of software in terms of:

1   costs (to the institution and user);
2   complexity (for the user);
3   control (including privacy and personalization);
4   clarity of use;
5   Common Technical Framework (computer interoperability; scalability, etc.); and
6   features (for the teacher, student, and administrator).

The types of online software reviewed are indicated in Table 4.2. Many of the software products have evolved since the original reviews, and their classification in the Table refers to the functions they fulfilled at that time. The history of these reviews illustrates the relatively high attrition rate (approximately 30%) of software products for online education during the last decade: i.e., the large number of brands that have emerged and disappeared, necessitating changes of approach to which teachers and students have to adjust. Figure 4.1 compares the number of products in each category at the time of review with the number available currently. These data cannot be generalized to the total pool of products, for new ones have continued to become available during the testing period, and many of the most

TABLE 4.2 Number of educational software products compared (2002–11).

Online software products	*Asynchronous (e.g., wikis, conferencing)*	*Synchronous (chat)*	*(Attrition, 2002–11)*
Text (stand-alone products)	40 (−11)	13 (−5)	30%
Integrated packages (text/audio/ video)	90 (−29)		32%
Other	39 (−5)		13%
TOTAL		**182 (−50)**	**27%**

Key: Bracketed figures indicate the number of products no longer available. [a] 'Other' category includes authoring, accessibility, polling, and editing tools.
Source: Author.

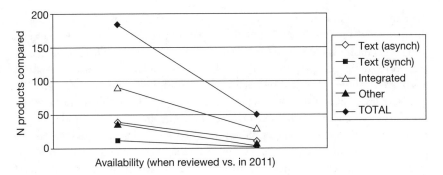

FIGURE 4.1 Attrition of software products reviewed.

Source: Author.

recent ones have not been evaluated in the series. It is evident, however, that asynchronous text-based software has been more popular than synchronous text based software over the ten-year period, despite the integration of many such products into hybrid packages and learning management systems. The 70 evaluation reports underlying this analysis can be inspected online, representing the opinions of distance education students specifically about the benefits and disadvantages of particular applications.[36] The product reviews provided by *Edutools.org* are more comprehensive, although do not specifically represent the needs of DE students.[37]

The consistent advice of the educational literature to keep teaching and learning practices simple has not been followed by many of these software designers. As online applications have grown increasingly complex, teachers and students have reported that they find them increasingly confusing.[38]

> Students have lost control of their learning process and activities, while the LMS vendors/administrators (and by implication instructors) have increased their control over a fixed style of learning that fails to evolve.[39]

An identical problem, Hotrum indicates, has been traced back to 1911, when the industrial psychologist, Frederick Taylor, suggested that workers' tasks should be systematically dissected into discrete elements and made more efficient according to 'scientific' principles.[40] The Luddites would have disliked Taylor. His views encouraged the development of mechanized workplace approaches that increased management control and failed to take account of individual working styles, just as theorists have since overlooked individual learning differences in attempting to generalize about educational performance.[41] "The development and implementation of learning management systems in distance education has proved to be similar (to Taylorism) in intent and effect," states Hotrum.

The software evaluation studies have also indicated a consistent preference on the students' part for online methods that allow them to interact in real time with their teachers. This preference contradicts those who recommend a 'paradigm shift' away from teacher-centered methods, and it indicates the importance of not using asynchronous methods in isolation. Such conclusions have been reported in numerous studies since the 1980s, although the recent educational media literature has proved as unfocussed and inconclusive as that of the previous educational TV era. Bernard *et al.* collated 862 reports of studies conducted from 1985–2002, measuring the effects of different DE methods on achievement, attitude and/or retention.[42] They established that 232 of the published reports satisfied reasonable criteria for a reliable comparison. The team showed that the conclusions of these studies contradicted one another to such a high degree that no overall effect, either positive or negative, could easily be identified on any of the outcome measures. On isolating the results of 'asynchronous' DE studies from those of 'synchronous' ones, however, Bernard and team observed more consistent conclusions among the studies. Asynchronous techniques were found to have more positive effects on student attitudes when they were used in conjunction with interactive media such as the telephone; and positive effects of DE in general (asynchronous as well as synchronous) were found to be increased by methods that encourage face-to-face or mediated contact between the students, and with the teacher. The conclusions derived by Bernard *et al.* from this meta-analysis favored the judicious selection of teaching methods for specific situations, and the need to ensure that "excellence and effectiveness take precedence over cost efficiency." These conclusions corroborate those of Chu and Schramm in the 1960s, and the aptitude-treatment interaction (ATI) observations of Salamon, Snow, and Clark in the 1970s and 1980s. It may also be noted that these findings are identical to the conclusions of the 'essentialist' educators, eclipsed in educational literature since the 1930s.

Despite the evidence that synchronous techniques offer significant benefits in DE, however, online conferencing practices are proving relatively slow to embrace them. This is not because the necessary software is unavailable or particularly expensive. A wide range of audio and video software is easily downloadable by which teachers and students can interact with each other in real time, face-to-face and often at no cost, at the furthest ends of the globe.[43] Voice over internet Protocol (VoIP) methods date from the development of the 'packet network' technique in 1974;[44] and the first commercial internet audio software became available in 1995 when *VocalTec* launched its *Internet Phone* freeware for one-on-one, online audio interaction over 28 kbps internet connections. That application was a technical breakthrough though by no means user-friendly, requiring the participants to communicate their IP addresses to one another before each session. A graphic user interface (GUI) was introduced into online conferencing by *ThePalace* software, also in 1995. Although not providing audio communication, *ThePalace* featured synchronous text-conferencing in chat rooms decorated by graphic images. The computing sciences department at the writer's DE university immediately applied this software and its community-building features in its online courses. Such methods were not adopted by less technically-minded colleagues at the university until 1998, when an online audio service named *Firetalk* overcame the set-up and usage complications of other products, and rapidly became popular as a means of creating online DE communities.[45] This product provided clear audio transmission, free of charge, between many people simultaneously, and the writer used it in the same year to talk to his Canadian students from Japan. Even with a delay of up to 15 seconds between signal and response, the experience represented an encouraging milestone, for it was now evident that the impersonal nature of DE communication could be reduced by live, cost-free online audio interaction. *Firetalk's* developers rapidly eliminated the lag-time problems, and in 2000 the writer used the product to enable his DE students in Canada to talk to an audience of broadcasters in Johannesburg. Even for sophisticated South African TV and radio practitioners, it seemed astonishing to exchange 19th-century gold rush stories in real time with a student in the Yukon.

By 2001, numerous audio and video-conferencing products (e.g., *HearMe* and *CU-SeeMe*) had become available, many of them combining A/V conferencing features with previously 'stand-alone' applications (e.g., text-chat, whiteboards, polling, co-browsing, and other shared tools). Some services provided dedicated 'chat room' services for a minor charge, while others (e.g., *Yahoo Messenger* and *MSN Messenger*) offered free services. The latter products were rapidly adopted by millions of international users, though with the disadvantage that a student might have to navigate through often disreputable non-educational discussion areas in order to enter a dedicated educational forum. Guidelines for conferencing participants and moderators have been well documented,[46-47] and sophisticated online conferencing methods have been developed in Norway and Sweden using broadcast-style TV techniques and special effects to clarify the educational content.[48] These methods have yet to be widely applied in DE, however. It will be interesting to see if the economic recession of the early 21st century will put an end to educational uses of the more complex commercial packages, which often provide surprisingly few extra features compared with their cost-free, open-source rivals. In the developed and developing worlds alike, uncomplicated audio-conferencing products such as *iVocalize* and *Skype* may become staples in e-learning, while, for activities requiring a more complex graphic interface, pioneering packages such as *ThePalace* can still be downloaded and used free of charge.

Currently, however, these are still 'the asynchronous years' in global education. There are practical reasons for teachers' hesitancy to develop synchronous approaches, and for institutional decisions not to build synchronous options into learning management systems.

1 Synchronous methods allow teachers as well as students less freedom to work at the times they prefer.

2   As with unjustified educational uses of social media, some users prefer not to reveal themselves synchronously via microphones and webcams without being given clear justification for doing so.

3   Many teachers do not have the time to develop the often complex skills of moderating synchronous conferences, which require careful protocols and practice.[49]

4   Efficient teacher-moderator practices in synchronous conferencing include the use of an assistant to coordinate participants' questions and comments via a text-box. Such assistance is often unavailable.

5   Policy-makers (for example, at the DE institution where the writer has taught) have from time to time discouraged the use of synchronous teaching methods on the grounds that they reduce the flexibility for which DE was created, and can create technical and scheduling problems for the students.

It is certainly important to warn students before they enroll in a course about synchronous activities (e.g., online video-conferencing) that may be incompatible with their facilities or schedules. Yet DE students in the east and west are requesting greater levels of interactivity in their online learning, and it is equally important to adopt course features (e.g., social networking activities) that provide this for them.[50] In western-style education, the evolution towards an online methodology that routinely alternates between synchronous and asynchronous communication, as appropriate, has been expedited by institutional support for server-based conferencing packages such as *Elluminate*, a Canadian product, and *Marratech*, a Swedish product, although the software licenses of these products tend to be expensive. The costs of online services such as *Paltalk* and *iVocalize* are minimal by comparison; and inexpensive products that do not require high internet bandwidth and a complex technical infrastructure are proving valuable for DE in developing countries. The *Skype* freeware, with its simple telephone-style interface and relatively few extra gadgets, has rapidly become the most universally recognized online audio/video communication tool worldwide. It is to be hoped that the years ahead will not be predominantly asynchronous in DE, and that the widely available and cost-effective real-time communication methods will be increasingly used owing to their cost-effectiveness, and as a counter to the common criticism that DE is impersonal and does not involve efficient teacher–student interaction.

A Web-based Bubble

The development of global education, however, is currently obstructed by the incompatibility of international distance education technologies. Assisted by the communications media, contrasting minds have developed that set different regions of the world apart from one another.

a) *Low-income nations in Africa and Asia have retained educational television and other traditional media, to overcome their students' lack of internet access in urban as well as rural regions.*

Multi-campus and distance education universities such as Indira Gandhi National Open University (IGNOU) in India, and the Monterrey Institute of Technology and Higher Education (ITHE) in Mexico, have led the world in the development of telephone-based (ISDN) conferencing since the 1980s. These are the *developed* nations with regard to that particular educational medium. Meanwhile, China and India, accounting for over a third of the world's population, have become the developed world with respect to educational video. In the internet age, the Open University of China (OUC) and the China Agricultural Broadcasting & TV School (CABTVS), each with 3 million students, continue to produce, update, and distribute thousands of video-on-demand materials to their students on VCDs and DVDs. These nations are the developed world with respect to educational video. The example of these world leaders in DE is rapidly being emulated in other parts of Asia. For example, the Virtual University of Pakistan (VUP), established in 2002, televises its courses and uses the internet to download open-source video productions from around the world for distribution to its students. The VUP President, Naveed Malik, stresses that this approach provides his students with the benefits of being taught by leading scholars from around the world.[51]

Another notable example of a multimedia education provider is the Open University of Indonesia (Universitas Terbuka: UT).[52] Indonesia is the fourth most populous nation in the world with a population of 237 million people spread across 33 provinces and 69,065 villages in 15,000 islands.[53] Its Open University is currently ranked as the seventh largest 'mega-university' in the world (Table 1.1). UT makes its 1,000 courses available at a distance through 37 regional offices and 8,000 examination rooms in 572 cities.[54] All of the course materials are distributed in print-based packages, 25% of which also include at least one multimedia element in the form of audio, video, radio and TV broadcasts, and computer and web-based materials. The design and distribution of each course is supported by a course development team containing one or more academic specialists, an instructional designer, and media staff usually based in UT's in-house studios. Course delivery is assisted by the National Radio Station Network (NRSN), and by 7,000 regional student advisors. Online versions of selected courses are available, primarily in the urban centers, though the *UT-Online* web site, home of online materials, exercises and tutorials, TV programs, a digital library and e-book store, academic counseling, and registration and examination facilities. The current proportion of students with the facilities or online skills needed to access the online facilities, however, is only 5%. For the millions of would-be students in the geographically remote parts of Indonesia, UT's courses using the traditional media are the only option. The cost of open and distance-based tuition at UT is estimated at 30% of that charged by conventional Indonesian universities.

b) *High-income Asian institutions provide course materials via a comprehensive convergence of traditional and online media, as appropriate to their students' needs in different situations.*

In affluent Asian nations (e.g., Japan, South Korea, and Taiwan), the traditional and online educational media have converged. The University of the Air in Japan (restructured in 2007 as the Open University of Japan, OUJ) has delivered its courses by satellite television and FM radio since 1985. Its research division, the National Institute of Multimedia Education (NIME), pursued an innovative program of studies dealing with these media's educational usage and with the potential of new media including virtual reality and 3D television. The writer first observed the daily schedule of Japan's satellite-based educational TV in 1998. In a Tokyo TV studio, vigorous young lecturers broadcast live to an estimated 300,000 students throughout Japan. At that time, the Japanese government was urging its universities to develop internet-based delivery methods, although many academics were reluctant to redirect their attention from the media that had given them a large student audience for many years. The OUJ's restructuring ten years later has retained the traditional media while allowing online media to develop in parallel with them, thereby avoiding the abandonment of tried-and-tested educational TV methods that has occurred in western nations. The 18 'cyber-universities' of South Korea also provide a sophisticated integration of live and recorded multimedia. In 2009, the writer was asked to give a spontaneous lecture at Kyung Hee Cyber-University (KHCU) in Seoul. He spoke for 30 minutes, seated at a TV news–style desk, and five minutes later was presented with an impressively packaged DVD recording of it. Academics at the Korean cyber-universities prepare each of their weekly lectures for recording and distribution via internet TV; and Taiwanese universities have been using similar real-time 'multicast' methods since the mid-1990s.[55]

Institutions in other Asian regions are poised to apply this convergent model. For example, the Multimedia University in Malaysia (MMU), owned by Telekom Malaysia, is developing online and traditional media techniques for use on the nation's Multimedia Super Corridor.[56] MMU's teaching and research departments cover a primarily engineering-oriented spectrum of approaches, and 'creative multimedia' issues ranging from the design of web-based and cellphone displays to educational and cultural applications of film, animation and theatre.[57] Similar convergences of television and the internet are being examined in Hong Kong[58] and Singapore.[59] With their unparalleled convergence of traditional and online media countries in East and South-East Asia have thus become the developed world of educational media during the last decade, combining synchronous and asynchronous approaches in its teaching as a matter of daily routine.

c) *Western institutions have adopted and subsequently abandoned a series of educational media during the last 50 years.*

By the early 1990s, the technologies of global education had evolved to a high level of compatibility and in relative harmony with one another. At that time, with educational TV, radio, and tele-conferencing facilities in common, it was relatively easy to develop global educational collaborations, as in the case of a joint doctoral program in which the writer was involved between Canada and China. The turning point came in the mid-1990s, with the advent of online methods and the closure in western institutions of traditional media facilities such as those described above. This led to the dismissal of a generation of producers and designers based on the mistaken assumption that fewer employees would now be needed in the development of online education, and that traditional media experience would be irrelevant in that context. It also created a new research and development era which is repeating the trial-and-error process of the 1960s. In the late 1990s, one of the writer's doctoral supervisees in Canada was a visiting scholar from Asia, manager of a massive university tele-conferencing installation there, catering to a million students. The student returned home to work on her thesis, which was about the efficient use of video-conferencing in distance education. A tele-conference would have been the ideal vehicle for the thesis' final defense, and the candidate had the facilities and skills to mount an expert long-distance presentation. Unfortunately, the Canadian university did not have the infrastructure or the inclination to allow this, and the candidate was required to attend the examining session in person, at great personal expense. Fifteen years on, the educational delivery systems of North America and Asia are still incompatible, and compared with the advances being made in Asian institutions, today's western-style distance education system can only be described as undeveloping. In addition, academics in general have failed to apply a century of recommendations as to how these systems should and should not be used. Today's economic climate has made the prospect of global collaboration appealing to educators, but if they cannot adapt to colleagues in other cultures, for whatever reason, they stand little chance of meaningful discussion with them.

Asian educators are generous to their western visitors in suggesting that the 50-year history of technological development in western institutions has generated an advanced tradition of pedagogical expertise. Some of them clearly believe that this is so, and hasten to apply the recommendations of western educators on the assumption that they are appropriate for Asian conditions. Others, however, appear to realize that they are not appropriate: that the high-bandwidth graphics of 'virtual world' software, for example, are unlikely to be accessible for most of their students for years to come. In discussions with such educators, the writer has privately concluded that their generous comments with regard to western expertise are a courtesy that cannot be taken literally. He has formed this conclusion on the basis of visits since 2004 to universities, colleges, and ministries in 20 Asia-Pacific countries. In moments of friendship and trust, developed over perhaps half-a-dozen visits, his hosts have told him about western consultants who have demonstrated no awareness of local conditions and have recommended the adoption of completely inappropriate western practices; who are not old enough to have acquired hands-on experience of the traditional educational media that remain the only means of reaching most Asian students; and who have demonstrated their sophisticated virtual-world applications at Asian conferences, insensitive to the fact that the audience knows they will never be locally usable. Meanwhile, Asian teachers and students speak of the high respect accorded to teachers in their cultures—a value which seems poignantly foreign in today's western culture. Asian educators should heed the risk that 'learner-constructed' methods may erode that value.

d)   *Other nations have the choice of whether to adopt western or Asian distance education models.*

The educational potential of open and distance learning is also perceived in Africa, Eastern Europe, and the Middle East, though not as yet realized on any appreciable scale. A notable exception is the University of South Africa (UNISA), established in 1873 and located in Pretoria. Occupying one of the most spectacular university buildings in the world, UNISA uses a comprehensive range of traditional media and has a growing emphasis on online delivery. According to the current *Wikipedia* 'mega-universities' ranking, its 250,000 students make it the 22nd largest university enrollment in the world.[60] The African Virtual University (AVU), in operation since 1997, claims a comparable wide range of traditional and online media facilities. By late 2002, however, the AVU was delivering only three courses, using recorded video and involving no student-teacher interaction. By 2006 it was serving only 3,000 students.[61] Reporting these statistics, Laaser has described the AVU's mission statement ("To bridge the digital divide and knowledge gap between Africa and the rest of the world") as "ridiculously unrealistic and ideological." Juma has reported that in 2007 even educational administrators in Africa remained "digitally isolated";[62] and in 2009, any tendency towards optimism in describing DE across Africa was dispelled in a bitter description by Muhirwa,[63] not only of inadequate facilities and untrained teachers, but also of the "poor social dynamics, dominance, and arrogance" and teacher-student miscommunication that attempts at media-based education can generate. Muhirwa concludes, however, with a constructive proposal for international distance education (IDE) in Sub-Saharan Africa (SSA):

> With political will, pedagogy, instructional design know-how, and only a fraction of the resources dedicated to ICT-based IDE, it would be possible to transform traditional media such as radio and video into productive educational technologies in SSA and in oral cultures around the world.

Such writers are to be lauded for their honesty in an educational literature characterized all too often by rosy claims that reflect the writers'
fond hopes more than reality.

So isolation takes two forms in contemporary distance education. At the one
extreme, educators and students in low-income nations feel isolated from the rest
of the world because they lack internet access. This situation was predicted by
Venezky in a comparison of the internet age with that of the medieval banqueting
hall, in which the rich sat near the salt while the poor sat too far away to reach
it.[64] "Comparable to those who sat below the salt are those today who have
limited or no WWW access. They sit offline, disconnected" (p. 67). At the other
extreme, western educators have allowed the internet to isolate them from the
traditional approaches that serve the majority of students in the rest of the world.
From 2004–10, the writer supervised a series of DE research and development
projects in 13 Asian nations, from Mongolia to Indonesia, and from Pakistan to
the Philippines. Sponsored by the International Development Research Centre
(IDRC), and coordinated by its PANAsia division in Singapore, each of the
9 projects was conducted by collaborators in 3–4 countries.[65–66] This network
initiative, named 'PANdora', has demonstrated the deep divisions between DE
approaches in the world, and the concern of educators and policy-makers across
Asia to develop methods capable of making education and training available to
hundreds of millions of students in urban and rural regions. The projects have
included detailed needs assessments and pilot-test evaluations sensitive to local
needs and conditions, and have resulted in the development of approaches including mobile learning, shareable course materials, open-source learning management systems, and appropriate DE 'best practices'. The initiative has also examined
the hurdles to be overcome in global education, making its allusion to the
troublesome Pandora's Box of Greek legend highly appropriate.

A major hurdle is the doubt expressed across the region by parents, teachers,
and decision makers that impersonal DE technologies can ever be as educationally
effective as face-to-face teacher-student interaction. Back at home in Canada after
six years of Asian travel, in indiscrete moments with his fellow distance educators,
the writer has taken to describing western DE as isolated from the rest of the
world in a "web-based bubble". This view does not seem to go down too well
with western colleagues! Yet teaching and research collaborations between western
and other educators currently require the greatest level of adjustment from the
westerners, who need to develop traditional media skills that have been marginalized in North America and Europe since the 1990s. Teachers elsewhere
typically have experience with both old and new media, and are better equipped
than their western counterparts to develop media-based DE for all of the world's
regions. At the bottom of the legendary Greek box, however, lay hope. In the
effort to overcome global barriers to education, hope may lie in the fact that in
one sector at least most regions do share a common technology. For, while closing

the facilities for teaching by television, institutional managements have tended to retain video-conferencing for their administrative purposes. So the facilities and technical support skills needed for global education are still in place in many western educational institutions, though would probably need to be 'dusted off' in order to be capable of supporting today's teaching as well as administrative functions. The unification of international approaches to education thus has a viable technological foundation.

Practical Evaluation Guidelines

As 20th-century research has consistently indicated, educational development needs flexible as opposed to generalized approaches, teacher-student interaction, and constant evaluations of teaching and learning in specific situations, The development of educational media has not been well served by the century's studies overall, however. Hooper (1975) described the educational computing field as one of half-truths and ambiguities, and the computer as a "sacred cow", assumed to be educationally useful on the basis of little clear evidence. He argued for the need to take this problem in hand.

> As innovators, we are told that too much ambiguity is dangerous, and so the slogans and sacred cows are born. It is about time some of the sacred cows were well and truly milked.[67]

(Hooper actually likened educational scholarship to a "slag heap" (p. 94), on which a mishmash of inconsistent approaches and conclusions are thrown together.) The undisciplined nature of DE research specifically was further criticized by Moore (1985); and Farrell (2001) described the evolution of DE technologies as 'dysfunctional.'[68] Bernard *et al.* (2004) summarized numerous criticisms of research and reporting standards, listing eleven reasons that lead them to reject 630 studies from their meta-analysis of DE effects before settling on 232 studies that were capable of direct comparison. Such stringent analytic criteria might well discourage the important research and evaluation effort; and they should not. For studies conducted in specific situations are likely to yield useful conclusions, yet may not be comparable with other studies across a range of situations. Analytic and meta-analytic methods reduce principles and perspectives to relatively simple levels, and it is essential for evaluation studies to be conducted in a complex range of situations in order to move the DE field forward. At the practical level, situation-specific studies may also be required by funding agencies to establish whether or not project funding has been well spent. They may be conducted at the beginning of the project (as in needs assessment), during the project (formative evaluation), and/or at the project's conclusion (summative evaluation). In studies of this type, precautions need to be taken to avoid common problems.

Design of Evaluation Instruments

Evaluative studies typically involve presenting participants with questions and/ or statements inviting a response in terms of, e.g., agreement and disagreement. Such measures can be presented as, for example, items in a printed or online questionnaire, or as points to be covered in an interviewer's checklist. The rigor of the evaluation instrument can be protected by the following procedures.

1   *Explanation of study.* An important aspect of research and evaluation studies is that participants are often extremely anxious about the ways in which the data they give might be used against their interests. Whether in a printed questionnaire, or in a face-to-face interview/discussion, the evaluator should begin by explaining his or her identity and involvement in the study, the study's purpose, the identity of the organizations involved in the study, and the study's sponsor. The purposes for which the participants' responses will be used should be described. The participants should be assured that their responses will be both *anonymous* and *confidential*, and will not be used for any purpose beyond those of the study—as, for example, in decisions about student grades, teacher promotion, etc.

2   *Instructions about participation.* The participants should receive general instructions at the beginning of the study about the types of information that will be collected (e.g., personal, prior knowledge/learning, attitudes). At each stage of the study (pre-test, post-test, etc.), these instructions should be repeated, to reassure the participants that the same rules and procedures apply throughout.

3   *Time required for participation.* The participants should be accurately informed in advance about the amount of time they will be expected to provide. This information should be given in the face-to-face and/or written instructions presented at the beginning of the study. Not to provide the participants with this advance information could be regarded as exploitative, even in the absence of any conscious negative motives.

4   *Informed consent.* In certain situations it may be decided that the above explanations should be presented in a written statement of 'informed consent' requiring the participants' signatures, in order to record that they have understood and accepted the study's conditions.[69] This may be considered important when, for example, participants are paid for their contribution to the study: e.g., to anticipate and resolve disputes about payment. In other situations, however, involving, for example, rural participants who are unfamiliar with the research and researchers, written/signed statements might prove intimidating. The benefits and drawbacks of formal consent statements should be carefully weighed in advance of the study.

5   *Types of test item.* The most common types of information collected during evaluation studies are:

a) Personal details (e.g., age; gender; education), typically collected by multiple-choice items.

b) Descriptive information (e.g., about an educational medium's ease of use), typically collected on multi-point scales (Good to Poor; Easy to Difficult, etc.).

c) Attitudes (e.g., to issues discussed in a presentation), typically collected on multi-point scales requesting the participants to agree or disagree with particular statements.

6 *Multiple-choice items* (female/male; 25 years or less/26–35/36–45/46 or older; grade levels, etc.).

a) These items usually require one response only. Other items (e.g., occupation) may require more than one response. The number of responses required should be clearly stated before each question or set of questions.

b) Online questionnaire and quiz items should be carefully programmed to allow one or more response(s) as appropriate.

c) For simplicity's sake, the number of response options for a single item should not usually exceed 10.

d) Care should be taken to ensure that alternative responses do not overlap (as in this example: 26–35 years/35–45 years).

7 *Descriptive scales.* The most common descriptive scale in evaluation studies is the *semantic differential,* designed to allow the participant to describe something in terms of "shades of meaning".[70]

a) A seven-point semantic differential scale is typically used, with the midpoint carefully worded as appropriate to the study (Neutral; Don't Know; Neither; Not appropriate; etc.).

b) Care should be taken to ensure that the responses on each side of the midpoint have equal weighting, both verbally and in number. In this example, three positive options are equally weighted against three negative ones: Very Good; Good; Quite Good; (mid-point); Quite Poor; Poor; Very Poor.

c) Extreme responses (e.g., Excellent; Very Poor Indeed) are often avoided by participants, and their use can restrict the responses to the less extreme options around the middle of the scale.

d) Most descriptive scales carry positive and negative levels of meaning. When a series of scales is presented, some should read from positive to negative (e.g., Good to Poor), and others in the opposite direction (Poor to Good). The sequence of scales should be determined at random, with approximately half in each direction. This procedure avoids 'response bias': i.e., accidentally biasing participants towards either a positive or a negative response.[71]

8 *Attitude scales.* The most common attitude measure is the *Likert-type* scale, designed to allow the participants to express different levels of, e.g., agreement and disagreement.[72]

a) In creating attitude statements, wordings should be avoided that require complex and confusing 'double negative' responses (e.g., "I disagree that cellphones are not familiar tools").

b) The wording of any one attitude item should be limited to a single statement. An item containing more than one statement (e.g., "The cellphone is a familiar tool, and text-messaging is easy to use") may generate different attitudes for each sub-statement, which would be impossible to record on a single scale.

c) A five-point Likert scale is typically used, with the midpoint carefully worded as appropriate to the study (Neutral; Don't Know; Neither; Not appropriate; etc.).

d) Care should be taken to ensure that the responses on each side of the midpoint are worded with equal weighting (e.g., Agree; Agree Slightly; (mid-point); Disagree Slightly; Disagree).

e) Extreme response options (e.g., Agree Strongly; Disagree Strongly) are often avoided by participants. Such wordings can restrict the range of responses to less extreme options around the middle of the scale.

f) The response options of a cluster of attitude statements should be worded in the same sequence (e.g., Agree to Disagree; or Disagree to Agree). This avoids confusion for the participants.

g) The sequence of scales should be determined at random, with approximately half in each direction. This procedure avoids the type of response bias noted in 7d) above.

9   *Other types of evaluation item.*

a) *Rank-order.* It may occasionally be useful to create evaluation items that require the participants to place different objects or ideas in order: e.g., "Please give the following cellphone features a value from 1-10 (where 1 is Most Useful, and 10 is Least Useful): Telephone | Texting | Internet | Camera | Calculator." Rank-order items of this kind, however, are often misunderstood by participants, and should be avoided if there is another way to obtain the information.

b) *Open-ended items.* These should be kept as simple as possible, and the blank space for responses to them should be as brief as possible, to indicate the length of the response that is appropriate. Participants dislike long, open-ended questions which do not specify whether a single-line or an essay-type answer is required.

c) *Controversial items.* Some participants can object to being asked for information that they regard as private (e.g., salary; political preferences). Such items should only be included when they are essential to the study, and they should be justified in a statement on the evaluation instrument itself. If such items cannot be avoided, it may be tactical to present the section in which they occur (e.g., personal information) at the end of the questionnaire, to avoid annoying participants before they have provided the other information required by the study.

10   *Combined items.* If more than one type of item (e.g., 6 to 9 above) is used in a study, the evaluation instrument can become tedious and confusing. To avoid this:

    a)   individual types of item should be presented in clusters: descriptive statements in one, attitude scales in another, etc.; and

    b)   each cluster should be preceded by instructions containing a sample item and the type of response that would be appropriate.

Analysis and Reporting of Data

11   *Descriptive statistics.* The most basic statistical analyses in evaluation studies involve:

    a)   the total number of specific responses to an item (e.g., female participants = 48; males = 32);

    b)   the total number of responses to each item on a descriptive or attitude scale;

    c)   the average number of responses by a group of participants on a descriptive or attitude scale;

    d)   the percentages of responses in different categories (e.g., females = 48/80 (60%); males = 32/80 (40%); and

    e)   combinations of the above (e.g., the number of female participants agreeing vs. disagreeing with a particular statement).

Computer packages for statistical analysis commonly generate the above simple descriptive results side-by-side with more complex results (e.g., standard deviations), regardless of whether all of these measures are actually essential to the study. The more complex statistics should be not included in the analysis or subsequently reported, unless their relevance is clear and their meaning is fully explained.

12   *Inferential statistics.* More complex statistical analyses involve drawing conclusions ('inferences') about, for example, the extent to which two groups of participants (e.g., female and male) give 'significantly different' responses to an item. Such questions involve higher levels of statistical analysis not always required in basic research and evaluation studies. For the record:

    a)   when inferential analyses are required, the data obtained from measures such as those described above are usually *non-parametric*; and

    b)   appropriate non-parametric statistics may include the Chi-square, Wilcoxon, and Mann–Whitney U tests. Simple procedures can be found online for conducting these analyses.

    c)   The term 'significant' should be reserved to describe levels of *statistical significance* in research and evaluation reports, and other terms—e.g., a 'substantial' difference—should be used when a non-statistical meaning is intended.

13 *Tables and Figures*. Most quantitative evaluation studies require a descriptive summary of the results in terms of frequency totals and/or average scores, though only when these are meaningful and central to the discussion. These may be presented:

a) in the body of the report, as Tables, or, when extensive data were collected though not all reported, in Appendices; and

b) in Figures, as graphs. Computer packages for statistical analysis commonly generate a range of graphs (line diagrams, bar diagrams, pie-charts, etc.) for every test item. These should only be included if they contain meaningful information that cannot be adequately expressed in a simpler form (e.g., a table). For example, a pie-chart illustrating the female/male breakdown of a participant group adds no useful information to the simple statement 'Female participants = 60%; Males = 40%'.

14 *Percentage scores and decimal points*. Computer packages commonly generate far more specific information of these types than is actually useful or meaningful, as in the following examples.

a) Percentage scores are usually superfluous when the number of participants is small (e.g., 10 or less). For example, a description of the males in a group of participants as '89%' can be easily recognized by statistically minded readers as signifying that the group contained only 9 persons, including 8 males.

b) In particular situations—e.g., analyses involving a large number of participants—it may be useful to accept computer-generated statistics involving decimal places (e.g., '88.9%'), though it is rarely useful to include two decimal places (e.g., '88.89%'). As a rule, statistical quantities including decimal places can be rounded up or down to the nearest whole number.

c) Computer packages for statistical analysis can also generate results that are complete nonsense (e.g., a group average score of 1.25, 'where 1 = Female and 2 = Male')! The evaluator should guard against uncritically retaining meaningless results of this kind.

15 *Reporting the study*. In the social sciences, a standard set of conventions for reporting research and evaluation studies has been defined by the American Psychological Association (APA format).[73] Otherwise, the precise rules and procedures may differ between the organizations requesting the report (funding agencies, journals, conference organizers, etc.). In general, the results of a study should follow this basic sequence:

a) *Introduction*. The general background to the study is described (e.g., the national and local context in which it takes place; similar work reported previously; and justification for the current study). In general, all of the relevant literature sources should be introduced in this section.

b) *Methodology.* The procedures adopted for data collection, sampling, and statistical analysis should be described in sufficient detail for the study to be replicated by others in future.

c) *Analysis and Presentation of Results.* The relevant and meaningful results should be presented in tabular and graphical formats as appropriate. Results lacking a clear meaning should not be reported unless alternative results were specifically expected. The presentation of results in this section should avoid editorial comment and interpretation.

d) *Discussion of Results.* The meaning of the results is interpreted in relation to the study's objectives. Explanations can be suggested for results that were expected though not actually observed. Ideally, the literature sources used to explain the results should have been introduced in the previous Introduction section, because the introduction of new literature evidence in the Discussion/Conclusions sections can look like an afterthought. The Discussion section is appropriate for the presentation of recommendations.

e) *Conclusions.* The overall conclusions of the study are summarized by paraphrasing the most meaningful findings and recommendations reported in the previous sections.

By following such checklists, an evaluation study may not only fulfill the immediate needs of specific applied projects but also, by accident if not design, the rigorous criteria of generalizable scientific research.

Summary

A century of research has generated solid foundations for global education projects. Recurring conclusions have emphasized the importance of direct communication between students and with the teacher via synchronous (real-time) as well as asynchronous (delayed) methods. These foundations have been obscured by successively simpler educational principles, and by open and distance learning practices that sacrifice real-time interaction in favor of the flexibility and convenience of asynchronous methods. Evaluation studies illustrate the wide range of cost-effective methods available for both types of interaction; but major differences have opened up between the uses of online and traditional media in western and Asian education. The importance of situation-specific and culturally sensitive evaluation studies raises the need for practical evaluation guidelines.

5

THE POWER OF MANY

Double-Edged Swords

Online institutions are familiar with the criticism that they have sacrificed academic quality to quantity and automation. The Asian PANdora network's studies have determined that, in each of Bhutan, Pakistan, and Sri Lanka, over half of the 3,000 students surveyed believe that they could "learn more from books than from a computer or other technologies."[1] In Cambodia, Laos, and Vietnam, interviews with 450 teachers, students, policy-makers, and members of the public, reveal hopes that distance education can help to solve national educational and economic problems, but doubts that it can ever be as good as face-to-face education.[2] The majority of 533 teachers and students surveyed in China are similarly dubious about the value of online learning, and decline to use it even when it is available to them.[3] These criticisms are polite compared with those of DE's arch-critic, David Noble. Distance educators still smart at the attacks by Noble in a series of books and articles during the 1990s and early 2000s. The "technozealouts . . . forge ahead", he argued, without evidence for their claims that the new media enhance educational standards or productivity, and without appreciable demand from teachers and students.[4] Recalling Reid's analysis 50 years ago of commercial operations that dispense costly though worthless academic qualifications ("degree mills"),[5] Noble listed educational institutions—some academically credible, others less so—that in his opinion were on their way to degree and diploma mill status. "The overriding commercial intent and market orientation behind these initiatives was made explicit," he concluded (p. 30), causing credible distance educators to howl with rage at being tarred by the same brush as diploma millers.

The criticisms still flourish ten years later, true to Noble's prediction. A 2010 documentary on PBS-TV has accused the burgeoning US market in 'for-profit' online education of excessive student fees, improper recruiting tactics, reliance on non-tenured, part-time teaching faculty, and monotonous online learning routines dominated by asynchronous, text-based discussion.[6] Pina (2010) argues that legitimate DE institutions continue to outnumber the diploma mills, but that "conditions which allow diploma mills to thrive appear to be ingrained in the culture of higher education" (p. 125) and need to be addressed.[7] Meanwhile, educational monitoring groups update their records of educational quackery on an almost daily basis, alleging that hundreds of "online colleges crank out fake diplomas and phony college degrees at a dizzying pace";[8] and credible educators are encouraging the use of the internet for 'massive open online courses' (MOOC) attended by thousands of students. In a climate already critical of DE's automated and impersonal nature, such initiatives are inviting criticism, and receiving it. For example:

> (I) see the MOOC as the technology-driven, socially-networked version of the cattle-herd lecture hall courses so prevalent on college campuses today. Herding 500 students in a course is still herding 500 students in a course, even if try to put a modern technology spin on it.[9]

In this climate of doubt, credible online educators ought to keep track of any way in which their services might be criticized. An obvious first target for the critic is their reliance on a medium that offers little or no guarantee of privacy. A simple command on PC computers ('traceroute') reveals that every e-mail sent and web site visited can be instantaneously screened in dozens of locations. With the help of the PANdora network, the routes of attempted web-site hits were traced from a dozen Asian countries.[10] At a minimum, 7 web servers were involved in the routes from source to target, as in the case of a web hit made from a university-based computer in Lahore, Pakistan, to a web host in Islamabad, Pakistan. By contrast, web-page requests from a university in Phnom Penh, Cambodia, to another university in the same city involved 10 'hops' between web servers, because their route took them through Hanoi in neighboring Viet Nam. Even more indirect was the route taken by hits from China (Beijing) to Ulaanbaatar (Mongolia), which typically involved 15 hops through Hemden (USA) and Tomsk (Russia). One of the more complex routes is shown in Figure 5.1, describing the outward route of a web hit from Lahore to Phnom Penh (via Islamabad, Chieti, Bochum, Virginia, and Hanoi), and the return route (via Hanoi, Beijing, three states in the USA, and Islamabad). Eventful routes of this kind were commonly identified in the 2007 study, and remain in place four years later.

The study also recorded the lengths of time taken by web hits as indicated by the traceroute method.[11] These appeared related to web-site design techniques. The most rapid hits were associated with the HTML option of the *Moodle* learning management system (10–19 seconds from request to display). The more recent PHP version of *Moodle* took up to 39 seconds to display. If a traceroute attempt

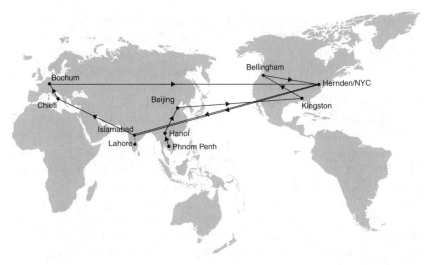

FIGURE 5.1 The world travels of a web hit from Pakistan to Cambodia.

Source: Baggaley & Batpurev, 2007b.

was unsuccessful after 3 minutes, it was abandoned. Ten of the study's 31 participants failed in all of their traceroute attempts, with results indicating that their online requests had successfully left the source computer but were always blocked on route. This mirrors the common experience of internet users in many Asian countries, as described by this patient academic in Bhutan:

> (A)ccess is still our main concern . . . Even if one has access, connectivity can be very poor. This week I experienced (this) in Phuntsoling. After one hour I still couldn't send one email . . . (W)e had Moodle installed on our server at Samtse, but then lightning struck and we were down for a month. Then the suggestion from the techies was to have Druknet (the ISP) host it. Even after moving it there, it went down on a number of occasions . . . So we decided to explore possibilities of hosting it elsewhere where we may receive better support and service. However, we have not been very successful so far.[12]

The traceroute study concluded that the low levels of web accessibility experienced across Asia are not primarily due to the use of inadequate computers, for all of the participants were using up-to-date institutional facilities. A more fundamental reason appeared to be the complex routings taken by the web hits, some of them apparently determined by political or economic factors. This raises concerns about the security of e-mails and web-page selections that travel through three or more continents on the way to their destination sometimes a mile up the road, or in a neighboring office. The study recommended the development of new routes, internet Exchange Points (IXPs) and mirror sites for educational usage in the regions with poor accessibility. It also urged that online programmers should resist the common temptation to design educational applications that require ever more bandwidth ('bandwidth creep').[13] Succumbing to the temptation of devising complex but less efficient techniques invites criticism from those wishing to cast doubt on the validity of DE claims in particular geographical regions.

So the techniques selected for online education, as well as poor accessibility, are obvious targets for criticism. All media can be used efficiently and inefficiently, and at worst they each have the potential to do harm as well as good. They are the "double-edged swords" described by 17th-century philosopher Robert Boyle in his analysis of methods "as well applicable to the service of Falsehood, as of Truth."[14] Film and television have carried violent and potentially harmful content throughout their histories, and commonly design their messages to be persuasive with specific demographic groups (e.g., the female teenager; the young professional). Today's online media, however, because of their added interactive element, have an unprecedented power to direct their messages not just at general social groupings but at specific individuals. The receivers of online information can be identified in relation to:

a)   the history of their previous online activities;
b)   the personal profiles they have placed in online social media databases; and
c)   the unique internet protocols (IPs) by which their computers publicly identify them each time they log on.

The double-edged effects of social networking tools have been discussed in the political arena for a decade. Rheingold[15] described the ability of like-minded individuals to assemble almost instantaneously in "smart mobs", aided by online and mobile technologies that combine "computation, communication, reputation, and location awareness" (p. 169). He detailed the dramatic results of social media coordination, as in the case of the Filipino President, Joseph Estrada, forced from office in 2001 by a million protesters coordinated by text-messaging. He described this process as a type of 'swarming'—"massive outbreaks of cooperation" demonstrating "the power of the mobile many." The same effects occurred during the writing of this book in 2011, in the use of social media to coordinate the overthrow of successive Middle Eastern governments. The social media are a dramatic example of the "knowledge is power" principle discussed earlier; and, as knowledge is relative to one's prejudices, the messages of the social media can be as double-edged as those of any medium.

Social media tools offer powerful effects in education. *Twitter* has been recommended as a useful way of establishing instant contact with like-minded people in deciding on lesson plans, book and resource recommendations, and in hosting book clubs;[16] and an enlightened example of *Twitter* use is currently enabling Chilean medics to coordinate organ transplants.[17] *Facebook* activities are developed for purposes including the reduction of high-school dropout rates[18] and the building of student self-esteem.[19] In conjunction with 'location-aware' services such as *Brightkite*,[20] *Foursquare*,[21] and *Loopt*,[22] these services are used to mount 'social media treasure hunts' in which journalism students explore their cities equipped with cellphones, laptops, and location-tracking global positioning systems (GPS), gaining experience in tracing individuals and online information about them.[23] Major suppliers including *Facebook*, *Twitter* and *Gmail* streamline their services via strategic alliances that allow users to link their personal accounts in an 'aggregated' database of personal details. Adding the *Recognizr* facial recognition software to one's cellphone makes personal tracking even easier, allowing subscribers to point their cellphone cameras at passers-by in the street and to download their identities, addresses, and other personal details within seconds.[24-25] Depending on who wields the sword, this double-edged information can be used to assist someone in distress, or to rob his home before he returns there.[26] The social media search skills used for educational activities also facilitate online activities ranging from stalking, bullying and blackmail to, in a recent extreme case, the luring of an Australian teenager to her death by a *Facebook* contact (defined by the service as a 'friend').[27] Meanwhile, services such as *Anonymizer*[28] and *MuteMail*[29] disguise the location and identity of the online sleuth, protecting the innocent and the guilty alike.

This "dark side" of the new social media is discussed by Evans (2010).

> In many ways, we're drunk on social media. The reality is there's a dark side to social media that people need to seriously start thinking about now. Every tweet, update, video and blog post is micro-chapter of your public profile that anyone can access. Sure, it's information that is created for friends, family and colleagues but it's also out there for other people with less virtuous interests.[30]

The evidence of such risks can easily be overlooked. One would not easily have guessed at the intrusive potential of the *Recognizr* software, for example, by looking at the web site on which it was launched, which stressed the tool's uses for legitimate purposes only by students, professionals, and college alumni associations. (A year later, the company that developed this software has been sold, and the original *recognizr.com* location doesn't mention this application at all.) Social networking products commonly identify themselves with credible users in this way: e.g., *Second Life*[31] with educational institutions including Harvard University and the UK Open University; and *Facebook* and *Twitter* with credible professionals, broadcasting networks, companies, and social organizations. At the other extreme, *Second Life* has been shown to host activities including child pornography,[32] prostitution,[33] and illegal gambling[34] and, while the supplier states its concern to curb such activities,[35-37] the ease with which a casual *Second Life* surfer can find them indicates lax scrutiny. Information is readily available on how to optimize the design of a *Facebook* page for political and marketing purposes;[38–40] and comparable instruction is needed to educate the public about the risks of social software generally.[41] Web sites such as *PleaseRobMe*,[42] *QuitFacebook*,[43] and *AThinLine*[44] have emerged to promote this awareness, and agencies including the US Electronic Privacy Information Center (EPIC),[45–46] and Canada's Office of the Privacy Commissioner (OPCC)[47] have instructed social media providers to tighten their procedures in order to safeguard users' security. *Facebook*'s response has been to make modifications to its services and site design, while still leaving the responsibility for secure configuration of user accounts to the individual subscribers. In the words of the company's 25-year-old chief executive, Mark Zuckerberg (2009): "(We) understand that everyone's needs are different . . . the best way for you to find the right settings is to read through all your options and customize them for yourself."[48]

The small print of *Facebook*'s 5,000-word Privacy Policy (section 3) indicates that the default setting for a new account is no-privacy, and that subscribers need to make a conscious effort to change this:

> Facebook is designed to make it easy for you to find and connect with others. For this reason, your name and profile picture do not have privacy settings. If you are uncomfortable with sharing your profile picture, you should delete it (or not add one).[49]

The current default settings expose the details of one's online status, biography, family, and personal relationships to general view. Religious and political views are exposed to one's 'friends' and their 'friends', while certain information can be restricted to friends only. So the friends' personal details are exposed through one's account, if they have not configured their accounts to prevent this; and users have no way to choose which of their friends' friends should be allowed to see their details. Zuckerberg has recently announced the addition of location-tracking software to *Facebook*, so that users can know "where a person is and to personalize what's around them."[50] This will increase the ability of teachers and students to locate like-minded people for educational purposes, and will enable customized advertising to be targeted at individuals based on their interests and tastes. If *Facebook*'s new tracking software has the same functions as the 'location-aware' services, one can assume that it will also increase the precision of online stalking.

These issues are not ignored in the latest academic writings about the social media. Thelwall & Stuart have discussed the personal security risks of using *MySpace*, a major social networking site of the early 2000s until its market share was overtaken by *Facebook*. *MySpace* too has come under fire for lax policies potentially exposing users to online predators, and the company has taken steps to remove known pedophiles from its user lists. Despite the evidence common to numerous social media sites, commentators currently seem to prefer not to come down on one side of the argument or the other.

There is no simple answer as to whether MySpace has made life more or less safe for teenagers . . . and it is not clear whether MySpace's publically removing identified pedophiles will create a false sense of security or raise awareness of the need to be careful.[51]

Pedigree of a Plagiarized Piece

The commercialization of online techniques has been successfully opposed in the last decade by the developers of open-source software (OSS) and open publishing approaches. In the previous chapter, it was argued that proprietary software products can restrict the flexibility of the teaching and learning process. OSS approaches, by contrast, are more easily customized to the needs of specific situations. These same approaches have led to a loss of quality control, however, as indicated by reports of open editing biases in the popular *Wikipedia* information source,[52] and by that repository's own self-description as "the free encyclopedia that anyone can edit."[53] Increases in student plagiarism have been widely attributed to the increased ease of online 'copying and pasting';[54] and a corresponding increase in plagiarism has also been observed in the publishing practices of academics.[55] The ease of online referencing has also had a discomforting impact on the current writer's practices. The reference list of this book, for example, contains an unusually high proportion of citations in the year of writing (2010–11), which would have been impossible before the expansion of online resources. While it is satisfying to have access to such a large amount of up-to-date material, it is worrying that so many of the sources increasingly cited are 'blogs' by unknown and unaccredited people rather than quality-assured traditional sources. The four-year 'shake-down' period whereby submitted articles were reviewed, published in print, absorbed, and cited in subsequent articles, is a thing of the past.

To a teacher, editor or journal reviewer, the warning signals of plagiarism can be easy to detect. A writer of a journal submission may betray plagiarism in the opening paragraph, with a phrase such as "this book will discuss." A plagiarized paper may also be longer than required, or may contain multiple styles of expression, off-topic emphases, and off-beat literature references.[56] It can still be impossible to recognize the source of the material plagiarized, however. To assist in this, a wide range of online 'plagiarism checking' products and services have emerged (e.g., *AntiPlagiarism, CaNexus, CopyCatch, DupliChecker, FindSame, iThenticate, ScanMyEssay, Turnitin, Viper, WordCheckSystems*). In 2005, the writer uploaded a suspect student paper to the checking service, *Turnitin.com*.[57] Within minutes, it provided clear evidence of the online sources of information that the student had copied without acknowledgement, and of the many occasions the same work had been submitted in other academic courses. This case revealed the various types of denial that a student can offer when accused of plagiarism, and generated a firm but fair policy for handling such cases at the writer's former university.[58] On that occasion, the analysis focused on the mentality of the plagiarist. Data provided in *Turnitin*'s 'originality report', however, allows one to dig more deeply into the often surprising history of the plagiarized material itself. For, if an online publication or passage is worth plagiarizing, it may have been plagiarized in its own right from an even earlier source. Options in the originality report allow one to dig deeply into the history of the material, revealing sources hidden by those with which the plagiarized content overlaps. The digging process resembles the search for an ancestor in a family history database, and the secrets revealed may be illustrated in the following genealogical terms.

- *Birth*: the moment at which material is published;
- *Genetic trace*: evidence of the material's origin in other sources;
- *Parent*: a person with previous authorship of at least part of the material;
- *Marriage*: the union of several materials originating in different sources;
- *Death*: the deletion and disappearance of material;
- *Orphan*: material derived from sources since deleted;
- *Generation*: the period from the birth of reused material to its reuse in other material; and
- *Ancestor*: a source from which material originated one or more generations ago.

As in family history research, plagiarism checking can establish the *pedigree* of the material and its sources; a historical account that remains on record even after the sources themselves have disappeared from online view.

A Birth is Announced

During the writing of this book, the writer used *Turnitin.com* to investigate another student assignment (Paper/X) that recently arrived on his desk, bearing several plagiarism hallmarks. The unoriginality report gave the paper a 'similarity index' of 72%—the extent to which sections of it were the same as other material in the *Turnitin* database. The report also highlighted the exact passages that the student had copied, color-coded to indicate their original sources. *Turnitin* appears to have an encyclopedic amount of material in its repository, trawled from the internet and supplemented by the documents uploaded to it for analysis. It should be noted, however, that its similarity index is a useful but fallible estimate of originality, and that to accept it uncritically could do a student injustice. *Turnitin* provides three analysis options to ensure a more accurate reading by excluding:

1   *quoted passages*: if a passage is cited in quotation marks, *Turnitin* will not classify it as potentially plagiarized;
2   *bibliography*: if a bibliography item is cited in a standard publication format (e.g., APA or Chicago style), it is likely to be the same as in previous publications, and will not be classified as plagiarism; and

3   *small matches*: different authors may create the same word sequences (strings) by chance, and strings may be excluded from the analysis if less than a specified word length.

The criteria for these exclusions are also fallible, however. For instance, when a paper's formatting convention uses indentation to indicate a quoted passage rather than quotation marks, the *Turnitin* user must add quotation marks to the uploaded paper in order to exclude the passage from the analysis. The rationale for the acceptable word length of a string is also arbitrary. For the current analysis, a generous 50-word cut-off was specified, to prevent the analysis from identifying hundreds of previous publications as overlapping with the uploaded document. A detailed analysis of academic plagiarism by Decoo stresses that a no-word limit provides the most thorough check. Deliberate plagiarists, Decoo indicates, may not stop at paraphrasing a few lines, but may reword whole articles phrase by phrase.[59] Even a generous 50-word cut-off does not seem to prevent genuine plagiarism from being uncovered, however, for many copiers do not seem to stop at the 50-word limit in taking material from other sources.

More important in a *Turnitin* analysis is the need to distinguish between a) overlaps between Paper/X and online sources; and b) overlaps between online sources and each other. In the absence of this evidence, the originality report can give the superficial impression that Paper/X was copied from numerous sources, whereas in fact it may have been copied from a single source which in turn copied it from others. This separation function is provided by *Turnitin*'s "Show highest matches together" display. The levels of similarity between Paper/X and previous sources in the current analysis, as estimated by the *Turnitin* report before and after these exclusions, are given in Table 5.1. After all four types of exclusion, the cumulative overlap between Paper/X and the remaining sources is estimated as 63%, including overlaps (51%) with other papers in the *Turnitin* database, mainly

TABLE 5.1 Cumulative similarity estimates (%) before and after *Turnitin* exclusions.

Exclusions	Similarity index (%)	Similarity by source (Turnitin *estimates*)		
		Internet sources	Publications	Papers
Before exclusions	100	78	4	100
1) After exclusion of previous upload	72	72	4	56
2) After exclusion of quoted passages	70	70	4	55
3) After exclusion of bibliography	63	63	3	51
4) After exclusion of 50-word matches	63	63	3	51

Source: Author.

by students who submitted the same material in assignments at other universities and colleges.

Parents are Identified

At this point, Paper/X was re-examined in order to determine whether or not its reuse of previously published material constituted deliberate plagiarism. A paper with a high level of similarity to other sources may have acknowledged them in unconventional ways. One of the writer's students, for example, on being told that an assignment looked as though it might have been plagiarized, submitted a revised version that the *Turnitin* analysis identified as having a *higher* amount of overlap with other sources than before the revision. The student simply did not understand how to attribute the sources correctly. Paper/X, however, reused page after page from other sources without acknowledging them in any form. Under the "Show highest matches together" setting in its *Turnitin* analysis, 119 sources were listed. This was not taken as evidence that the student had pains-takingly copied information from 119 online sources without acknowledging them; for it was clear from the dates of copying that the passages used in Paper/ X had also been copied into 119 other sources known to the *Turnitin* database. The publication dates of the other sources listed by *Turnitin* showed that this occurred both before and after the date on which Paper/X was submitted for grading.

This list of 119 sources was not exhaustive, however. In its "Show matches one at a time" display, the *Turnitin* report indicated that many of Paper/X's sources were completely or partially "hidden by one or more sources in the cumulative report." To reveal these hidden sources, the analyst has to return to the "Show highest matches together" display, and to exclude each source from the analysis in turn. At this point in the current analysis, the number of sources overlapping with Paper/X rose to 149. Some were unique sources, while others were different versions of web sites updated over time and retained in the internet's cache memory. As one is increasingly warned, nothing deleted from the internet ever truly disappears;[60] and, as will be shown below, it is a simple matter to check on versions of a web site that have long since disappeared from general view. Overlaps between Paper/X and 52 unique web sites were identified, as indicated in Table 5.2. This analysis shows that Paper/X's main parent, with which it had the highest percentage overlap, was an entry in *Wikipedia*. Nine other web sites had already used this source, usually with attribution. The *Turnitin* report showed that elements of the material had also been used in student papers submitted to 23 different educational institutions.

Wikipedia was not the only parent of Paper/X, however, for the student had evidently used unattributed material from several sources. According to the *Turnitin* analysis, the paper used independent material updated at *WiredSafety.org* in April 2009, at least some of which had also appeared in the earliest known

TABLE 5.2 Cumulative similarity estimates (%) after exclusions of other sources.

	Overlapping web sites	Similarity (%) after exclusion	Similarity by source (Turnitin estimates)		
			Internet sources	Publications	Papers
1	en.wikipedia.org	63	63	3	51
2	www.medbib.com★	63	63	3	51
3	www.answers.com★	63	63	3	51
4	www.fuhz.com★	62	62	3	51
5	www.ahooldus.ee★	62	62	3	51
6	www.globalwarmingart.com★	62	62	3	51
7	wiki.healthhaven.com★	62	62	3	51
8	Encyclopedia.vbxml.net★	62	62	3	51
9	www.evanzo.com★	62	62	3	51
10	www.callwiz.com★	61	61	3	51
	(...)				
35	www.wiredsafety.org	52	27	3	38
	(...)				
45	www.wiredkids.org	35	15	3	34
	(...)				
52	www.auburnmountain.com	4	2	3	10

Notes: The remaining overlaps after row #52 are predominantly with student papers.
★These web sites have reused some or all of the #1 source page at *Wikipedia.org*
Source: Author.

ancestor of material in Paper/X—a November 2002 version of *WiredKids.org*. It seems that one of the two 'wired' sites used material that had previously appeared on the other; and, as both were created by the same organization, one would not characterize this as plagiarism. The original versions of all three sites have since been deleted, as much if not all internet material may die catastrophically in the future. The plagiarized sections in Paper/X may therefore be described as orphans, the offspring of a marriage between parents since deceased.

Family history records—e.g., the *International Genealogical Index* (IGI)—are similarly incomplete, and the connections between its separate entries often have to be inferred with less than complete certainty. Popular TV genealogy programs rarely demonstrate the caution that is needed in verifying a family connection, and the possibility that the researcher may easily identify the wrong record as the ancestor among the many alternative records.

A Pedigree is Established

Despite their deletion from general view, the history of many web sites can be examined via the *Wayback Machine*, an online archive currently containing 150 billion pages from 1996 to the present day.[61] The archive states that the *WiredKids* site dates back to 2000, and *WiredSafety* to 2002; and it traces the pages reused in Paper/X to June 2004. The most recent versions of these sites that could be located are dated May 2004 and July 2005 respectively. It can be assumed that the *WiredKids* passage was reused by the same author(s) on the *WiredSafety* site. The *Wayback Machine* traces the material plagiarized from *Wikipedia* to July 2004, although its content does not overlap with that of the other two sites.

The chronological details provided by *Turnitin* were then compared with the date that Paper/X was submitted for grading. Twenty-two internet cache versions of the *Wikipedia* entry were identified, accounting for over half of Paper/X's content. In the week before its submission, Paper/X's similarity with the *Wikipedia* entry was at its highest, suggesting that the page had evolved to that level of overlap in the course of successive *Wikipedia* updates, and that it evolved away from similarity with Paper/X thereafter. *Turnitin*'s chronological record indicated that the *Wikipedia* material was used in 51 web sites and student papers before Paper/X was submitted for grading, and in 23 other sources subsequently. The information in the *Turnitin* report suggests a probable 'family tree' of Paper/X's plagiarized pieces, containing two direct 'parents' (*Wikipedia* and *WiredSafety*) and a 'grandparent' (*WiredKids*): Table 5.3. The rate at which the unoriginal pieces were reused by different writers, according to the *Turnitin* record, escalated

TABLE 5.3 Ancestry of the unoriginal passages in a student paper.

Dates of the plagiarized material		*The material's family tree*
January 2001	*Wikipedia.org* is founded.	Wikipedia.org
May 2004	*WiredKids.org* adds the material that was later found in Paper/X.	WiredKids.org
June 2004	The *WiredKids.org* material is also published at *WiredSafety.org*.	WiredSafety.org
By November 2009	The *Wikipedia* material is used in 34 sites and submitted online to 17 institutions.	51 other sites use the material
November 2009	Paper/X is submitted for grading	Paper/X
December 2009 -> October 2010	The *Wikipedia* material is used on another 17 sites and submitted online to another 6 institutions.	Another 23 sites use the material

Source: Author.

between 2002 and 2010. Their reuses rose from an average of 7 per year between November 2002 and November 2009, to 23 in the year from December 2009 to October 2010.

Skeletons in the Closet

The extensive quasi-genetic traces evident in Paper/X, and the student's failure to acknowledge its sources, clearly indicated conscious plagiarism. The *Wikipedia* and *WiredKids* passages qualified as plagiarized pieces with an eventful legacy. The *Turnitin* analysis was not exhaustive. There was no way of knowing, for example, how many times the same materials may have been copied from offline sources and/or submitted as hard copy. Other analyses by the writer have shown that student material can derive from a variety of sources, including the student's own previously submitted work, and from 'course materials repositories', a euphemism for 'cheat sites' from which copy-ready assignment material can be purchased. To his knowledge, plagiarism and cribbing rarely occurred among the writer's students, possibly because of university statements that make it plain to them that plagiarism-checking methods may be used in the assessment of their work. He has frequently noted obvious plagiarism in journal submissions sent to him for peer-reviewing, however. So far, *Wikipedia* has emerged as the most commonly plagiarized source in the writer's checks. It is the easiest and often the most up-to-date reference site, although its pages usually lack evidence of their sources and originality. *Wikipedia* is currently ranked by *Google* as the fifth most frequently visited web site in the world.[62]

The Uncritical Mass

With regard to personal security and that of intellectual property, the internet is neither more dangerous nor safe than the average motorway, and it is wise to have a sense of road safety in both contexts. One would not normally lead one's students onto a busy highway without first warning them about the traffic conditions. Currently, however, warnings about the security risks of online practices, expressed by government agencies and other concerned observers, seem plaintive and unavailing in the face of the apparent acceptance of these practices by countless credible institutions, academics, political leaders, and other professionals. The massive public use of online techniques seems to give some students and teachers the impression that they are risk-free. Raising concerns about the personal security of social media at a 2010 educational meeting, the writer was asked, "Why should I be concerned when everyone is using them?" The answer to this question is another question: in requiring your students to use these methods in their courses, do you preface the activity by reminding them how to configure their software for personal security? At a purely selfish level, this precaution may at least protect the teacher and the institution from liability if a student's compulsory social media activities have negative personal consequences.

For some students and teachers, there appears to be similar confusion as to the general academic conduct expected of them in the online age. In recent years, for example, the writer and his colleagues have noted a practice by some students of openly hiring 'professional academic editors', contrary to the University's conduct codes. Similar practices have arisen in journalism owing to the open availability of press releases and wire copy, and have been nicknamed 'churnalism'.[63] At the time of writing, a Cardiff University study has estimated that 80% of British press coverage is now wholly or partly based on unoriginal material instead of on original research and writing.[64] In education, the lines between plagiarism, acceptable copying and ghost-writing seem to have been blurred by the increased availability of open educational resource practices, which also facilitate the reuse of previously published material. It seems ironic that educators should be unconcerned about risks related to online media which have become so obvious in other social contexts. As Rheingold has said: "it would be foolish to presume that only benign outcomes should be expected from smart mobs" (p. 164).

The public has had an ambivalent response to dawning dangers throughout history, expressing views variously described as representing "the wisdom of the crowd" and "the madness of crowds." "Every age has its peculiar folly", said Charles MacKay in his 1841 classic about popular trends, "some scheme, project, or phantasy, spurred on by the love of gain, the necessity of excitement, or the mere force of imitation."[65] As Surowiecki has noted, a collective decision can be formed rapidly by a powerful 'aggregating' mechanism,[66] as in the coordination of "smart mobs" by cellphones and social media. Faced by a trend that others are embracing enthusiastically, an individual often needs personal evidence in order to be sure of its negative implications. To break with a collective decision, one requires personal information about the possible risks attached to it, as might be gained from a close family member who has experienced the dangers previously. An effective counter to the problem of student plagiarism, for example, is to encourage one's colleagues to check if material submitted to them has also been plagiarized. In this writer's experience, when to their indignation they discover that it has, the issue suddenly becomes meaningful to them and they take action against it. Surowiecki indicates that the ability to question a collective decision also depends on local knowledge: e.g., on recognizing that conditions are inappropriate for the innovations being recommended for it (as in the case of high-bandwidth internet methods being recommended for low-bandwidth users). Recommendations of western-style online education in Asian nations seem far less appropriate after personally experiencing the problems of internet connectivity there.

Even plagiarism becomes slightly easier to condone after experiencing at first hand the local conditions of many Asian partners. In his work on behalf of funding agencies, the writer has frequently conducted plagiarism checks of reports and proposals submitted by international educators, and has found page after page copied from earlier reports and proposals. As in the 'pedigree' of plagiarized material illustrated in the previous section, these reports often have a long ancestry of plagiarized material that can easily be identified. The phrase "X is a landlocked country", for example, immediately suggests material copied from *Wikipedia*! For students and teachers in many non-western countries, however, major problems arise from the fact that English is not their first language. Useful and rigorous academic work on their part can be denied its rightful place in the international literature solely because of their lack of adequate English writing skill. Their culture may admit to little or no awareness that copying other people's writings can be regarded as dishonest, and a cultural rationale may have developed that plagiarism is a compliment to the original writer. If the family of a student or teacher depends for its livelihood upon his academic success, online copying and pasting can come to be regarded as an honorable option. The writer's views on this were deeply influenced in a conversation with an Asian Vice-Chancellor to whom he had mentioned the problem of plagiarism in the region. The man spread his hands sadly and said, "Our students are poor: they have no ethics." This was not intended as it sounded. It signified that Asian students cannot *afford* western-style ethics, and would be neglecting their family's interests if they embraced them. As Alfred Doolittle says in Shaw's *Pygmalion*, the poor cannot afford "middle-class morality":

> I'm one of the undeserving poor: that's what I am. Think of what that means to a man. It means that he's up agen middle class morality all the time . . . What is middle class morality? Just an excuse for never giving me anything.[67]

Being sensitive to international conditions, however, does not reduce the need to deal with the threat that plagiarism represents to academic quality. The seriousness of the situation was stressed in a detailed analysis by Lathrop & Foss, dedicated to "honest students (whose) integrity and hard work need to be recognised, supported, and protected."[68] These authors examined the mentality of those who cheat as well as that of the online services that assist them by supplying unoriginal material; and they provided practical guidelines for addressing the problem at all educational levels. Ten years later, plagiarism is still described as a problem that is going from bad to worse. In international collaborations, a line needs to be drawn between the academic activities that may be acceptable in one culture but are not in others. It should be explained to partners that, in the west, plagiarism can have the same consequences for one's family income as not plagiarizing might have elsewhere, for the following reasons:

a)   western writers found responsible for plagiarism or condoning it may be disgraced, fired, and barred from publication in academic journals and/or future project funding;

b)   western writers who copy their own previously published work into a new report can also be accused of plagiarism because the earlier publication is the copyrighted property of the publisher;

c)   a journal's reputation can suffer if it is found to have published plagiarized material;

d)   a development agency may lose its reputation if it is found to have awarded funding based on proposals containing plagiarism; and

e)   the appearance of plagiarism can arise even when it is not deliberate.

Georgetown University's conduct guidelines leave its student in no doubt on this: "If you came from a country where the definitions of plagiarism are different, then you have some catching up to do here."[69]

International partners can be reassured, however, that plagiarism and the appearance of it can be avoided by using the appropriate conventions for acknowledging the unoriginal material's source, and for inserting quotation marks around previously published passages. These conventions need to be taught to one's students. Critical interpretation skills are necessary for them to assess suspect and low-quality material before citing it, and unoriginal material should at least be paraphrased in students' own words, as per the skills of past generations. Such skills do not appear to be a high priority in today's schools, judging by the low quality that many of today's university students bring to the task of preparing assignments and crediting their sources. In this light, teachers and students should discuss the current arguments in favor of educational activities which re-combine other people's work in 'remixes'[70] and 'mashups',[71] and the fact that such practices are apparently not yet "subject to formal definition by any standards-setting body."[72] If these issues are not discussed, students may gain the clear impression that old values which respected the intellectual property of others are now passé. A powerful focus for student discussion is the steady supply of ethical issues brought to public attention by web sites such as *CheatingCulture.com*.[73] Students and project partners may also be required to 'turn in' their written material using services such as *Turnitin* in order to check for accidental plagiarism. They need to be shown how to assess the findings of such services reliably, however, for plagiarism-checking services can yield persuasive data needing careful interpretation. Unfortunately, detailed plagiarism analysis procedures of the type used in the previous section are repetitive and time-consuming (a half-day or more per paper), and few teachers have the time for this. It is to be hoped that companies such as *iParadigms* (the developer of *Turnitin.com* and *iThenticate*) will develop streamlined data-mining packages allowing educators to conduct such analyses routinely.

Once personal and local knowledge of threats to safety and quality have been shared with a critical mass of others, the uninformed crowd may begin to be transformed into a wise crowd. Social media polarize people, however, as efficiently as they coordinate them. For every smart mob, an opposing mob may form, each perceiving itself to be the wise group. This was illustrated by a sociometric analysis of the US political 'blogosphere' during the 2004 Presidential election, which revealed two tightly defined clusters of online opinion, liberal and conservative, each reinforcing its own views with little reference to those of the other group (Figure 5.2).[74]

> (S)ome people believed that the blogosphere might bring us together politically ... If the hope was that these two groups would talk to each other, the blog network reveals that these hopes have been utterly dashed . . . (P)olitical information is used more to reinforce preexisting opinions than to exchange differing points of view.[75]

There is no reason to suppose that social media will have more beneficial effects in education than they have had in the political arena, unless they are carefully guided towards specific purposes. If their uses lack a pedagogical rationale, the new media are likely to evolve on the basis of uninformed collective wisdom as their predecessors did. In the way that a popular trend can arise from a critical mass of opinion, so it may equally be formed by an *uncritical mass* that drives it

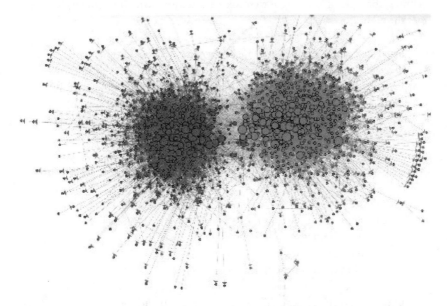

FIGURE 5.2   The political 'blogospheres' of the 2004 US Presidential election.

Key: Liberal blogs on the left of the diagram, conservative on the right.
Source: Adamic & Glance, 2005.

forward without clear justification; and if their purposes seem aimless, the media themselves are likely to take the blame and be marginalized when the development fails. The notion of the uncritical mass has not received much academic or popular attention. Even *Wikipedia*'s articles, currently numbered at 3.6 million,[76] do not deal with it. Freedman has considered the idea in relation to "the uncritical audiences that indulge" gregarious speakers at academic conferences;[77] and Fiske & Hartley rejected the idea in insisting that media audiences should be credited with having a range of reactions to messages.[78] They were correct in placing this emphasis because, in the 1970s context in which they were writing, 'mass communication' viewpoints had overlooked the individual differences that occur within audience reactions. Forty years on, the opposite seems to be occurring, with insufficient attention paid to the uncritical acceptance of new communication media and messages. The news media, once the domain of expert interviewees, are now filled with the comments of passersby in the street and anonymous bloggers who feel they have something to say. So the 'uncritical mass' may be an idea whose time has come!

To criticize and change one's views can be difficult, as Mezirow has shown in his analysis of the 'transformative learning' process.[79] The process involves changes in the understanding of a) oneself; b) one's beliefs; and c) one's behavior. To change the opinions and/or behavior of others is at least as difficult, requiring the kind of strategic effort required by health education campaigns, discussed earlier. For example, the six-stage approach to smoking cessation devised by Prochaska *et al.*[80] goes through:

1 *precontemplation*, in which general awareness of the issue is increased;
2 *contemplation*, whereby the individual imagines being in the changed situation;
3 *preparation*, building belief that the effort to change can be successful;
4 *action*, in which the change is implemented and socially supported;
5 *maintenance*, whereby temptations to revert are continually resisted; and
6 *termination,* when the change is stable.

Mezirow describes similar steps in his elaboration of the 'transformative' process[81]:

1 elaborating existing frames of reference;
2 learning new frames of reference;
3 transforming points of view; and
4 transforming habits of the mind.

Numerous classic project failures have been due to the lack of rationales and change strategies such as these, and have occurred precipitately. MacKay described the notorious banking collapse known as the 'South Sea Bubble'. Formed in 1711, the South Sea Company had sold its stock on the promise of rationales and promises that were not fulfilled. The investments grew ever more risky, until by 1720 they were no longer sustainable, and the bubble burst. MacKay's account indicates that projects cannot survive on over-optimism and hyperbole alone.

> Nations, like individuals, cannot become desperate gamblers with impunity . . . But in this false spirit has history too often been written. (The popular rationales) have been dilated on, and told over and over again, with all the eloquence of style and all the charms of fancy: while the circumstances which have most deeply affected the morals and welfare of the people have been passed over with but slight notice, as dry and dull, and capable of neither warmth nor colouring. (p. 74)

Back in the present, the American teen idol, Miley Cyrus, recently attempted to convince her fans that popular rationales about social media may not be as colorful as they appear. In an interview, she explained that she had terminated her online account at *Twitter.com* because, unguardedly disclosing her location in a *Twitter* message or 'tweet', she had caused herself and her hotel to be surrounded by an unruly mob of fans.

> That's because you announce everything you're doing . . . friends on the internet (are) not cool, not safe, not fun and most likely not real . . . I'm telling kids, 'Don't go on the internet. It's dangerous, not fun, and it wastes your life' . . . I (now) have a personal life.[82]

Such celebrities can play a valuable role in explaining the need for caution in the adoption of new media. Unfortunately, this particular teenage star missed the opportunity to be a role model for very long, by reopening her *Twitter* account when fans expressed outrage at her unfashionable decision.[83] For now at least, the 'uncritical mass' appears to have defeated her on that issue.

A Giant Structure

Useful lessons can be drawn from plans that go awry. At the inaugural meeting of the United Nations' Internet Governance Forum (IGF) in 2006, it was announced that the World Wide Web now had full language translation capabilities.[84] The report was welcomed as evidence that the internet can be used to unite all nations in a common language; that it is the equivalent of the Tower of Babel, built circa 3000 BC;[85] and that modern engineers have now succeeded in replicating the Tower.[86] This interpretation seemed to miss the point that the original Tower of Babel fell down, reputedly because God was angry at mankind's arrogance in building it. For their punishment, the people were scattered into diverse nations, and their common language was divided into many (Figure 5.3). The resemblance

FIGURE 5.3 The Tower of Babel

Source: Foster, 1914.

between this image and the tower later designed by Vladimir Tatlin (Figure 3.15) is unmistakable.

As with the internet 5,000 years later, credit for the Tower of Babel was claimed by numerous political factions. The consensus of opinion suggests that Iraq (formerly Babylon) was the Tower's location, and that the building effort was led by the Hamites under Nimrod.[87] The question arises as to whether the new online version of the Tower will be more successful than the original. Analogies between the Tower of Babel and the internet commonly suggest that it will not. Anderson has argued that the internet, like the Tower, "makes life simpler, yet more complicated; it brings us together, yet pushes us apart."[88] Wilks (2001) criticized the World Bank's Knowledge Bank project, and its Development Gateway initiative in particular, as a Babel-like activity creating "an illusory atmosphere of consensus and universality, while proclaiming 'diversity'."[89] Guri-Rosenblit made a similar allusion to the Tower in relation to the need for an integrated technological approach in higher and distance education.[90] Evidently, the creation of a common international communication platform still has some way to go. At the IGF's Hyderabad meeting in 2008, the chair of the Cyber-security and Cyber-crime symposium announced:

Yesterday, I think there were about 80 headsets missing after the session (It's) important to hand them back so that they can be recharged. If we lose 80 headsets after each session, we will not be able to hand them out anymore, and you will not be able to listen to our interpreters.[91]

The more one considers historical events, the more the differences between competing versions of them become apparent. It usually emerges that little has changed in human nature over the centuries, and that modern opinions are shaped by personal motives as they always have been. The Tower of Babel is therefore not only an apt metaphor for the internet's potential as a giant worldwide tool, but also a means for some updated reflection on how the future of online education may be shaped by human nature, as the Tower's fate was sealed previously.[92]

The Tower was a ziggurat or 'raised place', like many others in the Mesopotamian region.[93] The Bible's verdict is that the project was a success—too much so, in fact, and that God destroyed it, being offended by the hubris of a building that touched the skies and would encourage the people to think they could "do anything they want."[94] Apparently, the ancients were familiar with the "knowledge is power" principle, and with the fact that leaders might destroy their community development projects, as Stalin and other 20th-century leaders have since suppressed the projects of visionaries such as Dziga Vertov. Judaic texts give a similar account in which God destroys the nations' common language and disperses them across the earth. The Qur'an provides an account of a tower built in Egypt by the Pharaoh to confront the God of Moses; and the Book of Mormon adds a western-centric postscript in which God preserves the common language and leads the people to America. From these different perspectives, locations, and outcomes, five themes emerge.

1   *For better and for worse.* The ancient ziggurats and the internet are viewed as having similar benefits for humanity—the ziggurats as places of divine worship, and the internet as a giant structure by which diverse cultures can be unified and global education forged. These claims have been put into context by internet critics. In Stoll's words: "There are no simple technological solutions to social problems . . . Access to a universe of information cannot solve our problems: we will forever struggle to understand one another."[95] The ziggurats' construction has also been attributed to political motives: the need for high places where the elite could escape from floods,[96] and for secure places where the priests could conduct their rituals unobserved.[97] The least sympathetic descriptions of ziggurats resemble the modern-day critiques of the Burj Khaifa in Dubai: e.g., as "a monument for an era of credit-fuelled over-consumption—irresponsible and unsustainable" (Bedell, 2010). The internet today, like the Tower, is similarly described as a high place where elites can operate without interference from those who lack online access,[98] and as a secure place for covert interests and practices.[99] Distance educators

have excellent opportunities to advance the internet's potential for good; and the worldwide web's inventor, Sir Tim Berners-Lee, defends it as a tool for "helping humanity . . . any innovator can dream up an idea and set up a web site at some random place and let it just take off." He also stresses, however, the need to build "systems that help organizations become accountable . . . that respect users."[100] Thus, Berners-Lee indicates that, as with all media, the internet is neither better nor worse than the skills and intentions of its users.

2   *On again off again.* The development of the Tower was apparently a series of trial-and-error experiments with different techniques, some successful for a time, though all ultimately thwarted by political interests. After its original collapse in the 3rd millennium BC, the Tower was rebuilt by Nebuchadnezzar II (605–562 BC), and crumbled again after the Persian invasion of 478 BC.[101] Internet governance is in a similar period of flux at present. Since the announcement at the IGF Conference in 2006, internet designers have lamented the lack of a unified infrastructure, and the proliferation of technical protocols and terms: "everyone is trying to build a better mousetrap" (Ditter, cited by Amos, 2006).[102] As a deterrent to this division of labor, and in an attempt to deter nations from setting up their own independent root servers, the Internet Corporation for Assigned Names and Numbers (ICANN) has recently abandoned its requirement for internet domain names to be spelled in western characters.[103] It may equally be suspected, however, that this new measure will hasten the 'confusion of tongues' associated with the Tower, and the internet's loss of focus as a unified global structure. This development would restrict global education initiatives.

3   *Which world?* To the author(s) of Genesis, the world extended from the Mediterranean and the Black Sea to modern-day Iran and the Arabian peninsula, and no further.[104] Today, a similarly blinkered view is shown by those who recommend online education in developing nations despite its inaccessibility there. Web-based methods still flourish, in western-style education at least; but in other regions, they are faltering. Nations including China and Japan are making political efforts to kick-start online education in preference to traditional TV methods, though academics there are concerned that traditional media expertise and penetration will be lost to cost-ineffective alternatives.[105]

4   *What common language?* Of course, there never was a common language—at least not when the Tower was built in the 3rd millennium BC. Seely indicates the diversity of languages that already existed in the region at that time. Thus, the Tower of Babel has received an unfair reputation as the project that provoked a divine decision to divide one language into many; and the assumption has prevailed that it was named after the Hebrew term 'babel' meaning confusion. Yet it is also identified with Babylon, which as Dietz points out, has been translated as "gateway of the gods."[106] The educational internet has similarly been represented as both a gateway of opportunity and

a conduit of chaos. Pictures if not words are becoming the internet's common language. In the week this section of the book was written, photos of a gang rape in Vancouver were circulated on *Facebook* and other social media sites, escalating the victim's humiliation to an appalling international level.[107] If western-style online education and its tools are not better controlled than this, we need not feel surprised if other nations refuse to let their people access them, and decide that a multiplicity of divided internets is the only option.

5 *Warning signals.* Archaeological evidence indicates that the Babylonian ziggurats were strongly built with baked brick.[108] Judging by the barrage of hazards the Tower of Babel faced in Judaic, Greek and Roman texts,[109] it was singularly robust, withstanding high winds, fire, floods, and subsidence before finally falling. Perhaps the high priests, like the *Titanic* crew, became blasé as their Tower survived successive disasters, and failed to spot the warning signals of the end that was approaching. Warning signals have been indicated earlier in the book about the use of online methods in education: the decline and closure of online communities that results from loss of student interest; loss of student control caused by learning management systems; and student frustration in being required to use social media in their courses without a clear rationale. A cost-conscious educational administrator might invoke any one of these studies as an excuse to slash online resources, as decision-makers in the 1990s marginalized educational television. In other fields, the internet and worldwide web would doubtless have longer staying power, with little attention being paid to the demise of their educational subsector. According to the conclusions of numerous educators cited in this book, the need for evidence of pedagogical validity is central in the adoption of new online methods, and failure to act upon it is a critical misjudgment.

It takes a humorist to make the events of the past seem truly immediate. Goldstein (2009) speculates about how the builders of the Tower of Babel got on with their lives after the Tower fell:

> And so they cooked up new ideas . . . Li wanted to build the world's longest wall; Costa wanted to build a place where hundreds of people could sit in a circle and watch marvelous events; (and Mibzar) opened the world's first language school.[110]

So it is with the diversity of approaches in global education, for which the teachers and students are regularly required to master new tools. "The field appears to have a constant identity crisis, defined by a developmental deluge of pedagogies and technologies, depending on the favoured course delivery methods of the day".[111] It is cautionary to consider the possibility that global education might also be unrealistic and unsustainable, Babel-like. The internet and the Tower have both been described as facilitating the best and worst of human goals; as the outcome of cyclic success and failure; as an idea developed in one part of the world without regard for others; as a technology that began with diverse languages and ended without unifying them; and as a project that barrels onwards without paying attention to warning signals. Dowling (1996) cited the following optimistic analyses by educational media commentators:

- "one of the most magnificent instruments for raising the quality of teaching";[112]
- "an instrument for general adult education, it could significantly upgrade the common culture";[113]
- "no innovation has marched so quickly and confidently into the field of learning. It moves into the future of American education as a major resource";[114] and
- "a medium with so much potential, with so many needs to meet, and so many plans being made for it."[115]

These statements were not made about the internet, however, but were written between 1952 and 1962 about the advent of educational television. Dowling expressed the hope that online education would avoid a similar fate through the development of solid educational practices: "Television's failure to transform education was not technological," he wrote. "Television failed to meet the pedagogical needs of the educational community."[116] Perhaps online educators will learn from the lessons of the past, and will be more successful. Writers such as Dowling and Goldstein tread a lonely road in using the lessons of history to point to the uncritical optimism of the present; but even giant structures and grand designs can fail, and suddenly.[117]

Summary

All media carry benefits and risks. Online education relies on international communications with flawed technical quality, and on software programming and packaging techniques that reduce accessibility. The positive value of open resources in education is associated with an increase in academic plagiarism. The benefits of social media contrast with their personal security risks, and their powerful coordinating role is observed in the phenomenon of the 'smart mob'. The value of popular trends depends on whether they are adopted by informed groups or by an 'uncritical mass'. Popular critics of technology-based education commonly focus on its negative effects, and distance and online educators need to address these concerns in order to avoid the fate of flawed schemes throughout history.

6

HARMONY AND COUNTERPOINT

The Man who Mystified Moscow

> On one canvas is a huddle of objects painted with varying degrees of skill, virtuosity and vigour, harshly or smoothly. To harmonize the whole is the task of art.[1]

The effects of communication media are polarized in education as in politics and the arts; and analysts in each of these areas use similar methods for examining them. As the cubists analyzed their art forms into their component parts and synthesized them in new forms, so educators have analyzed the formal elements of their craft, and developed principles for their use. Like the constructivists in art, they have designed diverse technologies. One particular group of artists, the Futurists, developed the foundations for this multimedia world, developing the 'divisionism' technique of analyzing light and color into dots and stripes (1910). In their *Manifesto of the Futurist Painters* (1910), the Italian artist Umberto Boccioni and his colleagues criticized conventional art for not fully representing the dynamism of the world. Instead of celebrating "old canvases, old statues and old bric-a-brac," they said, it should express:

> the tangible miracles of contemporary life—the iron network of speedy communications which envelops the earth, the transatlantic liners, the dreadnoughts, those marvelous flights which furrow our skies, the profound courage of our submarine navigators and the spasmodic struggle to conquer the unknown.[2]

Simultaneously, the Russian Futurists sought to express hidden dimensions of meaning underlying multiple media—the visual arts, music, literature, photography, typography, architecture, theatre and film. A leading proponent of the new movement was Wassily Kandinsky. The painter had been deeply moved by a 1911 performance of music by Arnold Schoenberg, and perceived that the musical rules Schoenberg discussed in his book *Theories of Harmony* (1911), coincided with his own understanding of visual art form. "Sound, color, words!" he wrote. "In the last essentials, these means are totally alike" (p. 257). In his 1911 book *On the Spiritual in Art*, Kandinsky developed the notion that all artistic forms are created according to the same intellectual process, regardless of their medium. He had amassed a detailed awareness of the properties, contrasts, and symbolism of color since his childhood 40 years earlier, and he differed from many visual artists in having also developed a sensitivity to the properties of musical tone. In the *Blue Rider Almanac* (1911–12),[3] Kandinsky collated 140 works of art and detailed comparisons of visual and musical form; and in the same year he began work on his *Compositions*, in which he "painted music" on canvas, reproducing aural ideas of harmony and discord in visual terms of line and color—1911 had been a remarkable year.

Another Russian artist, the composer Alexander Scriabin, extended the analysis and synthesis of multimedia communication to an even more complex level. He perceived systematic connections between impressions gained by different senses, and sought to communicate them via a multimedia synthesis that would harmonize all arts and cultures, and herald "the birth of a new world"[4]—an artistic goal not unlike the global goals of educators today. In 1910, Scriabin toured as a pianist on a Volga river steamer, just as Vertov later travelled on the Volga and the rail routes of Russia with his educational film process. Simultaneously, Scriabin planned a giant theatrical event to launch his orchestral epic, *Prometheus: Poem of Fire*. The musical themes, harmonies and keys of *Prometheus* consistently expressed the moods he perceived in each of them, in an attempt to create a peak experience. Thus, themes that he perceived as 'bright' were simultaneously accompanied by correspondingly 'bright' musical harmonies and keys. The hidden dimensions of sound that Scriabin believed he had tapped were too varied to be experienced in terms of brightness alone, and had additional qualities that he compared with visual hue. To help the audience understand this complex system of associations, Scriabin planned to reinforce the moment-by-moment moods of his symphonic piece via a light-show of shifting colors projected from a *clavier à lumières,* or 'color organ'. But the machine proved too difficult and costly to build, and in 1911 the premiere of his work went ahead without it.

With *Prometheus*, however, Scriabin had completely mystified the artistic community of Moscow, and not in the spiritual way he intended. The work was received with bewilderment, and the composer was mocked as a mad mega-lomaniac. He recouped by moving to India, where he planned an even grander production, *Mysterium*, to be performed in the Himalayas by an estimated 2,000 musicians, singers, dancers, and technicians spraying perfumes. Music, color, dance, scents, and their audience would all be 'harmonized' by the event and the epoch would be changed. Sadly, as Tatlin dreamed of a giant communications

Tower a few years later, and as Vertov dreamed of an empire-wide scheme on the railroads to educate rural Soviets, Scriabin's plan was unfulfilled. In 1915, he died from blood poisoning following a cut lip; and, as is so often the case when it is too late, the artistic community of all Moscow came out for his funeral. Twenty years later, the Stalinist regime branded the Futurists as agents of anarchy, and suppressed their tradition as well as the mobile learning methods of Vertov and Medvedkin.

The story of Scriabin deals with one of the most curious of media schemes, and is an inspiring example of the depths of intellectual analysis and the heights of synthesis of which multimedia are capable. Sadly, it also provides a reminder that some media rationales are simply too far advanced to be intelligible in their day. As with Vladimir Tatlin, Scriabin had a multimedia plan that was too grandiose at the time to either be understood or implemented. As with the Russian Futurists and the *agit-prop* of the Soviet railroads, his ideas were perceived as anarchic and not to be tolerated. As Scriabin mystified Moscow 100 years ago, so he still seems to discomfort academics today. His case is frequently discussed in the fringes of the scientific literature as a classic example of *synaesthesia*, the association of images gathered by different senses.[5] Despite a massive list of celebrated artists and thinkers who have demonstrated synaesthesia in one form or another,[6] Scriabin's claim to synaesthesia is to this day described as dubious, and synaesthesia itself as the product of an overworked imagination, or of a tendency to florid rhetoric and lavish metaphors, or of a mystical mentality, or as some form of neurological malfunction that confuses the senses.[7-8] Each of these theories may be true in individual cases. Yet in individuals including Scriabin, associations between particular musical notes, keys and colors follow a more logical system, and have suggested to psychologists and acoustics specialists that descriptions of musical sounds in terms of color reveal the aural equivalent of full color vision. They have also been linked to 'perfect pitch', the ability of some musicians to recognize and recall individual musical notes and keys in the same way as a 'normal' person identifies visual color.[9-10] The implication of this theory is that most people's failure to perceive the 'colors' of sound, and to recognize them in the same way as a color, is the equivalent of aural color blindness;[11] and Scriabin's particular 'aural color vision' has been shown to have an acoustical basis arising from the practice of tuning the western keyboard and orchestra according to the 'equal temperament' principle.[12-13] Critics for whom these properties of musical sound are beyond their personal spectrum are not in a good position to judge whether claims to synaesthesia by such as Scriabin are genuine or not.

Thus the artistic world generates the same kinds of unresolved debate as the field of education, between esoteric thinkers and an uncritical mass that fails to understand their concepts. Scriabin clearly hoped that his theatrical light-show would be a mobilizing force that would make the logic of his multimedia vision recognizable to all, and would create a peak experience to unite the world. He obeyed the instinct of a natural teacher in designing a color keyboard to illustrate his multimedia rationale, via standard educational principles of repetition and reinforcement. Osgood had the same communicative instinct when he developed the 'semantic differential' technique, mentioned earlier as a common social-science measurement technique.[14] Osgood devised the 7-point scale and its analytical methodology in his doctoral research, as a way to describe and quantify his personal associations between music and color. Dittmar, representing cultural anthropology, suggests that synaesthesia may be a normal psychological state with valuable communication and orientation functions, and that it is misinterpreted in western culture and discouraged in children in the same way as left-handedness.[15] Cytowic has provided a reassuring service to synaesthetes in his writings on the topic.[16] A reader of his account of types of synaesthesia possessed by millions told him: "I ran to my husband shouting 'See . . . I'm not nuts!'" Another wrote to him: "When I told people about hearing colors as a child, they looked at me like I needed to be committed. I stopped talking about it a long time ago." Today's online media are bringing this esoteric class of people together, through the Synaesthesia Associations of the USA, the UK, Belgium, Germany, Australia and New Zealand, and via an eclectic web site created by Hugo Heyman which provides inter-Association coordination.[17] Heyman's site has a goal similar to those of the 20th-century Futurists, "To develop a synesthesia culture by connecting art and synesthesia." It also attempts the synaesthetic communicator's greatest challenge, "To connect synesthetes and their synesthetic experience with interested non-synesthetes worldwide."

This last goal—to communicate synaesthetic experiences to non-synaesthetes—may be difficult for them to attain. The online media bring like-minded people together more easily than they bridge the gaps between differently-minded people, as with the liberal and conservative bloggers of Table 5.2. Social media may aggregate groups overnight, but not if they have different views. The need for a harmonizing strategy is apparent; but 'harmonizing' is a political act in its own right, and has been so from the earliest uses of the term. The scales and melodies of western music are based on seven sets of musical notes (*harmonias*), formulated in ancient Greece and named after major tribes. Harmony in the original Greek sense did not signify the sounding of notes simultaneously but the sounding of selected notes in an unaccompanied melody (monophonic music). Each harmonia had its own character or *ethos*, perceived today in the contrasting qualities of, for example, brightness and energy (major keys) and darkness and sadness (minor keys); and in *The Republic*, Plato defined these tonal attributes in political terms.[18–19] The fact that he came from the Dorian region may have influenced his opinion that music written in the Dorian harmonia suggests "the utterances and accents of a brave man who is engaged in warfare," and that it should be played to troops to make them feel stronger. The fact that the Phrygians had a history of being conquered, first by the Lydians and then the Persians, may have prompted Plato's recommendation that the Phrygian style of music was appropriate listening for a man "engaged in works of peace." Playing the right music to people at the right time could have an inspirational effect, he argued—the same kind of mobilizing effect as achieved by social media today.

The problem with the harmonias, however, was that the musical instruments of ancient Greek times were tuned according to principles of mathematical perfection laid down by Pythagoras; and these prevented more than one musical key from being played at once. So a single piece of music was incapable of representing more than one tribal culture at a time. As with today's social media, a musical work in ancient Greece could reinforce the mood of an individual culture but could not bridge the gap between cultures. In the late 16th century, this problem was solved in China and Europe simultaneously by the development of a compromise. The *equal temperament* system sacrificed the mathematical perfection of musical harmonies in favor of a new tuning method that allows different notes to be played simultaneously, and enabled instruments to modulate continually between different musical keys. This solution created greater scope for musicians to play many layers of sound at once (polyphonic music), and gave rise to the notion of harmony as it is typically understood today. Equal temperament has been the standard method of tuning western instruments and orchestras ever since, and has created a strange new musical sensation in the process. For the compromise system involves a process of subtly mistuning the intervals between musical notes, at a level of accuracy that most musicians can only attain to within a margin of error; and the fallibility of this process leads to a build-up of error in particular musical keys. These may be the acoustic properties of tone sensed by synaesthetes such as Scriabin; and it is only since the development of the equal temperament system that such music and color associations have been reported. Today's music tuner has electronic gadgets to remove the error from temperament calculations, and it will be interesting to see if reports of key-color synaesthesia decrease from now on.

Modern ideas of harmony do not accurately represent their tradition in the physics, history, and psychology of music, therefore. The current idea that educational practices can be 'harmonized' between world cultures typically rests on the blithe notion that a state of perfect harmony exists which can either be attained or imposed, so that the cultures can move forward together in unison. Adapting to another culture's ways may require forfeiting one's own ways, however, as with equal temperament—an idea to which neither party may be willing to agree; and the ancient Greek understanding of 'harmonia' is a goal more easily fulfilled within cultures than between them. While the members of a unified culture may maintain a relatively harmonious mutual understanding through aggregating forces such as music, the greatest unification between cultures is more likely to be an acceptable, equal-tempered compromise, or 'imperfect harmony'. Intercultural initiatives that aspire to a higher ideal than this are unlikely to achieve an 'equal tempered' unity, as Russian artists found a century ago. They hoped that the power of their multimedia technologies and designs would be sufficient to achieve global understanding. When their plans proved impractical, they met with

blank incomprehension; and when they had powerful social results they encountered powerful opposition. Their rationales were intrinsically sound, however.
They aimed to create inspirational experiences leading to unifying effects, but
failed to anticipate the power of the uncritical mass to resist ideas that it could not
understand. Nonetheless, at the right point in the development cycle, the
multimedia instincts and vision of artists such as Scriabin and Kandinsky remain
useful teaching models for today.

Imperfect Harmony

The working title for this book was *To Teach the World*, after the 1971 Coca-Cola
advertising jingle. The writer realized, however, that the idea of teaching others is
a sensitive one, often perceived in other cultures as presumptuous, patronizing,
and imperialistic. In addition, the next phrase in the song ("to sing in perfect
harmony") reflects a fine ideal but, as shown by the history of global communication
schemes, it is unrealistic in practice. This perception has been formed in the course
of the writer's projects as a researcher, teacher, examiner, consultant, and funding
agency adviser around the world. Living in other cultures for extended periods
of time, and working with their people, gives an entirely different impression
than the tourist acquires by dipping into a city or village for a few days or hours.
Lasting impressions of 20 Asian nations include the enthusiastic determination of
the Cambodian people, so remarkable after their brutal period of repression; the
steady, determined evolution and exquisite culture of Chinese society; the thrift
and ingenuity of Mongolia, as found in remote schools and hospitals in the Gobi
desert; the special *joie de vivre* of Malaysia, with its three major ethnic groups living
in a state of enviable 'imperfect harmony'; and above all the love of each country
for its own culture. One nation stands out from the others visited: Bhutan, whose
gentility and genuineness it is fervently hoped will not be lost with its increasing involvement in the world. Television and the internet arrived in Bhutan as
recently as 1999, and internet cafés were soon to be found throughout the capital,
Thimphu.[20] When television arrived in the Canadian Arctic in 1972, it was found
to have changed social and educational attitudes within a year, but also to have
decreased the people's perception of their own value compared to that of other
peoples.[21] A decade later, young people in the same communities were observed
to have lost their personal 'locus of control', and to have one ambition—to move
south to the major cities of Canada and the US.[22] The lessons of history warn us
that sad consequences are also likely in Shangri-Las such as Bhutan.

So an educator must approach collaborative projects in other nations with a
heavy sense of responsibility, and knowledge of the many pitfalls that face international initiatives. Ignorance and insensitivity to the other culture can so easily
be suspected even when not intended. A successful project depends on so much
more than meeting a congenial person at a conference who shares an interest in
collaboration. If one is attached to an educational institution, it is necessary first

to establish institutional interest in the project which, as discussed in Chapter 2, may not be easy. A series of exchange visits may first be needed, possibly involving one's students and colleagues, to build an institutional sense of ownership of the project. All stages of the project are likely to require funding, and the sensitive issue of which partner pays the first travel bills may in its own right be sufficient to derail the initiative. If the initial hurdles can be overcome, the project is likely to need a consolidating agreement protecting all parties' interests. This too has potential pitfalls. In one case, the writer realized that an educational partnership between Canada and China would not go ahead unless the Canadian university's legal office could change the usual terms of its partnership contract. The institution's standard wording required the partnership to be governed by the jurisdiction of the Canadian province. To expect a major university representing the Government of China to submit to the legal interpretations of a small Canadian province was clearly unrealistic. If the Chinese partners had ever seen the draft clause, they would probably have found it sufficiently insulting to prevent them from dealing with that particular institution again. The solution was to postpone the activities that required the offending clause, and to concentrate initially on activities that did not require it, in order to create time for discussing more flexible jurisdictional arrangements.

The need for partner institutions to have a legal agreement at all may also require careful negotiation. In the North American mentality, a written understanding is essential to protect collaborating institutions from, for example, financial liability and intellectual property violation. In collaborations involving shared research ideas and course materials, such precautions are wise. To a partner in another culture, however, the suggestion that such problems are feasible may immediately imply a lack of trust. The creation and maintenance of trust between nations has been obstructed over the years by the prejudicial labels 'developed' and 'developing'. The use of these terms allows prospective North American partners to be perceived in other cultures as having an attitude of superiority and omniscience, which would in any case be completely unjustified. A patronizing attitude can be tolerated in visiting western academics, because they hold the key to understanding the western literature and publication in it; but only for so long. On the other hand, after determined, productive discussion, both partners may sincerely believe that legal problems could never arise, because the project discussion would not have been allowed to reach its final consolidating stage if trust and friendship were not evident on both sides. The emphasis on intercultural trust is consistent with Maxwell's motto: "People do not care how much you know until they know how much you care" (p. 121);[23] and western-style project agreements can both protect and jeopardize a project if they are not worded in a manner that allows trust to be maintained.

[I arrived in an Asian city to advise an international development project described by its North American funders as "an engine for capacity development." My hosts asked me what this meant. It was easy enough to explain that a capacity-building project can be described as an 'engine' if it proceeds 'under its own steam' once it is 'on track'. The project was harder to justify in terms of capacity development, because the local team clearly had solid capacity already, both personally and collectively.[24] I told them that all 'capacity development' means is 'training', though not necessarily to drive train engines. After that, every time someone had a good idea, we made train noises and shouted 'Capacity!' It may sound as though not much work was done, but I suspect we were more successful than if we hadn't been able to laugh at high-sounding verbiage.]

At one time, the anthropologist Margaret Mead was thought to have commanded the trust of the Samoan people sufficiently to have been able to write an authoritative account of their 'coming of age' ceremonies. Mead visited Samoa as a 23-year-old in 1924. Her published analysis of the sexual activities of the island's adolescent girls shocked many western readers, though was inspirational for the new field of anthropology.[25] Mead continued to write about other cultures in the years ahead, using language that today seems insensitive—for example, in her *Cooperation and Competition among Primitive Peoples* (1937), which described the "defective structure" of "primitive societies" compared to that of "western civilization".[26] Whether or not the Samoan girls perceived a patronizing attitude in Mead, they apparently decided to have some fun with her. After her death, another anthropologist, Derek Freeman, visited the island and met some of Mead's interviewees, by then grandmothers. They assured him that the promiscuous stories they had told her were false. "She must have taken it seriously," said one of them:

> but I was only joking. As you know, Samoan girls are terrific liars when it comes to joking. But Margaret accepted our trumped up stories as though they were true.[27]

Mead was no longer alive to answer Freeman's allegations, and the reliability of his data has been criticized on her behalf as vigorously as he criticized her work. In 1973, however, Mead did admit that it had been a mistake to assume that Samoans would not read her book.

> I did not include Samoan young people as possible readers for two reasons, one because those about whom I wrote, although they themselves wrote letters in Samoan, read no books, and second, because I was discussing their own lives … and did not have to tell them what life was like in the villages.[28]

On perceiving the crassness of some western visitors to other regions through the eyes of the local people, in living and working with them, it is easy to feel less than proud of being a westerner. At the same time, when working in other cultures, it is necessary to preserve one's own cultural priorities when they are challenged, as in the case of the plagiarism issue discussed earlier. Once collaborative projects are confirmed and underway, financial issues may become a particular source of discord, and the control and management of project funds can disrupt even the best-laid plan. The universal thirst for project funding, and for the personal and institutional kudos it brings, can be the main driver of collaboration for western and eastern partners alike, and may precede any serious thinking about the project's actual topic. If the responsibility for administering project funds is not shared coequally by the partners, the collaboration may flounder. The partner holding the funds may refuse to disburse them until receiving evidence that the other partner's work is under way; and the other may be unwilling to do the work until funding is on its way. Neither of the partners may trust the other even within the same culture, let alone when one of them is on the other side of the world; and a delay in the project's work by one partner may cause impossible problems for the other's schedule. In desperation, partners sometimes resort to subcontracting the work in secret to agencies unknown to the project funding agency; and the subcontracted agencies may imperfectly understand the project's scope and objectives. Project agreements are wise to anticipate money management, scheduling, and subcontracting issues, albeit by way of sensitive wordings as opposed to standard templates that fail to work well in all of the cultures involved.

In general, the challenge of coordinating global education initiatives can be complicated by an often unpredictable range of personal and political motives. The following classification of collaborative motives is largely subjective, and withholds national identities for obvious diplomatic reasons.

a) *Keen to explore existing methods, as appropriate.* Many of the writer's Asian partners willingly apply evaluative methods of the type highlighted in Chapter 4, in order to ensure that the proposed methods are appropriate in their regions.

b) *Keen to accept outside funding but not acting on it.* A recent analysis of distance education (DE) development in Indochina has revealed an inverse relationship between external research funding and project implementation.[29] One nation in that region has received much external assistance for DE development, and has done little with it. Viet Nam on the other hand has accepted relatively little external support for DE research and development, and yet has developed the most detailed DE-related policies and practices.

c) *Keen to apply existing methods, even uncritically.* It can be difficult to turn down the chance to be involved in a funded project, however much one may disagree with the proposal. Some partners are keen to apply a foreign approach while showing little concern to evaluate it. One may sympathize with this attitude in local conditions where any new method can be a cause for optimism. This was sensitively recognized by Schramm *et al.* in their observation that a teacher or educational institution can be "surrounded by scarcities (and) sometimes toys with the idea of trying less conventional methods such as 'new media'".[30]

d) *Spurning western advice and funding.* Some governments tend to decline external collaboration and funding in order to give the impression that their nation no longer needs it. It is tragic that political hubris can prevent people from receiving benefits that they urgently need.

So the increasing use of inappropriate western DE approaches in Asian countries can be due to more than the wish to be perceived as embracing new methods. Numerous other factors may lead partners into a project despite their better judgment that it has little or no chance of being useful. Technology-based education cannot afford to take this risk. DE already has a negative image in many regions,[31–32] and studies with a limited chance of success can harm the chances of more appropriate projects in the future. This possibility needs to be minimized by encouraging planners to anticipate ways of optimizing project outcomes. The International Development Research Centre (IDRC), for example, has made this a top priority by encouraging the formative evaluation activity of 'outcome mapping';[33] and each of the twelve sub-project reports in the IDRC's 2010 books about its Asian DE initiative discusses the steps taken to encourage sustainable policy and practice.[34–35] If partners are not responsible for anticipating these outcomes, expensive research will be impotent, and the litany of complaints about educational development initiatives (lack of infrastructure, training, effective materials, etc.) will fill the literature indefinitely.

The value of sharing materials, a trusting relationship, and an outcome with mutual benefits, is illustrated by the Britain–China relationship of 1793. The Emperor Qian Long sent King George III some lavish gifts, and an accompanying letter which showed that other nations can command the English language at least as well as the English can.

> I confer upon you, O King, valuable presents in excess of the number usually bestowed on such occasions, including silks and curios—a list of which is likewise enclosed . . . As your Ambassador can see for himself, we possess all things. I have no use for your country's manufactures . . . Swaying the wide world, I have but one aim in view, namely, to maintain a perfect governance and to fulfil the duties of the State: strange and costly objects do not interest me.[36]

The subtext to this letter is that Britain had been sending China some less generous goods of its own, illegal opium, and the Emperor's fury is clear in the courteous but barbed language of his full text. He made his lack of trust for the British Ambassador clear too, by sending the King the inventory checklist of gifts that the Ambassador would be bringing back to court with him! Britain continued sending China its unwelcome drugs, and the Opium Wars broke out a few years later.

Asian countries give their academic visitors truly exquisite gifts today, capable of becoming family heirlooms. They also exchange excellent gifts in visiting each other. It can be embarassing, therefore, to arrive at an Asian university armed with little more from one's western university than a ball-point pen or key-chain bearing the institutional logo. Perhaps western institutions believe that one's presence in the foreign land is gift enough. The western academic can always spend his own money on a gift at the airport, but a jar of maple syrup just doesn't cut it!

Today, international development projects are commonly guided by 'participatory action' approaches based on Mezirow's transformative learning approach: i.e., discussing frames of reference, adopting new frameworks, and developing compatible attitudes and habits.[37] In conventional educational situations, this process stresses separate roles for the teacher and learner.[38] While the teacher (or external facilitator) creates a climate of trust and sensitivity, the other participants are responsible for developing and maintaining it. In developing intercultural collaborations, however, advisory input by third-party experts may not be welcomed, for it may incorrectly imply that the main partners have differences of opinion that cannot be resolved without help. Collaborative projects can certainly be designed in which one partner takes an expert or facilitating role and the other a learning role; but such projects may not be sustainable beyond the point at which the learner decides that the expert has imparted everything worth learning. Lasting collaborations are those in which each party feels it can continue to benefit from the other indefinitely, and in which neither is defined as teacher or learner. Ultimately, the planning of collaborative projects needs to maintain the type of relationship stressed by Bishop Desmond Tutu in the South African 'truth and reconciliation' process.[39] Tutu has indicated that inter-cultural discussions can all too easily flounder owing to the inflexible assumption that one party needs to bend to the views and judgment of the other. The discussion between the parties should seek neither advantage nor one-sided gain; and the ultimate goal should be for each to leave the discussion feeling that its integrity is intact.[40] The process is less one of achieving 'harmony' in the modern sense, as of creating 'counterpoint', in which different musical voices combine in an interdependent whole.

Global Counterpoint

The concept of counterpoint evolved in the 16th century as musicians realized the artistic benefits of combining monophonic voices in polyphonic forms. Following the rules of counterpoint, musical lines with independent 'minds of their own' were no longer constrained to being heard separately (asynchronously) but could co-exist (synchronously). Musicians now had the choice of focusing on individual melodies, as in a unison line of Gregorian chant, or of exploring the synergy created when separate lines of music interact. The evolution from asynchronous to synchronous musical expression had taken 2,000 years, from the harmonias of the ancient Greeks to the contrapuntal styles of Palestrina. In the 17th century, Bach created new counterpoint forms in which different melodic voices each had their own integrity while yielding lush harmonies in combination with each another: 'synchronous' and 'asynchronous' effects co-existing. By the 20th century, composers had learned to express the discords of synchronous sound in counterpoint—the dissonances as well as the consonances between separate voices. The parallels expressed by Plato between musical form and cultural characteristics remained true throughout this evolutionary process, arriving at successive new levels. In a cultural exchange, one voice can dominate while others play a subordinate accompanying role. Two voices can co-exist with equal integrity, producing consonances and sometimes dissonances but always sharing a music-like bond that keeps them moving forward together. Old ideas can be examined and new ones developed, as in the complex contrapuntal rules of 'fugue', and in the 'transformative learning' practices of Mezirow and others. In multimedia conferencing, participants can share visual and auditory information as Scriabin attempted to communicate his synaesthetic experiences in *Prometheus: Poem of Fire*.

The music-culture parallel also extends to the notation systems used by musicians and communication analysts. On a conventional music sheet, the moment-by-moment experience is conventionally represented horizontally on a time-base; and the successive events are compared vertically as different musical notes. The variability of musical experience is the same as illustrated in the 'cubist' scheme of Figure 3.11, in which intensity of effect, fluctuation over time, and the consonant and dissonant effects of individual voices are contrasted. The same wide-ranging variations also occur in interpersonal contexts. Interactions between prior knowledge, attitudes, and teaching technique change continually from one moment to the next, and some form of continuous response measurement is needed in order to register them. While continuous responses are analyzed and interpreted in advertising and propagandist research, as has been discussed, they are relatively overlooked in educational research. Online, however, educators can use powerful 'data-mining' techniques to investigate these phenomena at little or no cost; and a range of multimedia technologies is available to them with the versatile potential of Scriabin's sound-and-light projector and Kandinsky's musical paintings. Synchronous online techniques have been available to enhance teacher-student and student-student interactivity since the 1990s, including response methods (polling) by which teachers can collect data from their students and provide them with instant feedback at no cost.[41–42] To date, however, synchronous methods common in online education do not represent the full range of interactive practices of which these technologies are capable.

Table 6.1 describes 12 levels of interactivity that are viable when online techniques (web browsing, e-mail, polling, etc.) are used by one or many students in transactions with packaged material or a teacher. The original notion of

TABLE 6.1 Twelve levels of educational media interactivity.

Capability of interactive software / Levels	Students	Teacher	Hand units	PC + internet	Cellphone 1G	Cellphone 3G	Cell + media hybrids
A) *Low level of student 'interaction' with pre-produced material*							
1 Online and offline material	One	No	n.a.	Yes	No	Yes	n.a.
B) *Asynchronous human interaction added*							
2 E-mail	One	Yes	n.a.	Yes	Yes	Yes	n.a.
3 Text forums	Many	Yes	n.a.	Yes	No	Yes	Viable
4 Q&A (no feedback)	Many	No	Yes	Yes	SMS	Yes	Viable
5 Real-time Q&A (no feedback)	Many	No	Yes	Yes	No	Yes	Viable
C) *Successively higher levels of real-time interaction*							
6 Text chats (synch)	Many	Yes	n.a.	Yes	Yes	Yes	Viable
7 A/V-conferencing (synch)	Many	Yes	n.a.	Yes	Audio	Yes	Viable
8 Q&A: feedback (synch)	Many	Maybe	Yes	Yes	Yes	Yes	Viable
9 Collaboration (synch)	Many	Yes	Yes	Yes	No	Yes	Viable
D) *Real-time continuous interaction involving combined media*							
10 Asynch (no feedback)	Many	No	Yes	Yes	Viable	Viable	Viable
11 Synch (no feedback)	Many	Yes	Yes	Yes	Viable	Viable	Viable
12 Synch (with feedback)	Many	Yes	Yes	Viable	Viable	Viable	Viable

Key:
Asynch: Asynchronous (not real-time, delayed interaction)
Synch: Synchronous (real-time interaction)
1G: 1st generation cellphones (text only)
3G: 3rd-generation cellphones (text and graphics)
SMS: Short message service (cellphone texting)
A/V: Audio and/or video
No: Useful software not conceivable for this technology
Yes: Useful software available for this technology
Viable: Useful software could be created for this technology
n.a.: Not appropriate or relevant to this technology

Source: Baggaley, 2009a, with revisions.

computer-based interactivity, as in the interactive videodiscs of the 1980s and their online equivalents today, only fulfill functions at *Level 1* in this classification scheme. This level relates to students 'interactions' with pre-recorded/programmed material, as in web surfing, though not directly with a teacher. Human interaction, regarded as the missing ingredient in many educational technologies, occurs in basic forms in *Levels 2–5*, via asynchronous techniques including e-mail, polling, and text-conferencing. At *Level 6*, a higher form of real-time interaction occurs in live text-chat activities; while *Levels 7–9* indicate the successively higher levels of interactivity achieved by adding audio, video, polling and other techniques to conferencing, polling, and 'social networking' software. *Levels 10–12* relate to new opportunities created by combining mobile phones and hand-held internet devices with other media (e.g., TV) to enable real-time, continuous response tasks and instant feedback of results to many students at once.

The 12 levels of educational media interactivity are further defined as follows.

1   The most basic level of interactivity occurs when a student *browses through computer-based materials or the web*, making requests that generate immediate displays of material. The 'interactive video' materials of the 1980s used this level of interactivity alone. No teacher is present.
2   More interactivity is possible when the student communicates asynchronously with a teacher, as via *e-mail*. In addition to the usual technology (computer with internet), a 1G cellphone with internet connection can be used with text-based e-mail software. With the development of graphic-based messaging software, designers have placed less emphasis on producing text-based materials for the more accessible 1G hardware.
3   A higher level of interactivity occurs when the teacher is able to communicate via text-based messages with many students asynchronously as in *online text-conferences and blogs*. If all the participants are not simultaneously present, analysis of responses is delayed. The displays are not usually possible on a 1G cellphone, though are possible in text/graphics on a 3G cellphone.
4   *Online question-and-answer polling* software has been available since the 1990s, allowing many students to answer multiple-choice, interval, or ranking questions simultaneously. In the basic asynchronous Q&A polling situation, no teacher need be present, and the students receive no feedback of results. Similar results can be yielded by SMS methods on the 1G cellphone.
5   *Systems for real-time polling* (also known as continuous response measurement) have been used in media and advertising research since the 1940s (Chapter 3). PC software has been available for this function since the 1980s. The responses are collected from many participants moment by moment, and analyzed *post hoc*, with feedback possible for the respondents in, for example, focus groups.
6   Synchronous text-based software allows a teacher and many students to interact in real-time via *live text-chat boxes*. Basic text-chat software has been

available for computers with internet since the 1990s. If graphic displays are not required, 1G cellphones can also be used.

7 Combinations of real-time *audio and/or video* and *text-conferencing* allow two-way interaction between the teacher and one student at a time, and one-way presentations by a teacher or student to many participants at once. Real-time text-chat boxes are commonly included in A/V conferencing software, and can be useful in conference coordination.

8 The software for *synchronous Q&A polling* is usually the same as at Level 5, with extra routines for instant analysis and feedback of results. Students answer multiple-choice, interval, or ranking questions, and feedback is given either by automated routines or by a teacher instantly interpreting the results.

9 Combinations of these interactive methods (web browsing, e-mail, live text chatting, Q&A polling, A/V and text-conferencing, and blogs) in social media packages, can be used in *online collaborative activities*, providing options for asynchronous or synchronous interaction as appropriate. These interactive methods are commonly labelled 'Web 2.0'.

10 Continuous analyses of audience responses to a recorded presentation were commonly used in programmed learning research from the 1950s to 1980s. Hand-units, web-based, and/or cellphone keypads can now be used to collect student responses. The presentation can be revised subsequently without synchronous feedback being provided for the respondents.

11 When continuous responses to a live presentation (e.g., a TV broadcast or a lecture) are collected, the teacher can react tacitly to an instant analysis of the responses in adjusting the presentation in real time. For example, if students give continuous responses showing failure to understand the lecture at specific moments, the teacher can repeat or clarify related points.

12 The highest level of interactivity occurs when continuous responses are instantly analyzed and the results continually fed back to the students and the teacher. The students can compare their responses with those of other students, and the teacher can improvise with follow-up questions, comparing new responses with prior data in order to gain insights into individual and sub-group responses.

The viable cells in Table 6.1 indicate the viability of numerous interactive applications of the traditional and modern educational media not yet fully developed. The real-time polling applications of political and advertising research have previously used customized hand-unit technologies only.[43] The same techniques can now be developed via internet and cellphone applications, as in Figures 3.5 and 3.6, in order to make any educational medium interactive. If real-time polling software is developed for text-based as well as graphic-capable phones, it will be possible to use them in combination with television delivery, for example, for students who lack internet access and advanced computer hardware. Using the cellphone to collect real-time responses to live and recorded presentations, the teacher can collect and analyze student responses moment by moment, provide instant feedback of results as appropriate, vary the presentation according to students' feedback, and generate follow-up questions and displays. Carefully designed data collection techniques and cautious statistical analysis are needed to ensure reliability and validity in the data.[44] The result is continuous, two-way feedback between the teacher and many students simultaneously which, owing to its nonverbal methodology, can be scaled to a large number of participants. Such systems can overcome the common criticism that technology-dependent education lacks teacher–student interactivity.

The web camera also tends to be under-exploited in online synchronous presentations. Many teachers and students prefer not to show themselves on their webcams, either because their moving images use too much bandwidth for their systems, or because they are simply irrelevant to the presentation, or for privacy reasons. In online lectures and conferences where the participants' images are considered useful, they tend to be reminiscent of the monotonous 'talking heads' shots of 1970s educational television. Yet most conferencing freeware packages contain 'whiteboards' that allow presentations to be illustrated with slides, movies, and 'web tours'. In addition, with a little simple HTML coding, an online teacher or assistant can 'cut' between webcam and other images provided by his students as a TV director selects the studio camera, so that the participants can at least see the name and location of the person talking. Audio-conferencing freeware combined with synchronized images can be used to mount TV-like discussions in this way.[45] Figures 6.1a and b show an online display containing control buttons used by a teacher to keep conference participants' displays synchronized with the audio. With applications of this type, a greater range of interactivity and clarity of exposition can be added to online presentations, at a level corresponding to #7 in the Table. In global project planning, such solutions can overcome distance, cost, and spontaneously arising problems. The extra effort required to produce this level of communication requires no more time nor skill than an illustrated

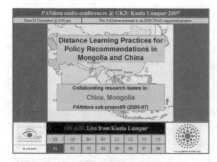 

FIGURE 6.1a TV-style live display.   **FIGURE 6.1b** TV-style speaker shot.

Source: Author.[46]

classroom lecture. Making even a small effort to personalize the online presentation in this way may help to build harmony within cultures, and counterpoint between them.

A Fugue State

When ideas take flight, they can be overwhelming, and the individual who experiences them may retreat into the dissociative disorder known in psychiatry as the 'fugue' state. They can also be uplifting, as in the musical fugues of Johann Sebastian Bach. Musical fugues take a single theme and subject it to 'discussion' by different instrumental and choral 'voices', via 'arguments' or counter-subjects. A fugue explores the numerous harmonies and counterpoints created by successive variations of the theme and vocal combinations. At interim stages, the main theme may return in 'false entries', as though parodying failed attempts by a conference moderator to get the discussion back on track. By the end of the fugue, numerous ideas have been examined. The styles of fugue in musical history resemble the 'best practices' of different cultural, teaching, and debating traditions; and the German composer Ernst Toch explored the parallel between musical and cultural characteristics specifically in his *Geographical Fugue* (1930), which provided a musical tour of major cities from Athens to Yokohama. Similar musical parallels were explored in two Walt Disney films. *Fantasia* (1940) begins with an orchestral performance of Bach's *Toccata & Fugue in D minor*, which illustrates the moods and layers of the work synaesthetically via increasingly abstract visual shapes, movements, and color combinations.[47] In Disney's *20,000 Leagues under the Sea* (1954), Captain Nemo (James Mason) played the same work on the organ in his submarine lair, becoming increasingly distraught as the work reached its climax.[48] Images of organ pipes and underwater scenes gave synaesthetic accompaniment to the music, as in *Fantasia*. In *Sinking of the Titanic* (1969), Gavin Bryars created a similar synaesthetic effect which he is still updating, in which the voices of the string quartet on the ship's deck gradually drift apart, illustrating the ship's disintegration in its descent to the sea-bed.[49]

The interplay of harmony and counterpoint in musical fugues mirrors the complexity of educational and intercultural discussions. Mediated by simple audio or webcam presentations in the impoverished audio-visual environment of an online conference, this complexity may be concealed, much as the old 'talking heads' formats of 1970s educational television failed to do justice to complex content. Complex online presentations can be clarified by enhancements to the webcam image, as in Table 6.2, and by 'chroma-key' techniques which electronically fuse images. These formats are the same as used in TV news broadcasts, and were used in educational television from the 1980s onwards. The fact that they are not yet common in online education demonstrates the extent to which current educational media formats have reverted to the undeveloped designs of 40 years ago.

TABLE 6.2 Webcam displays of interaction at a distance.

a) A blank cotton sheet
    (usually green or blue)
    behind the presenter
    in a lecture or video-
    conference allows the
    electronic combination
    (chroma-keying) of
    supportive images.

b) The presenter's image
    is chroma-keyed
    into an appropriate
    background image.

c) Images of the presenter and
    participants at a distance
    are chroma-keyed into a
    background image.

d) The presenter views a
    matrix showing the real-
    time responses of many
    participants to single
    questions or continuous
    presentations
    (Interactivity level 11).

e) The presenter views a second-by-second analysis of the participants' responses in an animated bar diagram (Interactivity level 11).

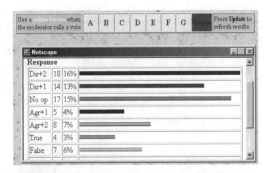

f) The presenter and participants receive continuous feedback of their responses on a chroma-keyed animated diagram, as appropriate (Interactivity level 12).

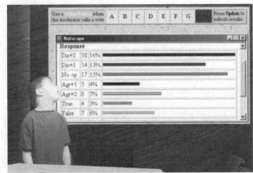

g) The participants' reactions to a presentation are continually compared on a second-by-second time-base chroma-keyed on the video image.

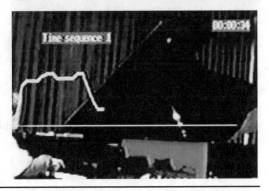

Source: Author.[50]

The costs for an individual (e.g., an online teacher) to create formats of this type are estimated in Table 6.3. For up to USD 350 per year at 2011 prices, an individual online teacher can operate a synchronous TV-style lecture facility with Q&A polling and instant audience feedback of results. As it is in the interests of online and distance education institutions to encourage interactive presentation styles, it would be reasonable for these costs to be institutionally covered. Server-side software or external services would be needed at the institutional level to

TABLE 6.3 Costs of synchronous visual formats (2011 estimates).

Equipment (lecture-style presentation)	Estimated costs of office teaching studio (USD)	
	Minimum	Maximum needed
Webcam	- Built into most computers: $0 - Separate webcam: $30	- Network (IP) camera: $100
Microphone	- Built into most computers: $0	- Wireless microphone: $50
Slide changer	- Standard computer arrow keys	- Hand-held remote: $50
Chroma-key software	- Downloadable freeware	- TV-style software: $400
Chroma-key background	- Blue/green-screen: $20	- Studio size screen: $150
Data collection and feedback (Q&A)	- Downloadable polling freeware - Free online polling services	
Data collection and feedback (continuous)	*(freeware not currently available)*	*(unpredictable without customization)*
Camera selection + live streaming software	- $100	- $400
Web server	- External (min.): $200 per year	
Media streaming server	- Free external multimedia services	
TOTAL COST per year	**- $350**	**- $1,150**

Source: Author.

coordinate simultaneous presentations of this type, involving many teachers and participants and frequent sessions. The costs would vary according to user numbers and multi-campus needs, and would be within the normal price bracket of external conferencing services.

A synchronous teaching solution such as this is the equivalent of Tatlin's Tower and Vertov's train for the present day. The media specialists of the post-revolutionary Soviet Union had goals strikingly similar to those of today's online educators: to make information more publicly accessible and intelligible over large distances, and to bring information to the people rather than making them go out of their way to find it. In cost terms, the Futurist schemes may have had little chance of success 80 years ago. Today, however, facilities for global communication are available in the home or workplace in most regions of the world, and chroma-key techniques are among the many ways in which their use can be improved. In conventional teaching institutions where classroom-style lectures are the norm, the addition of simple studio-type facilities for online lectures and teleconferences requires no major change of attitude or work style. In distance education institutions where teaching staff have become acclimatized to an asynchronous, primarily text-based routine for a decade or more, a shift to synchronous activities may be more difficult. These institutions should be reminded that, in the major Asian 'cyber-universities', live online lecturing of this type from video studios is already the norm. If western and non-western educators are to work together in efficient partnerships, they will need to adopt similar synchronous methods of communication, and the west will need to catch up in its use of them. It is to be hoped that, by the time this book is published, the march of time will have led to the integration of such options in standard online conferencing systems, and that these recommendations and estimates will have become obsolete!

Institutionally, the addition of time-honored synchronous practices to the distance education process may be achieved by the following approach. For want of a jargon term, it may be named the *fugal model*.

1   In order to catch up with other nations in their use of synchronous methods, western online teachers will need to adopt the practices and routines of campus-based teachers, preparing and giving lectures at regular appointed times, and specifying office hours at which students can contact them.
2   Lectures should be simultaneously delivered in dual mode (face-to-face and online), with identical support materials cost-effectively produced for both modes.
3   Student access should be provided to video-on-demand recordings of the lectures, as well as to their live versions—as already the practice in, for example, the cyber-universities of South Korea.
4   Each teacher could be provided with a chroma-key screen for folding into a laptop case during travels, permitting efficient synchronous conference presentations, international communication, and mobile teaching as well as mobile learning,
5   Teacher training will be needed in the new techniques, involving skills no more complex than are required in the preparation of a classroom slide presentation.
6   Institutional and union 'benchmarks' for the new practices will need to be defined, recognizing the greater amounts of time that synchronous activities make available for academic research, publication, and committee work.
7   The new synchronous practices and policies may be developed by distance education institutions operating independently, or in conjunction with conventional universities and colleges, or in being absorbed into conventional institutions.

Summary

Musicians have described the visual properties of sound; visual artists have seen the world in musical terms; and for 2,000 years melodic sequences have expressed cultural characteristics. Artists suggest that these synaesthesias reflect the consistent rules underlying all sensory experience. Rules of harmony and counterpoint have evolved expressing unity within individual cultures and differences between cultures. The musical fugue uses rules to examine the consonances and dissonances created when harmonies and counterpoints are juxtaposed. A century ago, Russian and Italian Futurists created multimedia techniques to make these constantly changing qualities more publicly accessible and intelligible; and new multimedia practices and policies may be developed today to enhance online interactivity and to facilitate modern global education.

7

THE PRISM OF HISTORY

Down on the Farm

The hardware and software of global education have evolved through regular cycles of development and decay. Pursuing the analogy between educational technology and artistic cubism, one can conclude that the educational media have evolved through two cycles since the 1970s, during which the traditional formats of television were analyzed, synthesized into educational formats, and communicated to the public in an effort similar to 'cubist constructivism'. In the 1990s, the new media were abandoned in favor of internet-based methods, and new new media began to be analyzed and synthesized. In the first decade of the 21st century, the media are at the low end of a new development cycle. Owing to the rapid emergence of technologies (the smart-phone, social media, etc.), new analytical phases are required constantly, and the research and development of this period has not yet succeeded in applying the latest new media in a globally acceptable manner. From Genghis Khan to *Facebook*, efforts to dominate the globe have been justified in terms of the benefits they will bring, while ignoring the dissonances created in the process. The 'asynchronous' processes of open and distance learning (e-mail, text-conferencing, etc.) are a case in point. Originally justified in terms of their convenience for students with scheduling problems, they have since contributed to the dissociated, impersonal state for which distance education is commonly criticized. Picasso summed up the process in his phrase, "Every act of creation is first an act of destruction", although in the educational context it would have been better if the traditional media had not been destroyed before the new ones have been found to work. Teachers and instructional designers can address this problem by embracing efficient new media in the current development cycle, while overcoming the incompatibility of their use in different parts of the world.

It is timely then to suggest an emphasis in the current cycle on synchronous media practices capable of raising online education to a level equaling and even improving on classroom-based methods. For millions of people, open and distance-based learning is the only option. All types of education have their good and bad teachers, and it is unfair to criticize DE for having its share of them; but DE cannot escape the fact that its options are limited and public appreciation of it low. By integrating traditional and new media in a flexible combination of live and recorded teaching events, institutions can cater to the world's students with increased efficiency. In the standard classroom, interactive techniques such as instant polling and feedback require expensive hardware and can be cumbersome to use. In online events, however, such tools can be cost-free and spontaneous, opening up possibilities not available in face-to-face education, which are already a reality in Asian 'cyber-universities'. For the benefit of intercultural discussion and exchange, these new designs need the creativity that drove cubist art onwards a century ago, and which has led musicians over the millennia to develop their systematic principles and practices of harmony and counterpoint.

Of course, proposals for change can fall on deaf ears in academic establishments, especially where the workload is stressful. Distance education is one such environment. The routine of asynchronous text-based teaching has become ingrained in habit for many distance educators, and suggestions to add the real-time personal touches that teachers and students have valued for centuries are likely to generate the same chorus of complaints as was heard in the 1980s when institutions replaced secretarial services with personal 'word-processors'. Many online teachers are right to point out that they are currently too overworked to find the time for retraining. Teaching students one at a time via e-mail, phone calls and online text-conferences can fill a ten-hour day or more. Without the facility to discuss student problems face-to-face, deserving students can be overlooked, and undeserving students can monopolize the teacher's time by their repeated requests for information already provided in the course materials. At best, good students survive in this ersatz classroom because their working styles are suited to independent study. At worst, low-achieving and possibly even dysfunctional students can cause serious problems for the other students and the teacher, in the absence of a face-to-face means to examine their problems in depth. In this context, an overloaded teacher may be completely reasonable to suggest that there is little or no time in the day to be trained in new skills.

The modern fashion for 'learner-constructed learning' is woefully idealistic in this situation. Although this book will probably be criticized for repeating the following indignant, provocative account of a student's 'constructivist' experience, the writer finds it typical of the way in which students have complained about other students in many of the online courses he has taught over 15 years. A DE teacher received this student complaint and circulated it to his faculty colleagues in December 2010.

(Although) I think you can learn and get a ton out of the program with minimal interaction with your peers and some people learn better that way, this should not be forced . . . for the first 3 years of my master's I can honestly say that I was in many classes with the same people, and a significant portion of them I'd consider border line mentally challenged . . . And the college thinks I should partner with these people and I'm going to learn more if I interact with them in message boards? I don't think so. The sick part is that there are probably tons of bright people in these courses but they, like me, hide and keep their mouth shut because the idiots run rampant and make the most noise like monkeys with pots and pans.

A solution sometimes suggested for dealing with student disagreements in collaborative projects is to introduce obligatory prior courses about project management; but even these cannot prevent a minority of students from making the work unpleasant for others by breaking project deadlines and manipulating others into doing unfair shares of the work. The only way to keep such projects on track, contrary to the general principles of the learner-constructed approach, is for the teacher to remain very much involved in monitoring the collaborative activities.

It is as well to take stock of opinions such as these in a climate which embraces learner-constructed methods on blind trust. The early 21st-century recession has generated quite feverish discussion of these issues in DE circles. In a 2010–11 online text discussion to which the writer was privy, a surprising 700 postings were made over a 5-month period by DE teachers and support staff who would normally have been too busy to type anything to each other for months on end. Their topics included budget problems, overload, hiring freezes, and suggestions of new course delivery media; and their often factious discussion revealed the urgency with which these professionals currently view the need for revitalization of the DE field. Numerous change ideas were proposed, though many of them seemed to plunge some colleagues into the type of fugue condition found not in the musical context but in the psychiatric state of dissociation. Some academics, predominantly younger ones, offered detailed ideas for new delivery techniques likely to increase efficiency and interactivity: social media, blogs, e-portfolios, etc. Some of these ideas were unoriginal and unrealistic, lacking experience of previous attempts to apply the same or similar techniques, while other ideas seemed worth exploring. In general, however, they failed to penetrate the world-weary attitudes of usually senior colleagues, which can halt a constructive discussion in its tracks. "Don't worry, X," a jaded senior colleague would say. "You are not the only one who does not understand." Another enthusiastic proposal would be dismissed with: "Y made a number of suggestions and assertions too numerous to take up", or with "Z, I admire your enthusiasm, but we should not lose sight of what we're trying to achieve." Academics are highly skilled at discarding one another's ideas undiscussed in this way, with the net result that discussion fizzles and change is indefinitely shelved.

> (T)hey had come to a time when no one dared speak his mind, when fierce, growling dogs roamed everywhere, and when you had to watch your comrades torn to pieces.[1]

The unfortunate fact is that DE teachers require technological skill in addition to subject matter expertise and an appreciation of educational psychology; and many of them simply do not have it. William Bagley's call a hundred years ago for teachers to receive systematic training in these issues goes ignored. The technological skills were simpler then than they are today, and he still argued that they needed to be trained! In addition, many DE teachers lack experience of conventional classroom-based teaching; and those who are most loath to relinquish their asynchronous ways often do not recognize the excessive workload they involve. They do not realize how uneconomical it is to answer the same questions daily in individual e-mails to different students; and they have never known the more efficient teaching routine of preparing for the weekly lectures, presenting them, and having a sizeable amount of time left over afterwards for research, writing, absorbing new teaching practices, and developing skills in the use of new technologies. They need to be convinced of the advantages of this routine, and to learn that adopting it is essentially no more complex than the 1980s' challenge of mastering the word-processor, or the 1990s' challenge of acquiring new e-mail and web-browsing skills. Junior academics whose proposals for change meet with academic put-downs can be reassured, fortunately, that their ideas' time will come, because senior colleagues do tend to retire fairly soon. Meanwhile, teachers who independently adopt synchronous practices in their courses, and do it well, are likely to have valuable lobbying support from their fee-paying students. Once online students have sampled efficient live interactivity in the online classroom, they can become powerful advocates for it. As in the WWI song, *How 'Ya Gonna Keep 'Em Down on the Farm (After They've Seen Paree)*, there may be no going back to the old 'asynchronous' ways after that.

Some educators, senior and junior alike, may not like this volume's criticisms of new media practices—poor uses of the wildly popular social media, for example, and insecure activities using virtual world software. Yet every medium ever invented is capable of being used badly, and such criticism should not be rejected undiscussed, especially when students are required to use the techniques without being tutored about their personal risks. With 750 million people currently using *Facebook*, criticisms of its capacity for endangering personal security are apt to be described by social media enthusiasts as one-sided 'polemics', even when the benefits of these media are highlighted as well as their drawbacks. Those who object to negative comments about their favorite medium can be reminded that polemics occur on both sides of an argument, as in Berg's reminder of the "polemical optimism" that accompanies new developments.[2] They can be reminded that the only way to expose developments advocated by people like Hans Christian Andersen's emperor, whose new clothes proved to be no clothes,[3] is to discuss the new ideas critically. Meanwhile, those who favor balanced discussion but fear they are alone in having negative views, can usefully rehearse their responses to the polemical optimism they may encounter when they 'go public' with their views. For instance:

- the *ad hominem* tactic that attacks the commentator rather than the comment;
- the *argument from authority* which refuses to consider a problem because others in authority have not yet warned about it;
- the *appeal to ignorance* which states that if something has not been proved to be false it must be true;
- *suppressed evidence and half-truths* which assist the appeal to ignorance and prevent balanced discussion;
- the *straw man* tactic designed to make an argument look foolish and easier to attack; and
- the *slippery slope*, down which either side may fall if discussion is not well regulated.

Such debating strategies are not necessarily used to mislead purposefully.[4] They can nonetheless cause awkward issues in intercultural discussions when one partner fails to understand the ways in which another culture forms its arguments. Educators interested in global education opportunities can make a useful study of these discussion tactics. In *Seven Pillars of Wisdom*, for example, T.E. Lawrence described the Arab culture, which he loved, as one whose people express themselves in "black and white . . . they pursued the logic of several incompatible opinions to absurd ends".[5] This style of argument was apparent in February 2011 during the writing of this book, when the Libyan ruler, Colonel Gaddafi, was opposed by rebels. "Why are they against me?" he asked the media: "the Queen of England has ruled for longer than me and she is still there." To assume that the Colonel was capable of black-white thinking, however, would probably be naïve, for he may have been skillfully combining the 'appeal to ignorance', 'suppressed evidence', and 'straw man' tactics to win the support of Libyans who do not realize that the ruling styles of Gaddafi and the Queen are not strictly comparable. Arguments about the remarkable mobilizing role played by the social media in national rebellions during the early 21st century are similarly one-sided, given the fact that 'knowledge is power' and subject to bias. Positive polemic arguments are as subject to bias and monochrome thinking as negative ones. Debating tactics are the province of no one world culture; and it is important for the shades of grey to be uncovered by a critical mass within and between the cultures, so that shallow arguments can be prevented from obstructing good ones.

With open discussion of the pitfalls of intercultural discussion as well as the benefits, a solid foundation can be created for the development of global education. A remarkable example of the potential of online media has been given by Bo Xie (2010). The *OldKids* internet Community in China was launched in 2000 to provide social and educational activities for the elderly, and has been described by users as "a Utopia." One wrote:

> In the mundane world, everything is about money . . . You can't get anything done without money. However, in the online world, even though we may not know each other [in real-life], we all are selfless . . . It makes me feel that there are true feelings in this world.[6]

Bo Xie is quick to acknowledge that such views may reveal the innocence of *OldKids* users, and that the Utopian nature of their online community may be an illusion rather than reality. In China, however, where controls over internet content are more stringent than in many countries, it is feasible that online communities such as *OldKids* are genuinely rewarding and safe. Whether or not one characterizes such controls as censorship, the *OldKids* network experience suggests that attention to the challenges of online communication can yield benefits. Working on this assumption, the current book has suggested research and evaluation methods for countering threats to online educational quality. These methods include plagiarism analysis, web-log analysis, and the continuous response methods used in advertising and political campaigning. Each of these areas, it has been suggested, carries its own ethical risks that should be considered in order to strengthen the integrity of online education generally. If the risks can be diffused, online education can be a laboratory for more precise investigation of teaching and learning than is possible in face-to-face environments.

A major challenge for educators at the outset of this new development era is to find ways of returning to the original open learning principles without creating new problems. As indicated at the start of this book, distance education evolved from a concern for community development in nations where communications and development are complicated by great geographical distance. In the world's two largest national landmasses, Canada and Russia, mobile learning methods have been used to overcome barriers to learning for a hundred years. In the west, the open learning movement has lost this community-minded focus, and a balkanized form of distance education has developed in the world—one region not knowing the other's practices or even using the same communication media—rather than the globalized approach that was emerging in the educational TV era. While the adoption speed of new technologies has increased around the world, the skills for developing and sustaining their use have not; nor have widely shared policies and procedures been developed for course-sharing and international student enrollment, and the specialized agencies needed to manage them (Perraton, 2007).

International forces and agencies do not seem to be operating with the intensity and extent, or with the speed and level of impact that would mark a fully globalised system.[7]

Without such mechanisms, the globalization of education by open and distance-based methods may all too easily be seen as a form of imperialism,[8] and the endless optimism of the distance education literature as a deluded unwillingness to accept that its mission is impossible. One way to start rectifying this perception will be to develop compatible, shared, highly interactive, and cost-effective global communication practices. The ultimate goal of the global discussion should be no less than that expressed by the film-maker Jean Rouch.[9] In 1960, Rouch dedicated his film *Chronique d'un été* to Dziga Vertov, who he felt had made an inestimable contribution to the world by inspiring 'cinema vérité', a style of film-making that could truly express truth. This view of film was far removed from the usual perception of the medium as a source of bias, and gave it credit for being capable of "magic . . . with a mysterious meaning."[10] Rouch urged that his films about West African communities should be

> seen by a large audience in the interests of humanism and global understanding, so that all people will realise, through the medium of film, that people all over the world are just like themselves.[11]

"There it is!"

In Peter Shaffer's play *Amadeus*, Mozart's latest opera receives this critique from the Emperor of Austria:

> I thought it was most interesting. Yes indeed. A trifle—how shall one say, Director? . . . Very well put. Too many notes . . . There are in fact only so many notes the ear can hear in the course of an evening.[12]

Readers of this book may share the Emperor's feeling that there "too many notes"—to which one might respond with Mozart that: "There are just as many notes, Majesty, neither more nor less, as are required." After a pause, the Emperor replies, "Well, there it is" and leaves the stage abruptly.

So a final word for the artists of the last century who have developed innovative media practices. The book has supported the notion that artists in different media use similar creative principles. They have common rules "through which individuals become social beings sharing codes and signs from a common pool . . . with historic depths".[13] Many of these visionaries held fervent spiritual views about the sources of their inspiration, believing, for example, that universal harmonic rules govern all experience. This does not imply, however, that they obtained their ideas from beyond their own intellects, whatever their personal views about their inspirations' origins. Nor should the credibility of their esoteric experiences be brought into question because they offered mystical explanations for them. Alexander Scriabin's 'colored hearing' has been disparaged since the premiere of his *Prometheus* epic in 1911 owing to the eccentric explanations he gave for it, not recognizing its acoustical basis. Yet anomalous phenomena have often explained normal ones. The modern understanding of color vision, for instance, evolved from the study of color blindness;[14] and as Jamieson points out, considering un-comprehended experiences enables "the necessary leap across the divide which separates the rational from the irrational".[15] Magic, said Sartre, is something that the imagination has perceived but that the mind has not yet explained;[16] and examining the ideas that have driven artistic innovation can suggest concepts that a century of analysis and synthesis has overlooked.

William Bagley in 1911 suggested that empirical researchers can only go so far in shedding light on educational processes, and that novelists should do more to help. The craftsmanship of education, he said, needs to be analyzed frankly in terms that:

> idealize the technique of teaching as Kipling idealized the technique of the marine engineer, as Balzac idealized the technique of the journalist, as Du Maurier and a hundred other novelists have idealized the technique of the artist . . . with the cant and the platitudes and the goody-goodyism left out, and in their place something of the virility, of the serious study, of the manful effort to solve difficult problems.[17]

The world of education can benefit from sturdy fictional representations. From the abusive Mr. Squeers in *Nicholas Nickleby* to Professor Dumbledore in *Harry Potter*, the techniques of teaching have received much thought-provoking literary attention. A role model for the researcher is the inductive thinker, Sherlock Holmes. Conan Doyle's detective could draw elaborate inductive conclusions about a person from clues that to others were imperceptible. In *A Study in Scarlet*, Holmes gives a detailed description of the process whereby deductive analysis and inductive synthesis allowed him to recognize that his friend Dr. Watson had just returned from Afghanistan.

> The train of reasoning ran, 'Here is a gentleman of a medical type, but with the air of a military man. Clearly an army doctor, then. He has just come from the tropics, for his face is dark, and that is not the natural tint of his skin, for his wrists are fair. He has undergone hardship and sickness, as his haggard face says clearly. His left arm has been injured. He holds it in a stiff and unnatural manner. Where in the tropics could an English army doctor have seen much hardship and got his arm wounded? Clearly in Afghanistan.' The whole train of thought did not occupy a second.[18]

Focusing the prism of history on 1910–11, as recommended by Virginia Woolf,[19] has revealed a similar cast of characters. These are assembled in Table 7.1, like the actors in the final scene of a 'whodunnit' mystery.

Equally deserving contributors will inevitably have been left out of this historical slice. The value of this particular cross-section of characters, however, is not just the ideas they generated but the ways they formed them. With the possible exception of the industrial psychologist Frederick Taylor, the one thing these particular people had in common is that *they all seem to have been thinking inductively*. The time was evidently right 'on or about December 1910', give or take a few months, for a certain kind of imaginative leap forward in artistic and cultural fields. The thinkers had done their homework, analyzing their crafts and their circumstances, and moved on more or less simultaneously to a new level. Their creative ideas have since been labelled analytical, synthetic, constructivist, futurist and the like, although such jargon was probably far from their minds when they formed their ideas. The influence of intellectual role models may have stimulated them, or they may have formed their ideas independently by a kind of spontaneous combustion, as appears to have been the case with Scriabin and Vertov. If any of these thinkers had paused to think deductively for a while, their ideas might have

TABLE 7.1 Events in 1910–11 and their actors.

Date	Event
1910	Halley's Comet pays a visit
1910	Arnold Bennett creates literary realism style in the first of his three *Clayhanger* novels
1910	Pablo Picasso pioneers analytical cubism in *Girl With a Mandolin*
1910	Albert Einstein answers the question "Why is the Sky Blue?"
1910	Carl Jung reports word association measurement in real-time
1910	The Italian Futurists develop 'divisionism' and publish their *Manifesto of the Futurist Painters*
1910	William Bagley co-founds the *Journal of Education Psychology*
1911	William Bagley publishes three books: *Classroom Management*, *Craftsmanship in Teaching*, and *Educational Values*
1911	Hermann Rorschach develops the inkblot method of projective testing
1911	Frederick Taylor publishes his industrial efficiency text, *Principles of Scientific Management*
1911	Arnold Schoenberg publishes *Theories of Harmony* likening music to visual form
1911	Wassily Kandinsky is visually inspired by a musical performance by Arnold Schoenberg, publishes *On the Spiritual in Art*, collates *The Blue Rider Almanac*, and starts work on his "painted music" *Compositions*
1911	Alexander Scriabin premieres the synaesthetic *Prometheus: Poem of Fire*

Source: Author.

proceeded down blind alleys; for deduction uses general hypotheses to draw narrow conclusions, while induction combines small ideas into new forms. Sadly, the price to pay for their inductive conclusions was that many of them were at best misunderstood and at worst derided. It would be nice to think that their ideas kept them feeling alive, but for those whose instinct was to communicate that may not have been so.

A few small ideas of this kind have driven the current work. Some of them have been mysterious to the author for many years, and their strangeness has provided a sense of purpose at times when it seemed the work would never be done. There is no easy explanation for the excitement of a whale-watching expedition, for example—not so much for the sight of whales but for the group experience of looking at them. On a recent sea trip off Vancouver Island, a dozen people came together from different countries, of different ages, and clearly with very different personalities. On the boat they said little to each other, but with the help of a young expert in whaling behavior, they soon learned that whales need a new intake of air every eight minutes; and they learned approximately when and where they could next expect to see a whale surfacing. When it did, they pointed in unison and chorused "There it is!" The same electricity was present in the 2000 online audio-conference between an audience of world-weary broadcasters in Johannesburg and the writer's graduate students across North America. "Hi from the Yukon," said one of the students to the South African audience's surprise, and they suddenly found themselves discussing the two cultures' shared 19th-century gold rush experiences. The sense of wonder emerged once again in a 2009 online video-conference between groups of doctoral students in Canada and China. Neither had probably ever believed that such a conversation would be possible in their lifetimes; and suddenly it was happening. Each group welcomed the other with eloquence and delight. Such unexpected electricity revitalizes the teaching and learning effort, and gives welcome evidence that its wonder is worth pursuing.

One final puzzle is worth mentioning, because it demonstrates that there is always a new level to fathom beyond the current 'event horizon', as physicists term it. Like whales in the sea, a pattern has recurred in the writer's statistical data since his student days. Never sought and always surfacing spontaneously in different contexts like an old friend, it resembles the yin-yang symbol with which this book opened. The symbol is present in the data summarized in the book, and of course in the many Asian countries which its philosophical connotations have influenced for millennia. The fact that the yin-yang symbol appears in so many diverse cultures suggests that it was traded between them along ancient communication routes. On the other hand, it may simply be a naturally occurring pattern in the reasoning styles of many people who have never influenced one another directly, and who have discovered the symbol for themselves. Those who have spotted it may not understand it, so may never mention it to others, as synaesthetes withhold their possibly not so rare intersensory experiences. The fact that the yin-yang image is so ubiquitous, however, suggests that there is a logical explanation for its sinuous shape; and all of these possibilities are a cause for wonderment.

But that's another story. "There it is!"

NOTES

1 The New Silk Road

1 EWGEC (2002).
2 O'Loughlin, E. & Wegimont, L. (eds.) (2007).
3 EDNA (2011).
4 UNICEF Canada (2011).
5 GENE (2011).
6 GCE-US (2011).
7 Zerjal, T. *et al.* (2003).
8 Ausubel, D. (1960).
9 Rahim, R. (2005).
10 Bacon, R. (1267), p. 204.
11 Innis, H. (1950).
12 Nostbakken, D. (1983).
13 CBC-TV (1960).
14 McLuhan, M. (1964).
15 Rosen, C. (2008).
16 McLuhan, M. (1962).
17 Miller, J. (1971), p. 132.
18 Orwell, G. (1949).
19 Orwell, G. (2010).
20 Bate, J. (1991).
21 Empson, W. (1930).
22 McLuhan, M. (1973).
23 Martin, N. (2008).
24 Rosenberg, S. (ed.) (1995), p. 392.
25 MuslimHeritage.com (2002–10).
26 Bernstein, J. (2008).
27 Knight, J. (1997), p. 6.
28 Daniel, J. (1996).
29 Wikipedia.org (2011b).
30 OUC (2010).
31 USO (2011).
32 Wikipedia Commons (2010a).
33 Jakupec, V. & Garrick, J. (eds.) (2000).
34 Melton, R. (1977).
35 Freedman, D. (2003), p. 66.
36 Goldwyn, E. (1974).
37 Perraton, H. (2007).
38 Daniel, J. (2010).
39 NIOS (2010).
40 OUUK (2010).
41 Morrow, R. (2006).
42 MacKenzie, N. (2005), pp. 711–723.
43 Taylor, J. (2001).
44 Skinner, B. (1958).
45 Kay, H. *et al.* (1968).
46 Taylor, J. (2010).
47 Thorne, K. (2003).
48 Carpenter, C. (1972).
49 Schramm, W. (1977).
50 James, J. (2004).
51 Pick, J. & Azari, R. (2008).
52 Baggaley, J. & Belawati, T. (eds.) (2010).
53 dela Pena-Bandalaria, M. (2007).
54 Wayodd.com (2008).
55 Wikipedia.org (2011e).
56 Librero, F. *et al.* (2007).
57 O'Reilly, T. (2009).
58 Luckin, R. *et al.* (2009).
59 Kear, K. (2011).
60 DIVERSE (2008).

61 Austin, L. & Husted, K. (1998).
62 Shearer, R. (2007).
63 McLuhan, M. (1964).
64 Baggaley, J. (1999).
65 DigitalBuzz.com (2010).
66 Banking.com (2011).
67 Kukulska-Hulme, A. (2005b), pp. 45–56.
68 Ally, M. (ed.) (2009).
69 James, S. (1996b).
70 Henny, L. (1976).
71 Henny, L. (1983).
72 James, S. (1996a).
73 Medvedkin, A. (1993).
74 Medvedkina, C. (1993).
75 Berger, S. (1990).
76 Baggaley, J. (1990).
77 Budzynski, M. (2007).
78 Dilke, O. & Dilke, M. (1994).
79 Mohan, G. (2008).
80 ISNAR/IDRC/CTA (2003).
81 Lewin, K. (1946).
82 Laurillard, D. (2008).
83 Vigyan Prasar (2011).
84 Science Express (2011).
85 Hirsch, Jr., E. (1996).
86 McLuhan, M. (1944).
87 Jackson, P. (2005).
88 Vertov, D. (1984).

2 Wax and Wane

1 Woolf, V. (1924).
2 Stevic, A. (2010).
3 Woolf, V. (1966).
4 Bloom, B. (ed.) (1956).
5 Vygotsky, L. (1962).
6 Bandura, A. & Walters, R. (1963).
7 Piaget, J. (1967).
8 Bruner, J. (1961).
9 Bruner, J. (1967).
10 Gagné, R. (1965).
11 Baggaley, J. et al. (eds.) (1975).
12 Dick, W. et al. (1978).
13 Fleming, M. & Levie, W.H. (1978).
14 Stufflebeam, D. et al. (1971).
15 Schramm, W. (1977).
16 Popham, W. (1988).
17 Pask, G. (1976).
18 Laurillard, D. (1987).
19 Schwier, R. & Misanchuk, E. (1993).
20 Skinner, B. (1938).
21 Lumsdaine, A. & Glaser, R. (1962).
22 Ausubel, D. (1963).
23 Scriven, M. (1967).
24 Flagg, B. (1990).
25 Merrill, M. (1980).
26 Reigeluth, C. & Stein, F. (1983).
27 Reigeluth, C. (1999).
28 Bruner, J. (1996).
29 Siemens, G. (2005).
30 Schumpeter, J. (1942).
31 Latchem, C. et al. (1999).
32 Latchem, C. (2006).
33 Carr-Chellman, A. (2006).
34 Reigeluth, C. & Carr-Chellman, A. (eds.) (2009).
35 Librero, F. (2010).
36 Carr-Chellman, A. (ed.) (2005).
37 Baggaley, J. & Belawati, T. (eds.) (2010).
38 Selwyn, N. & Grant, L. (2009).
39 Hughes, G. (2010).
40 Salmon, G. et al. (2010).
41 Swift, J. (1727).
42 Thom, R. (1975).
43 Woodcock, A. & Davis, M. (1978).
44 Berman, M. (1982).
45 James, S. (1996a).
46 James, S. (1996b).
47 La Rochelle, R. (1984).
48 Brunner, E. & Hsin Pao Yang, E. (1949).
49 Freire, P. (1969).
50 Rheingold, H. (2002).
51 Freire, P. (1970).
52 Bloch, J. (1995).
53 McMichael, P. (2008).
54 Samaranayake, V. et al. (2010).
55 Ramos, A. & Triñona, J. (2010).
56 McLuhan, M. (1964).
57 Miller, J. (1971).
58 Eaton, M. (ed.) (1979).
59 Blythe, M. (2011).
60 NIHCE (2011).
61 Baggaley, J. (2010).
62 Tomczak, M. (n.d.).
63 Binfield, K. (ed.) (2004).
64 Thomas, J. (2009).
65 Pynchon, T. (1984).
66 Thompson, E. (1963).
67 Hotrum, M. (2005).
68 Bonk, C. (2009).
69 Mishra, S. (ed.) (2010).
70 Baggaley, J. & Batpurev, B. (2007a).
71 Elias, T. (2010).
72 Lasar, M. (2009).
73 Noble, D. (1993).

74 Noble, D. (2002), p. 36.
75 Postman, N. (1993).
76 Vivian, J. (2010).
77 Lasswell, H. (1948).
78 Lashley, K. & Watson, J. (1921).
79 Hovland, C. et al. (1949).
80 Hovland, C. et al. (1953).
81 Chu, G. & Schramm, W. (1967).
82 Bugelski, B. et al. (1968).
83 Christiansen, R. & Stone, D. (1968).
84 Mielke, K. (1968).
85 Williams, R. (1974).
86 Cronbach, L. & Snow, R. (1977).
87 Salomon, G. (1979).
88 Selwyn, N. & Grant, L. (2009), p. 84.
89 Baggaley, J. (1999), p. 187.
90 Wayodd.com (2008).
91 Librero, F. et al. (2007).
92 Ally, M. (ed.) (2009).
93 Costhelper.com (2011).
94 Calimag, M. (2008).
95 Latchem, C. et al. (2008).
96 Blythe, M. (1988).
97 Hyman, H. & Sheatsley, P. (1947).
98 Davis, M. (2008).
99 Cambre, M. (1981).
100 Flagg, B. (1990).
101 Lesser, G. (1974).
102 Finch, C. (1993).
103 AudienceScapes.org (2010).

3 Why is the Sky Blue?

1 Reed, H. (1942), p. 92.
2 Zelevansky, L. (ed.) (1992).
3 Picasso, P. (1910).
4 Einstein, A. (1905).
5 Kern, S. (1983).
6 Miller, A. (2001).
7 Apollinaire, G. (1913).
8 Eisenstein, S. (1943).
9 Pudovkin, V. (1949).
10 Arnheim, R. (1954).
11 Zettl, H. (2011).
12 Baggaley, J. (1973).
13 Coldevin, G. (1976).
14 McGuire, W. (1986).
15 Shepherd, J. (1967).
16 Zettl, H. (1968).
17 Anderson, C. (1972).
18 Schramm, W. (1972).
19 Findahl, O. & Hoijer, B. (1977).
20 Millerson, G. (1972).
21 Metallinos, N. & Tiemens, R. (1977).
22 Naftulin, D. et al. (1973).
23 Abrami, P. et al. (1982).
24 Wurtzel, A. & Dominick, J. (1971–72).
25 Bates, T. & Robinson, J. (eds.) (1977).
26 Dieuzeide, H. (1977).
27 Wurtzel, A. & Rosenbaum, J. (1995).
28 Bates, T. (1995).
29 Bates, T. (2000).
30 Bates, T. (2005).
31 Baggaley, J. & Duck, S. (1976).
32 Baggaley, J. (1980).
33 Osgood, C. et al. (1957).
34 Kaiser, H. (1956).
35 Alfian & Chu, G. (1981).
36 Baggaley, J. et al. (eds.) (1987).
37 Metallinos, N. (1996).
38 Clark, R. (1983).
39 Kozma, R. (1994).
40 Zettl, H. (2010).
41 Kear, K. (2011).
42 Verleur, R. (2008).
43 Verleur, R. et al. (2007).
44 Verleur, R. et al. (2011).
45 de Boer, C. et al. (2010).
46 Verleur, R. et al. (2006).
47 Moor, P. et al. (2010).
48 Whewell, W. (1840).
49 Picasso, P. (1912).
50 Jung, C. (1907).
51 Monroe, P. (ed.) (1911).
52 Wikipedia.org (2011a).
53 Haupt, E. & Perera, T. (eds.) (2008).
54 Millard, W. (1992).
55 Stanton, F. (1935).
56 Baggaley, J. (1985).
57 Baggaley, J. (1987a).
58 Biocca, F. (1994).
59 Baggaley, J. (2009a).
60 Hyman, H. & Sheatsley, P. (1947).
61 Krech, D. et al. (1962), p. 240.
62 Baggaley, J. et al. (1990).
63 Baggaley, J. (1987b).
64 Baggaley, J. (1988).
65 Baggaley, J. et al. (1992).
66 Heider, F. (1958).
67 Taylor, L. (2010).
68 Shearer, R. (2008).
69 Jansen, B. et al. (2009).
70 Baggaley, J. (2002a).
71 Baggaley, J. & Ludwig, B. (2003).
72 Moreno, J. (1951).
73 Flanders, N. (1967).
74 Fahy, P. et al. (2001).

75   Vasconcellos-Silva, P. *et al.* (2003).
76   Annett, J. (1969).
77   Jamieson, K. & Birdsell, D. (1990).
78   Baggaley, J. (1997).
79   Rorschach, H. (1921).
80   Dictionary of Psychology (2010).
81   Milgram, S. (1963).
82   Orwell, G. (1949).
83   Baggaley, J. (1997).
84   Gray, C. (1986).
85   Picasso, P. (1923), pp. 270–271.

4 Building Global Practices

1   Bagley, W. (1911a).
2   Bagley, W. (1911b).
3   Bagley, W. (1911c).
4   Thorndike, E. (1921).
5   Cremin, L. (1961).
6   Bagley, W. (1938), pp. 241–256.
7   Wesley Null, J. (2003).
8   James, S. (1996a).
9   Chu, G. & Schramm, W. (1967), pp. 108–109.
10   Briggs, L. (1970).
11   Chickering, A. & Gamson, Z. (1987).
12   Scott, S. *et al.* (2003).
13   Schramm, W. *et al.* (1967), p. 172.
14   Elias, T. (2010).
15   Mackworth, J. (1969).
16   Postman, N. (1986).
17   Zillmann, D. *et al.* (1980).
18   Job, R. (1988).
19   Urban Dictionary (2011).
20   Jacobson, R. (1993), p. 338.
21   Cheal, C. (2009).
22   Hughes, G. (2010).
23   Carr, D. (2010).
24   Oliver, M. (2007).
25   Garber, D. (2004).
26   Carr, D. & Oliver, M. (2009).
27   Moore, K. & Pflugfelder, E. (2010).
28   Postman, N. (1996), pp. 39–40.
29   Berg, M. (1980).
30   Schramm *et al.* (1967), p. 172.
31   Robertson, H-J. (1998).
32   Noble, D. (1993).
33   Bagley (1911a), p. 216.
34   McKee, T. (2010).
35   Belyk, D. & Feist, D. (2002).
36   Educational Access & Accessibility (2011).
37   Edutools.org (2011).
38   Hotrum, M. *et al.* (2005).
39   Hotrum, M. (2005).
40   Taylor, F. (1911).
41   Russell, T. (1999).
42   Bernard, R. *et al.* (2004).
43   Baggaley, J. (2009b).
44   Cerf, V. & Kahn, R. (1974).
45   TMCnet.com (2000).
46   Salmon, G. (2004).
47   Anderson, L. & Anderson, T. (2010).
48   Knudsen, C. (2004).
49   Baggaley, J. *et al.* (2004).
50   Wikamanayake, G. *et al.* (2010).
51   Malik, N. (2010).
52   Belawati, T. (2010).
53   ICBS (2010).
54   Setjorini, L. & Adnan, I. (2010).
55   Chu, C. (1999).
56   MSCMalaysia.my (2011).
57   MMU (2011).
58   Yuen, W. & Chu, W. (2010).
59   Yeung, Sze Kiu (2010).
60   Wikipedia.org (2011b).
61   Laaser, W. (2006).
62   Juma, C. (2007).
63   Muhirwa, J-M. (2009).
64   Venezky, R. (2000).
65   Baggaley, J. & Belawati, T. (eds.) (2010).
66   Belawati, T. & Baggaley, J. (eds.) (2010).
67   Hooper, R. (1975), p. 101.
68   Farrell, G. (2001).
69   Psychology.com (2011).
70   Osgood, C. *et al.* (1957).
71   Cronbach, L. (1946).
72   Likert, R. (1932).
73   APA (2011).

5 The Power of Many

1   Wikramanayake, G. *et al.* (2010).
2   Doung Vuth *et al.* (2010).
3   Chen Li & Wang Nan (2010).
4   Noble, D. (2002).
5   Reid, R. (1959).
6   PBS-TV (2010).
7   Pina, A. (2010).
8   GetEducated.com (2010).
9   Crosslin, M. (2010) .
10   Baggaley, J. & Batpurev, B. (2007b).
11   Baggaley, J. & Batpurev, B. (2007a).
12   Jamtsho, S. & Bullen, M. (2007).
13   Young, M. (1999).
14   Boyle, R. (1661).

15 Rheingold, H. (2002).
16 Cole, S. (2009).
17 Rivera, E. (2011).
18 Constine, J. (2011).
19 Gonzales, A. & Hancock, J. (2011).
20 Brightkite.com (2010).
21 Foursquare.com (2010).
22 Loopt.com (2010).
23 Bradshaw, P. (2010).
24 Recognizr.com (2010).
25 Dillow, C. (2010).
26 Yamshon, L. (2010).
27 Dickinson, A. (2010).
28 Anonymizer.com (2010).
29 MuteMail.com (2010).
30 Evans, M. (2010).
31 Secondlife.com (2010a).
32 Connolly, K. (2007).
33 Lees, J. (2006).
34 Raby, M. (2007).
35 Ferret, W. (2007).
36 Linton, K. (2009).
37 Secondlife.com (2010b).
38 Goldfarb, S. (2009).
39 SocialMedia-Forum.com (2010).
40 SocialMarketingForum.net (2010).
41 O'Neill, N. (2010).
42 PleaseRobMe.com (2010).
43 QuitFacebook.com (2010).
44 AThinLine.org (2009).
45 EPIC (2010).
46 Raphael, J. (2009).
47 OPCC (2009).
48 Zuckerberg, M. (2009).
49 Facebook.com (2011b).
50 Schweizer, K. (2010).
51 Thelwall, M. & Stuart, D. (2010), p. 270.
52 Fildes, J. (2007).
53 Wikipedia.org (2011g).
54 Derby, B. (2008).
55 Errami, M. & Garner, H. (2008).
56 Baggaley, J. (2002b).
57 Turnitin.com (2010).
58 Baggaley, J. & Spencer, B. (2004).
59 Decoo, W. (2002).
60 Anderson, B. & Simpson, M. (2007).
61 Wayback Machine (2010).
62 Adplanner (2011).
63 Churnalism.com (2011).
64 Davies, N. (2008).
65 MacKay, C. (1852).
66 Surowiecki, J. (2004).
67 Shaw, G.B. (1916).
68 Lathrop, A. & Foss, K. (2000).
69 Georgetown University (2011).
70 Vasudevan, L. (2010).
71 McKendrick, J. (2009).
72 Crupi, J. (2009).
73 CheatingCulture.com (2011).
74 Adamic, L. & Glance, N. (2005).
75 Christakis, N. & Fowler, J. (2009), p. 206.
76 Wikipedia.org (2011d).
77 Freedman, T. (2008).
78 Fiske, J. & Hartley (1978).
79 Mezirow, J. (1991).
80 Prochaska, J. *et al.* (1994).
81 Mezirow, J. (2000).
82 Morgan, H. (2010).
83 HollywoodGossip.com (2009).
84 IntGovForum.org (2006).
85 Cornwell, J. (1995).
86 McCarthy, K. (2006).
87 Murphy, F. (1993).
88 Anderson, E. (1999).
89 Wilks, A. (2001).
90 Guri-Rosenblit, S. (2001).
91 Kummer, M. (2008).
92 Baggaley, J. (2011).
93 Crawford, H. (1993), p. 73.
94 Vision.org (2001).
95 Stoll, C. (1995), p. 50.
96 Oppenheim, A. (1977).
97 Crawford, H. (1993), p. 73.
98 Burnett, R. *et al.* (2010).
99 dmoz.org (2009).
100 Warman, M. (2010).
101 Krystek, L. (1998).
102 Amos, C. (2006).
103 Adkihari, R. (2009).
104 Seely, P. (2001).
105 Carr-Chellman, A. (ed.) (2005).
106 Dietz, O. (2004).
107 Bellett, G. *et al.* (2010).
108 Forbes, R. (1964).
109 Wikipedia.org (2011f).
110 Goldstein, J. (2009), p. 78.
111 McKee, T. (2010).
112 Newsom, C. (ed.) (1952).
113 Kurtz, E. (1959).
114 ICR (1962), p. 51.
115 ICR (1962), p. 3.
116 Dowling, S. (1996).
117 Basic English Bible (2004).

6 Harmony and Counterpoint

1 Kandinsky, W. (1911).
2 Boccioni, U. *et al.* (1910).
3 Kandinsky, W. *et al.* (1997).
4 Minderovic, Z. (2007).
5 McKellar, P. (1968).
6 Wikipedia.org (2011c).
7 Harrison, J. (2001).
8 Galeyev, B. & Vanechkina, I. (2001).
9 Carroll, J. & Greenberg, J. (1961).
10 Baggaley, J. (1974).
11 Bachem, A. (1950).
12 Isacoff, S. (2001).
13 Baggaley, J. (1972).
14 Osgood, C. *et al.* (1957).
15 Dittmar, A. (ed.) (2009).
16 Cytowic, R. (1993).
17 BSA (2011).
18 Plato (c. 400 BC).
19 Hammer, M. (2011).
20 Jamtsho, S. & Bullen, M. (2010).
21 O'Connell, S. (1975).
22 Coldevin, G. & Wilson, T. (1985).
23 Maxwell, J. (1993).
24 ISNAR/IDRC/CTA (2003).
25 Mead, M. (1928).
26 Mead, M. (1937).
27 Freeman, D. (1983).
28 Mead, M. (1973), p. xxvi.
29 Doung Vuth *et al.* (2010).
30 Schramm, W. *et al.* (1967), p. 13.
31 Chen Li *et al.* (2010).
32 Wikramanayake, G. *et al.* (2010).
33 Earl, S. *et al.* (2001).
34 Baggaley, J. & Belawati, T. (eds.) (2010).
35 Belawati, T. & Baggaley, J. (eds.) (2010).
36 Qian Long, Emperor of China (1793).
37 Bessette, G. (2004).
38 Mezirow, J. (2000).
39 Lawrence, C. (2011).
40 Karuna Center (2007).
41 Baggaley, J. *et al.* (2002).
42 Klaas, J. (2003).
43 Millard, W. (1992).
44 Baggaley, J. (1987a).
45 Baggaley, J. & Klaas, J. (2006).
46 PANdora-Asia.org (2007).
47 Walt Disney Company (1940).
48 Walt Disney Company (1954).
49 Bryars, G. (2011).
50 TubeTape.com (2011).

7 The Prism of History

1 Orwell, G. (1945).
2 Berg, M. (1980).
3 Andersen, Hans Christian (1837).
4 Thouless, R. (1953).
5 Lawrence, T.E. (1926), p. 36.
6 Boe Xie (2010), p. 250.
7 Perraton, H. (2007), p. 181.
8 Dodds, T. (2005), p. 121.
9 James, S. (1996b).
10 Rouch, J. (1979).
11 Rouch, J. (1955).
12 Shaffer, P. (1980).
13 Jamieson, H. (2007), p. 30.
14 Ladd-Franklin, C. (1929).
15 Jamieson, H. (1985), p. 46.
16 Sartre, J-P. (1972).
17 Bagley, W. (1911b).
18 Conan Doyle, A. (1891).
19 Woolf, V. (1924).

REFERENCES

Abrami, P., Leventhal, L. & Perry, R. (1982). Educational Seduction. *Review of Educational Research 52*(3), pp. 446–464.

Adamic, L. & Glance, N. (2005). *The Political Blogosphere and the 2004 U.S. Election: divided they blog*. Proceedings of the 3rd International Workshop on Link Discovery. New York: Association for Computing Machinery. Retrieved from: http://www.scribd.com/doc/7617566/Adamic-and-Glance-Political-Blogosphere-2004-Election.

Adkihari, R. (2009). ICANN's 'Tower of Babel' Decision May Prevent Net Schism. *TechNewsWorld* (October). Retrieved from: http://www.technewsworld.com/rsstory/68522.html?wlc=1287020071.

Adplanner (2011). *The 1000 Most-Visited Sites on the Web*. Retrieved from: http://www.google.com/adplanner/static/top1000/.

Alfian & Chu, G. (1981). *Satellite Television in Indonesia*. Honolulu: East-West Center.

Ally, M. (ed.) (2009). *Mobile Learning: transforming the delivery of education and training*. Alberta: AUPress.

Amos, C. (2006). TCP/IP-Ethernet Tower of Babel Breeds Confusion. *Automation World*, December. Retrieved from: http://www.automationworld.com/primers-2751.

Andersen, Hans Christian (1837). The Emperor's New Clothes. In *Eventyr, fortalte for Børn*. Copenhagen: C.A. Reizel.

Anderson, B. & Simpson, M. (2007). Ethical issues in online education. *Open Learning: the Journal of Open, Distance and e-Learning 22*(2), pp. 129–138.

Anderson, C. (1972). In search of visual rhetoric for instructional television. *AV Communication Review 20*, pp. 43–63.

Anderson, E. (1999). The Internet: 21st-Century Tower of Babel. *The Trumpet.com*, December. Retrieved from: http://www.thetrumpet.com/index.php?q=231.0.18.0.

Anderson, L. & Anderson, T. (2010). *Online Conferences: professional development for a networked era*. Charlotte, NC: Information Age Publishing.

Annett, J. (1969). *Feedback and Human Behaviour: the effects of knowledge of results, incentives, and reinforcement on learning and performance*. Harmondsworth, UK: Penguin Books.

Anonymizer.com (2010). *Anonymous Web Surfing and Online Anonymity Solutions*. Retrieved from: http://www.anonymizer.com.

APA (2011). *APA Style* (6th edition). American Psychological Association. Retrieved from: http://www.apastyle.org/index.aspx.

Apollinaire, G. (1913). *Picasso et Ses Papiers Collées*. Paris: Montjoie.

Arnheim, R. (1954). *Art and Visual Perception: a psychology of the creative eye*. Berkeley and Los Angeles: University of California Press.

Aspinall, A. & Smith, E. (eds.) (1996) *English Historical Documents XI*, Vol. 8, 1783–1832. New York: Routledge, p. 531.

AThinLine.org (2009). Help Define the Line between Innocent and Inappropriate. *MTV. com*. Retrieved from: http://www.athinline.org/.

AudienceScapes.org (2010). *Sesame Street Going Global*. Retrieved from: http://www. audiencescapes.org/resources/field-blog/sesame-street-going-global/sesame-street-going-global-635.

Austin, L. & Husted, K. (1998). Cost-Effectiveness of Television, Radio, and Print Media Programs for Public Mental Health Education. *Psychiatric Services 49*, pp. 808–811.

Ausubel, D. (1960). The use of advance organizers in the learning and retention of meaningful verbal material. *Journal of Educational Psychology 51*, pp. 267–272.

Ausubel, D. (1963). *The Psychology of Meaningful Verbal Learning*. New York: Grune & Stratton.

Bachem, A. (1950). Tone height and tone chroma as two different pitch qualities. *Acta Psychologica 7*, pp. 80–88.

Bacon, F. (1597). *Meditationes Sacrae*. London: John Windet.

Bacon, R. (1267). Opus Majus I. In R.B. Burke (trans.) *The Opus Majus of Roger Bacon*. Philadelphia: University of Pennsylvania Press.

Baggaley, J. (1972). *Colour and Musical Pitch* (Ph.D. thesis). University of Sheffield.

Baggaley, J. (1973). Analysing TV presentation techniques for educational effectiveness. *Educational Broadcasting International 6*(3), pp. 17–21.

Baggaley, J. (1974). Measurement of Absolute Pitch. *Psychology of Music 2*(2), pp. 11–17.

Baggaley, J. (1980). *Psychology of the TV Image*. New York: Praeger.

Baggaley, J. (1985). From Ronald Reagan to Smoking Cessation: the analysis of media impact. In B. Alloway & G. Mills (eds.) *New Directions in Education & Training Technology*. London: Kogan Page.

Baggaley, J. (1986). Formative evaluation of educational television. *Canadian Journal of Educational Communication 15*(1), pp. 33–43.

Baggaley, J. (1987a). Continuous response measurement in TV research. *Canadian J. Educational Communication 16*, pp. 217–238.

Baggaley, J. (1987b). *Not A Love Story: a summative evaluation* (unpublished report).

Baggaley, J. (1988). Perceived effectiveness of international AIDS campaigns. *Health Education Research 3*(1), pp. 7–17.

Baggaley, J. (1990) Media AIDS Campaigning: not just what you say, but the way that you say it! In R. Berkvens (ed.) *AIDS Prevention through Health Promotion*. Geneva: WHO.

Baggaley, J. (1997). Cross-cultural Uses of Media Research Technology. In M. Goldberg, M. Fishbein & S. Middlestadt (eds.) *Social Marketing: theoretical and practical perspectives*. Hillsdale, NJ: Lawrence Erlbaum Associates.

Baggaley, J. (1999). The Impact of Information Technology on National and Transnational Education. In S. Bond & J-P Lemasson (eds.) *A New World of Knowledge*. Ottawa: International Development Research Centre.

Baggaley, J. (2002a). *Integration of Polling, Conferencing and Server Log Analysis Methods*. Proceedings of 1st International Symposium on Educational Conferencing (ISEC). Alberta: Athabasca University.

Baggaley, J. (2002b). Plagiarism on a plate. *ScreenSeen* (Winter), pp. 12–13.

Baggaley, J. (2009a). Levels of Media Interactivity. In S. Mishra (ed.) *STRIDE Handbook on eLearning.* New Delhi: Indira Gandhi National Open University.

Baggaley, J. (2009b). Synchronous conferencing. In S. Mishra (ed.) *STRIDE Handbook on eLearning.* New Delhi: Indira Gandhi National Open University.

Baggaley, J. (2010). The Luddite Revolt continues. *Distance Education 31*(3), pp. 337–343.

Baggaley, J. (2011). A giant structure. *Distance Education 32*(1), pp. 133–140.

Baggaley, J. & Batpurev, B. (2007a). The World-Wide Inaccessible Web, Part 1: browsing. *International Review of Research in Open & Distance Learning 8*(2). Retrieved from: http://www.irrodl.org/index.php/irrodl/article/view/438/917.

Baggaley, J. & Batpurev, B. (2007b). The World-Wide Inaccessible Web, Part 2: Internet routes. *International Review of Research in Open & Distance Learning 8*(2). Retrieved from: http://www.irrodl.org/index.php/irrodl/article/view/447/910.

Baggaley, J. & Belawati, T. (eds.) (2010). *Distance Education Technologies in Asia.* New Delhi: Sage India/Ottawa: International Development Research Centre.

Baggaley, J., Brauer, A. & Glegg, L. (1990). AIDS education: the boomerang effect. *Studies in Educational Evaluation 16*, pp. 41–62.

Baggaley, J., De Schutter, A., Fahrni, P & Rudolph, J. (2004). Best practices in online conference moderation. *International Review of Research in Open & Distance Learning 5*(1). Retrieved from: http://www.irrodl.org/index.php/irrodl/article/view/164/245.

Baggaley, J., Duby, A. & Lewy, A. (eds.) (1987). *Evaluation of Educational Television.* Johannesburg: South African Broadcasting Corporation.

Baggaley, J. & Duck, S. (1976). *Dynamics of Television.* Westmead, UK: Saxon House.

Baggaley, J., Jamieson, G. & Marchant, H. (eds.) (1975). *Aspects of Educational Technology*, vol. 8. London: Pitman.

Baggaley, J., Kane, T. & Wade, B. (2002). Online polling services. *International Review of Research in Open & Distance Learning 3*(2). Retrieved from: http://www.irrodl.org/index.php/irrodl/article/view/89/168.

Baggaley, J. & Klaas, J. (2006). Video-conferencing with audio software. *International Review of Research in Open & Distance Learning 7*(1). Retrieved from: http://www.irrodl.org/index.php/irrodl/article/view/312/492.

Baggaley, J. & Ludwig, B. (2003). *Real-time Impact of Online Distance Education.* Proceedings of 4th International Conference on Information & Communication Technologies in Education. Athens: Research and Training Institute of East Aegean.

Baggaley, J., Salmon, C., Lewis-Hardy, R., Tambe, B., Siska, M., Jorgensen, C., Harris, R. & Jason, J. (1992). Automated evaluation of AIDS messages with high-risk, low-literacy audiences. *Journal of Educational Television 18*, pp. 83–96.

Baggaley, J. & Spencer, B. (2004). The mind of a plagiarist. *Learning Media and Technology 30*(1), pp. 57–64.

Bagley, W. (1911a). *Classroom Management: its principles and technique.* New York: MacMillan (1st edition, 1907).

Bagley, W. (1911b). *Craftsmanship in Teaching.* New York: MacMillan.

Bagley, W. (1911c). *Educational Values.* New York: MacMillan.

Bagley, W. (1938). An essentialist's platform for the advancement of American education. *Educational Administration & Supervision 24* (April), pp. 241–256.

Bandura, A. & Walters, R. (1963). *Social Learning and Personality Development.* New York: Holt, Rinehart, & Winston.

Banking.com (2011). *Social Media Statistics: By-the-Numbers, January 2011 (Part II).* Retrieved from: http://www.banking2020.com/2011/01/24/social-media-statistics-by-the-numbers-january-2011-part-ii/.

Basic English Bible (2004). *Proverbs 24:22.* Retrieved from: http://bible.cc/proverbs/24-22. htm.

Bate, J. (1991). Letter to the Editor. *London Review of Books 13*(2), 24 January.

Bates, T. (1995). *Technology, Open Learning and Distance Education.* London: Routledge.

Bates, T. (2000). *Managing Technological Change: strategies for college and university leaders.* San Francisco: Jossey Bass.

Bates, T. (2005). *Technology, e-Learning and Distance Education.* London: Routledge.

Bates, T. & Robinson, J. (eds.) (1977). *Evaluating Educational Television and Radio.* Milton Keynes: Open University Press.

Batpurev, B. (2006) Photograph of Mongolian Empire 800th Anniversary Festival, Ulaanbaatar. Personal communication, 26 August.

Bedell, G. (2010). Burj Khalifa – a bleak symbol of Dubai's era of bling. *The Observer* (10 January). Retrieved from: http://www.guardian.co.uk/culture/2010/jan/10/burj-khalifa-dubai-skyscraper-architecture.

Belawati, T. (2010). Cost effectiveness. In T. Belawati & J. Baggaley (eds.) *Policy and Practice in Asian Distance Education.* New Delhi: Sage India/Ottawa: International Development Research Centre.

Belawati, T. & Baggaley, J. (eds.) (2010). *Policy and Practice in Asian Distance Education.* New Delhi: Sage India/Ottawa: International Development Research Centre.

Bellett, G., Woo, A. & Crawford, T. (2010). Photos of teen's gang rape go viral on Internet. *Vancouver Sun* (16 September). Retrieved from: http://www2.canada.com/vancouversun/news/story.html?id=980425e4-bd9b-4838-90bc-a3e1178782ff.

Belyk, D. & Feist, D. (2002). Software evaluation criteria and terminology. *International Review of Research in Open & Distance Learning 3*(1). Retrieved from: http://www.irrodl.org/index.php/irrodl/article/view/70/141.

Berg, M. (1980). *The Machinery Question and the Making of Political Economy: 1815–1848.* Cambridge: Cambridge University Press.

Berger, S. (1990). *Medieval English Drama: an annotated bibliography of recent criticism.* New York: Garland.

Berman, M. (1982). *All that is Solid Melts into Air.* New York: Simon & Schuster.

Bernard, R., Abrami, P., Lou, Y., Wade, A., Wozney, L., Wallet, P. & Fiset, M. (2004). How does distance education compare with classroom instruction? A meta-analysis of the empirical literature. *Review of Educational Research 74* (Fall), pp. 379–439.

Bernstein, J. (2008). *The Lost Gold of Timbuktu* (Discovery Channel TV series: *Into the Unknown*, episode 6). London: Darlow Smithson Productions.

Bessette, G. (2004). *Involving the Community: a guide to participatory development communication.* Ottawa: International Development Research Centre.

Betanews.com (2008). *Rogers, Fido detail iPhone 3G plans for Canada.* Retrieved from: http://www.betanews.com/article/Rogers_Fido_detail_iPhone_3G_plans_for_Canada/1214589154.

Binfield, K. (ed.) (2004). *Writings of the Luddites.* Baltimore: Johns Hopkins University Press.

Biocca, F. (1994). Continuous Response Analysis (CRM): a computerized tool for research on the cognitive processing of communication messages. In A. Lang (ed.) *Measuring Responses to Media.* Hillsdale, NJ: Lawrence Erlbaum Associates.

Bloch, J. (1995). *Rousseauism and Education in Eighteenth-century France.* Oxford: Voltaire Foundation.

Bloom, B. (ed.) (1956) *Taxonomy of Educational Objectives: the classification of educational goals.* Susan Fauer Company.

Blythe, M. (1987). *A History of the Central Council for Health Education, 1927–1968* (M. Litt. thesis). University of Oxford: Faculty of Modern History.

Blythe, M. (1988). *Classical Dilemmas in Health Education Illustrated by the British Health Education Movement*. Paper to the 13th World Conference on Health Education (Houston, Texas).

Blythe, M. (2011). Personal communication, 25 January.

Boccioni, U., Carra, C., Russolo, L., Balla, G. & Severini, G. (1910). *Manifesto of the Futurist Painters. Poesia* (11 February), Milan. Retrieved from: http://www.unknown.nu/futurism/painters.html.

Boe Xie (2010). Perceiving an Internet Community as a 'Utopia': beliefs, norms, and resistance among older Chinese. In P. Zaphiris & Chee Siang Ang (eds.) *Social Computing and Virtual Communities*. Boca Raton, FL: Chapman & Hall.

Bonk, C. (2009). *The World is Open: how web technology is revolutionizing education*. San Francisco: Jossey–Bass.

Boyle, R. (1661). *Some Considerations Touching the Style of Holy Scriptures*. Cited by Markley, R. (1985). *Studies in Eighteenth-Century Culture 14*, 159.

Bradshaw, P. (2010). Teaching blogging: the Social Media Treasure Hunt. *Online Journalism Blog* (19 February). Retrieved from: http://onlinejournalismblog.com/2010/02/19/teaching-blogging-the-social-media-treasure-hunt.

Briggs, L. (1970). *Handbook of Procedures for the Design of Instruction*. Pittsburgh, PA: American Institutes for Research.

Brightkite.com (2010). *The simple way to keep up with friends and places*. Retrieved from: http://www.brightkite.com.

Broadbandreports.com (2008). *U.S. Beats Europe In 3G Device Penetration*. Retrieved from: http://www.broadbandreports.com/shownews/US-Beats-Europe-In-3G-Device-Penetration-97484.

Bruner, J. (1961). The act of discovery. *Harvard Educational Review* 31(1), pp. 21–32.

Bruner, J. (1967). *On Knowing: essays for the left hand*. Cambridge, MA: Harvard University Press.

Bruner, J. (1996). *The Culture of Education*. Cambridge, MA: Harvard University Press.

Brunner, E. & Hsin Pao Yang, E. (1949). *Rural America and the Extension Service*. New York: Columbia University.

Bryars, G. (2011). *The Sinking of the Titanic* (1969-). Retrieved from: http://www.gavinbryars.com/Pages/titanic_point.html.

BSA (2011). Association web site. Belgian Synaesthesia Association. Retrieved from: http://www.doctorhugo.org/synaesthesia/index.htm.

Budzynski, M. (2007). *Agitprop train*. Retrived from: http://www.youtube.com/watch?v=ck-7wqD2Zf0.

Bugelski, B., Kidd, D. & Segman, J. (1968). Imagery as a mediator in one-trial paired associate learning. *Journal of Experimental Psychology 76*, pp. 69–73.

Burnett, R., Consalvo, M. & Ess, C. (2010). *The Handbook of Internet Studies*. Chichester, UK: Wiley.

Calimag, M. (2008). *Philippine Carriers Willing to Reduce SMS Fees*. Retrieved from: http://www.zdnetasia.com/philippine-carriers-willing-to-reduce-sms-fees-62042804.htm.

Cambre, M. (1981). Historical overview of formative evaluation of instructional media products. *Educational Communication & Technology Journal 29*(1), pp. 3–25.

Canada.com (2008). *Ottawa demands explanation on text message charges*. Retrieved from: http://www.canada.com/topics/news/story.html?id=0c8ff864-2602-4772-80de-ed4e11af31f3.

Carpenter, C. (1972). Television or something else. In W. Schramm (ed.) *Quality in Instructional Television*. Honolulu: University of Hawaii Press.

Carr, D. (2010). Constructing Disability in Online Worlds: conceptualising disability in online research. *London Review of Education 8*(1), pp. 51–61.

Carr, D. & Oliver, M. (2009). *Second Life*, Immersion and Learning. In P. Zaphiris & Chee Siang Ang (eds.) *Social Computing and Virtual Communities*. London: Chapman & Hall.

Carr-Chellman, A. (ed.) (2005). *Global Perspectives on E-learning: rhetoric and reality*. Thousand Oaks, CA: Sage.

Carr-Chellman, A. (2006). *User-Design*. Hillsdale, NJ: Lawrence Erlbaum Associates.

Carroll, J. & Greenberg, J. (1961). Two cases of synesthesia for color and musical tonality associated with absolute pitch ability. *Perceptual &Motor Skills 13*, p. 48.

CBC-TV (1960). *The World is a Global Village*. CBC Television (18 May). Retrieved from: http://archives.cbc.ca/arts_entertainment/media/topics/342-1814/.

Cerf, V. & Kahn, R. (1974). A Protocol for Packet Network Intercommunication. *IEEE Transactions on Communications 22*(5), pp. 637–648.

Cheal, C. (2009). Student perceptions of a course taught in Second Life. *Innovate 5*(5). Retrieved from: http://innovateonline.info/pdf/vol5_issue5/Student_Perceptions_of_a_Course_Taught_in_Second_Life.pdf.

CheatingCulture.com (2011). *Fighting for a Fairer, More Ethical World*. Retrieved from: http://www.cheatingculture.com/.

Chen Li & Wang Nan (2010). *Attitudes to Distance Education in China*. In J. Baggaley & T. Belawati (eds.) *Distance Education Technologies in Asia*. New Delhi: Sage India / Ottawa: International Development Research Centre.

Chickering, A. & Gamson, Z. (1987). Seven principles for good practice in undergraduate education. *American Association for Higher Education Bulletin 39*(2), pp. 3–7.

Christakis, N. & Fowler, J. (2009). *Connected: how your friends' friends' friends affect everything you feel, think, and do*. New York: Back Bay.

Christiansen, R. & Stone, D. (1968). Visual imagery and level of mediator abstractness in induced medication paradigms. *Perceptual & Motor Skills 26*, pp. 775–779.

Chu, C. (1999). The development of interactive distance learning in Taiwan: challenges and prospects. *Educational Media International, 36*(2), pp. 110–114.

Chu, G. & Schramm, W. (1967). *Learning from Television: what the research says*. Washington: National Association of Educational Broadcasters.

Churnalism.com (2011). *Churn engine to distinguish journalism from churnalism*. London: Media Standards Trust. Retrieved from: http://churmalism.com.

Clark, R. (1983). Reconsidering research on learning from media. *Review of Educational Research 53*(4), pp. 445–459.

Coldevin, G. (1976). Comparative effectiveness of TV production variables. *Journal of Educational Television 2*(3), pp. 87–93.

Coldevin, G. & Wilson, T. (1985). Effects of a Decade of Satellite Television in the Canadian Arctic: Euro-Canadian and Inuit Adolescents Compared. *Journal of Cross-Cultural Psychology 16*(3), pp. 329–354.

Cole, S. (2009). 25 ways to teach with Twitter. *Tech&Learning* (4 June). Retrieved from: http://www.techlearning.com/article/20896.

Conan Doyle, A. (1891). *A Study in Scarlet*. London: Ward, Lock & Bowden.

Connolly, K. (2007). Germany investigates Second Life child pornography. *The Guardian* (8 May). Retrieved from: http://www.guardian.co.uk/technology/2007/may/08/secondlife.web20.

Constine, J. (2011). Gates Foundation Funds Inigral's Schools Facebook App for Keeping Students Enrolled. *Inside Facebook* (9 February). Retrieved from: http://www.insidefacebook.com/2011/02/09/gates-foundation-inigral-schools/.

Cornwell, J. (1995). The Alpha and the Omega. *Mazzaroth.com*. Retrieved from: http://www.mazzaroth.com/ChapterThree/TowerOfBabel.htm.

Costhelper.com (2011). *How much does text messaging cost?* Retrieved from: http://www.costhelper.com/cost/electronics/text-messaging.html.

Crawford, H. (1993). *Sumer and the Sumerians*. New York: Cambridge University Press.

Cremin, L. (1961). *The Transformation of the School: progressivism in American education, 1876–1957*. New York: Knopf.

Cronbach, L. (1946). Response sets and test validity. *Educational & Psychological Measurement* 6 (Winter), pp. 475–495.

Cronbach, L. & Snow, R. (1977). *Aptitudes and Instructional Methods: a handbook for research on interactions*. New York: Irvington.

Crosslin, M. (2010). Confessions of a massive open online course flunkie. *EduGeek Journal* (10 December). Retrieved from: http://www.edugeekjournal.com/2010/12/10/confessions-of-a-massive-open-online-course-flunkie/.

Crupi, J. (2009). Enterprise mashups. *SOA World* (11 January). Retrieved from: http://soa.sys-con.com/node/719917.

Cytowic, R. (1993). *The Man Who Tasted Shapes*. New York: Tarcher/Putnam.

Daniel, J. (1996). *Mega-universities and Knowledge Media: technology strategies for higher education*. London: Kogan Page.

Daniel, J. (2010). *Mega-Schools, Technology and Teachers: achieving education for all*. London & New York: Routledge.

Davies, N. (2008). Flat Earth News: an award-winning reporter exposes falsehood, distortion and propaganda in the global media. London: Chatto & Windus.

Davis, M. (2008). *Street Gang: the complete history of Sesame Street*. New York: Viking Press.

de Boer, C., Verleur, R., Heuvelman, A. & Heynderick, I. (2010). Added value of an auto-stereoscopic multiview 3-D display for advertising in a public environment. *Displays* 31(1), pp. 1–8.

dela Pena-Bandalaria, M. (2007) Impact of ICTs on Open and Distance Learning in a Developing Country Setting: the Philippine experience. *International Review of Research in Open & Distance Learning* 8(1). Retrieved from: http://www.irrodl.org/index.php/irrodl/article/view/334/792.

Decoo, W. (2002). *Crisis on Campus: confronting academic misconduct*. Cambridge, MA: MIT Press.

Derby, B. (2008). Duplication and plagiarism increasing among students. *Nature* 452(29) (6 March).

Dewey, J. (1897). My Pedagogic Creed. *School Journal* vol. 54 (January), pp. 77–80.

Dhanarajan, G. & Wong, T.M. (2007). Preserving Access to Lifelong Learning in the Digital Environment. In *Equity, Innovation, and Research for Distance Lifelong Learning*. Seoul: Korean National Open University.

Dick, W., Carey, L. & Carey, J. (1978). *The Systematic Design of Instruction*. Boston, MA: Allyn & Bacon.

Dickinson, A. (2010). Noma Belomesoff murder prompts Australian Facebook revolt. *The Courier-Mail* (17 May). Retrieved from: http://www.couriermail.com.au/news/technology/nona-belomesoff-murder-prompts-australian-facebook-revolt/story-e6frep1o-1225867931363.

Dictionary of Psychology (2010). *Informed Consent*. Retrieved from: http://dictionary-psychology.com/index.php?a=term&d=Dictionary+of+psychology&t=Informed+consent.

Dietz, O. (2004). *Geschichte Mesopotamiens. von den Sumerern bis zu Alexander dem Großen*, Munich: Beck.

Dieuzeide, H. (1977). Closing Address. In T. Bates & J. Robinson (eds.) *Evaluating Educational Television and Radio*. Milton Keynes, UK: Open University Press.

DigitalBuzz.com (2010). *Infographic: Twitter statistics, facts and figures* (12 May). Retrieved from: http://www.digitalbuzzblog.com/infographic-twitter-statistics-facts-figures/.

Dilke, O. & Dilke, M. (1994). The Adjustment of Ptolemaic Atlases to Feature the New World. In W. Hasse & M. Rheingold (eds.) *The Classical Tradition and the Americas*. New York: De Gruyter.

Dillow, C. (2010). Augmented Identity App Helps You Identify Strangers on the Street. *Popsci* (23 February). Retrieved from: http://www.popsci.com/technology/article/2010-02/augmented-identity-app-helps-you-identify-friend-perfect-strangers.

Dittmar, A. (ed.) (2009). *Synaesthesia: a 'golden thread' through life?* Essen, Germany: Verlag Die Blaue Eule.

DIVERSE (2008). *Developing Innovative Video Resources for Students Everywhere*. Retrieved from: http://csalt.lancs.ac.uk/diverse/.

dmoz.org (2009). Computers: Internet: Abuse. Dmoz Open Directory Project. Retrieved from: http://www.dmoz.org/Computers/Internet/Abuse/.

Dodds, T. (2005). Open and Distance Learning for Devloping Countries: is the cup half full or is it still half empty? In Y. Vissa, I. Vissa, M. Simonson & R. Amirault (eds.) *Trends and Issues in Distance Education*. Greenwich, CT: Information Age.

Doung Vuth, Chhuon Chanthan, Somphone Phanousith, Phonpasit Phissamay, Tran Thi Tai & Vu The Binh (2010). Distance Education Policy and Awareness in Cambodia, Lao PDR and Viet Nam. In J. Baggaley & T. Belawati (eds.) *Distance Education Technologies in Asia*. New Delhi: Sage India / Ottawa: International Development Research Centre.

Dowling, S. (1996). Internet Education: reform or false panacea? *Proceedings of the Annual Conference of the Internet Society*. Retrieved from: http://www.isoc.org/inet96/proceedings/c1/c1_1.htm.

Earl, S., Carden, F. & Smutylo, T. (2001). *Outcome mapping: building learning and reflection into development programs*. Ottawa: International Development Research Centre. Retrieved from: http://www.idrc.ca/en/ev-9330-201-1-DO_TOPIC.html.

Eaton, M. (ed.) (1979). *Anthropology − Reality − Cinema: the films of Jean Rouch*. London: British Film Institute.

EDNA (2011). *Global Education*. Education Network Australia. Retrieved from: http://www.globaleducation.edna.edu.au/globaled/go.

Educational Access & Accessibility (2011). *Software Evaluations*. Retrieved from: http://www.distedaccess.org.

Edutools.org (2011). *Providing Decision-making Tools for the E-D-U Community*. Retrieved from: http://www.edutools.info.

Einstein, A. (1905). Zur Elektrodynamik bewegter Körper. *Annalen der Physik* 17:891 (trans. *On the Electrodynamics of Moving Bodies*, by G. Jeffrey & W. Perrett, 1923).

Eisenstein, S. (1943). *The Film Sense*. London: Faber & Faber.

Elias, T. (2010). Universal instructional design principles for Moodle. *International Review of Research in Open & Distance Learning* 11(2), pp. 110–124. Retrieved from: http://www.irrodl.org/index.php/irrodl/article/view/869/1575.

Empson, W. (1930). *Seven Types of Ambiguity*. London: New Directions.

EPIC (2010). *Facebook Privacy*. Electronic Privacy Information Center. Retrieved from: http://epic.org/privacy/facebook/.

Errami, M. & Garner, H. (2008). A tale of two citations. *Nature* 451, 397–399, 24 January.

Evans, M. (2010). The Dark Side of Social Media and Privacy. *Mark Evans Tech* (21 February). Retrieved from: http://www.markevanstech.com/2010/02/21/the-dark-side-of-social-media-and-privacy.

EWGEC (2002). *Maastricht Global Education Declaration.* Europe-wide Global Education Congress. Retrieved from: http://www.coe.int/t/dg4/nscentre/ge/GE-Guidelines/GEgs-app1.pdf.

Facebook.com (2011a). *Company Timeline* (July). Retrieved from: http://www.facebook.com/press/info.php?timeline.

Facebook.com (2011b). *Facebook's Privacy Policy* (July). Retrieved from: http://www.facebook.com/policy.php.

Fahy, P., Crawford, G. & Ally, M. (2001). Patterns of interaction in a computer conference transcript. *International Review of Research in Open and Distance Learning 2*(1). Retrieved from: http://www.irrodl.org/index.php/irrodl/article/view/36/73.

Farrell, G. (2001). *The Changing Faces of Virtual Education.* Vancouver: Commonwealth of Learning (Chap. 8). Retrieved from: http://www.col.org/resources/publications/monographs/Pages/2001-changing.aspx.

Ferret, W. (2007). Second Life shuts down casinos. *The Inquirer* (26 July). Retrieved from: http://www.theinquirer.net/inquirer/news/1029004/second-life-shuts-casinos.

Fildes, J. (2007). Wikipedia 'shows CIA page edits'. *BBC News.* Retrieved from: http://news.bbc.co.uk/2/hi/6947532.stm.

Finch, C. (1993). *Jim Henson: the works—the art, the magic, the imagination.* New York: Random House.

Findahl, O. & Hoijer, B. (1977). *How Important is Presentation?* Stockholm: Sveriges Radio.

Fiske, J. & Hartley (1978). *Reading Television.* London: Methuen.

Flagg, B. (1990). *Formative Evaluation for Educational Technologies.* Hillsdale, NJ: Lawrence Erlbaum Associates.

Flanders, N. (1967). *Teacher Influence in the Classroom. Interaction analysis: theory, research, and application.* Reading, MA: Addison-Wesley.

Fleming, M. & Levie, W.H. (1978). *Instructional Message Design.* Englewood Cliffs, NJ: Educational Technology Publications.

Forbes, R. (1964). *Studies in Ancient Technology* (2nd ed.). Leiden, Netherlands: Brill.

Foster, C. (1914). *Bible Pictures and What They Teach Us.* Philadelphia, PA: A.J. Holman. Retrieved from: http://commons.wikimedia.org/wiki/File:Foster_Bible_Pictures_0025-1.jpg.

Foursquare.com (2010). *Find your friends. Unlock your city.* Retrieved from: http://www.foursquare.com.

Freedman, D. (2003). *Television Policies of the Labour Party 1951–2001.* London: Frank Cass.

Freedman, T. (2008). An uncritical mass. *The Educational Tchnology Site* (28 July). Retrieved from: http://terry-freedman.org.uk/artman/publish/An_Uncritical_Mass.php.

Freeman, D. (1983). *Margaret Mead and Samoa: The Making and Unmaking of an Anthropological Myth.* Cambridge, MA: Harvard University Press.

Freire, P. (1969). *Extensión y Comunicación* (trans. L. Bigwood & M. Marshall, *Extension or Communication* (1973)). New York: Continuum.

Freire, P. (1970). *Pedagogía del Oprimado* (trans. M. Ramos, *Pedagogy of the Oppressed* (2007)). New York: Continuum.

Gagné, R. (1965). *The Conditions of Learning.* New York: Holt, Rinehart & Winston.

Galeyev, B. & Vanechkina, I. (2001). Was Scriabin a synesthete? *Leonardo 34*(4), pp. 357–362. Retrieved from: http://prometheus.kai.ru/skriab_e.htm.

Garber, D. (2004). Growing virtual communities. *International Review of Research in Open & Distance Learning 5*(2). Retrieved from: http://www.irrodl.org/index.php/irrodl/article/view/177/259.

GCE-US (2011). *Global Campaign for Education: US chapter*. Retrieved from: http://www.campaignforeducationusa.org/.

GENE (2011). *Global Education Network Europe*. Retrieved from: http://www.gene.eu/.

Georgetown University (2011). *Honor, Commitment, and Community*. Retrieved from: http://gervaseprograms.georgetown.edu/honor/system/53508.html.

GetEducated.com (2010). *The Consumer's Guide to Online Colleges*. Retrieved from: http://www.geteducated.com/college-degree-mills.

Goldfarb, S. (2009). Top 10 Strategies for Running a Facebook Political Campaign. *All Facebook* (22 January). Retrieved from: http://www.allfacebook.com/2009/01/top-10-strategies-for-running-a-facebook-political-campaign.

Goldstein, J. (2009). *Ladies and Gentlemen, the Bible!* Toronto: Penguin Group.

Goldwyn, E. (1974). Access Television. *Educational Broadcasting International 7*(4).

Gonzales, A. & Hancock, J. (2011). Mirror, mirror on my Facebook wall: effects of exposure to Facebook on self-esteem. *Cyberpsychology, Behavior, and Social Networking 14*(1–2), pp. 79–83.

Gray, C. (1986). *The Russian Experiment in Art: 1863–1922*. London: Thames & Hudson.

Guri-Rosenblit, S. (2001). The Tower of Babel syndrome in the discourse on information technologies in higher education. *Global E-Journal of Open, Flexible and Distance Education, 1*(1), 28–38.

Hammer, M. (2011). *An Early Culture Critic Speaks Out*. Retrieved from: http://www.pianonoise.com/Article.Plato.htm.

Harrison, J. (2001). *Synaesthesia, the Strangest Thing*. Oxford: Oxford University Press.

Haupt, E. & Perera, T. (eds) (2008). Meumann-style ergograph. In *Museum of the History of Psychological Instrumentation*. Monclair, NJ: Montclair State University. Retrieved from: http://chss.montclair.edu/psychology/museum/x_393.htm.

Haveinternetwilltravel.com (2009). *The Philippines is the Text Messaging Capital of the World*. Retrieved from: http://www.haveinternetwilltravel.com/2009/01/10/random-factoid-the-philippines-is-the-text-messaging-capital-of-the-world/.

Heider, F. (1958). *The Psychology of Interpersonal Relations*. New York: Wiley.

Henny, L. (1976). Filmmakers as Part of a Revolutionary Intelligentsia. In A. Gella (ed.) *The Intelligentsia and the Intellectuals*. Beverly Hills, CA: Sage.

Henny, L. (1983). Video and the Community. In P. Dowrick & S. Biggs (eds.) *Using Video: psychological and social applications*. New York: Wiley.

Hirsch, Jr., E. (1996). *The Schools We Need and Why We Don't Have Them*. New York: Doubleday.

HollywoodGossip.com (2009). Fan to Miley Cyrus: return to Twitter or I murder a kitten! *Hollywood Gossip* (30 October). Retrieved from: http://www.thehollywoodgossip.com/2009/10/fan-to-miley-cyrus-return-to-twitter-or-i-murder-a-kitten.

Hooper, R. (1975). Computers and Sacred Cows. In J. Baggaley, H. Jamieson & H. Marchant (eds.) *Aspects of Educational Technology VIII*. London: Pitman.

Hotrum, M. (2005). Breaking Down the LMS Walls. *International Review of Research in Open & Distance Learning 6*(1). Retrieved from: http://www.irrodl.org/index.php/irrodl/article/view/212/295.

Hotrum, M., Ludwig, B. & Baggaley, J. (2005). Open Source Software: fully featured vs. 'the devil you know'. *International Review of Research in Open & Distance Learning 6*(1). Retrieved from: http://www.irrodl.org/index.php/irrodl/article/view/213/296.

Hovland, C., Janis, I. & Kelley, H. (1953). *Communication and Persuasion: psychological studies in opinion change*. New Haven, CT: Yale University Press.

Hovland, C., Lumsdaine, A. & Sheffield, F. (1949). *Experiments on Mass Communication: studies in social psychology in World War II (Vol. 3)*. Princeton, NJ: Princeton University Press.

Hughes, G. (2010). Social software: new opportunities for challenging social inequalities in learning? *Learning Media & Technology 34*(4), pp. 291–305.

Hyman, H. & Sheatsley, P. (1947). Some reasons why information campaigns fail. *Public Opinion Quarterly 11*(3), pp. 412–423.

ICBS (2010). *Results of Population Census 2010*. Indonesia Central Bureau of Statistics. Jakarta: Government of Indonesia. Retrieved from: http://dds.bps.go.id/eng/download_file/SP2010_agregat_data_perProvinsi.pdf.

ICR (1962). *Educational Television: the next ten years*. Stanford University: Institute for Communication Research.

Innis, H. (1950). *Empire and Communications*. Oxford: Clarendon Press.

International Telecommunication Union: www.itu.int (2008). *Indonesia Leads Southeast Asia in 3G CDMA Subscriber Growth*. Retrieved from: http://www.itu.int/ITU-D/ict/newslog/Indonesia+Leads+Southeast+Asia+In+3G+CDMA+Subscriber+Growth.aspx.

IntGovForum.org (2006). *First IGF Meeting: Athens, Greece*. Internet Governance Forum. Retrieved from: http://www.intgovforum.org/cms/athensmeeting.

Isacoff, S. (2001). *Temperament: the idea that solved music's greatest riddle*. New York: Knopf.

ISNAR/ IDRC/ CTA (2003). *Evaluating Capacity Development: experiences from research and development organizations around the world*. Ottawa: International Development Research Centre.

Jackson, P. (2005). *The Mongols and the West: 1221–1410*. New York: Pearson/Longman.

Jacobson, R. (1993). Sailing Through Cyberspace: counting the stars in passing. In L. Harasim (ed.) *Global Networks: computers and international communication*. Boston, MA: Massachusetts Institute of Technology.

Jakupec, V. & Garrick, J. (eds.) (2000). *Flexible Learning, Human Resource and Organisation Development: putting theory to work*. London: Routledge.

James, J. (2004). *Information Technology and Development*. New York: Routledge.

James, S. (1996a). Educational Media and 'Agit Prop': I. The legacy of Vertov. *Journal of Educational Media 22*(2), pp. 111–123.

James, S. (1996b). Educational Media and 'Agit Prop': II. The Vertov Process Repatriated. *Journal of Educational Media 22*(3), pp. 161–173.

Jamieson, H. (1985). *Communication and Persuasion*. Beckenham, UK: Croom Helm.

Jamieson, H. (2007). *Visual Communication: more than meets the eye*. Chicago, IL: Intellect Books.

Jamieson, K. & Birdsell, D. (1990). *Presidential Debates: the challenge of creating an informed electorate*. New York: Oxford University Press.

Jamtsho, S. & Bullen, M. (2007). Distance education in Bhutan: improving access and quality through ICT use. *Distance Education 28*(2), pp. 149–161.

Jamtsho, S. & Bullen, M. (2010). Development of ICT-based Distance Education in Bhutan. In J. Baggaley & T. Belawati (eds.) *Distance Education Technologies in Asia*. New Delhi: Sage India/Ottawa: International Development Research Centre.

Jansen, B., Spink, A. & Taksa, I. (2009). *Handbook of Research on Web Log Analysis*. Hershey, PA: IGI Global.

Job, R. (1988). Effective and ineffective uses of fear in health promotion campaigns. *American Journal of Public Health 78*(2), pp. 163–167.

Jonassen, D. (1991). Objectivism versus constructivism: do we need a new philosophical paradigm? *Journal of Educational Technology Research and Development 39*(3), pp. 5–14.

Juma, C. (2007). Give African Universities Free Internet Access. Nairobi: *Business Daily* (11 October).

Jung, C. (1907). On psychophysical relations of the associative experiment. *Journal of Abnormal Psychology 2*, pp. 247–255. Retrieved from: http://sidis.net/galvanicjung1.htm.

Jung, C. (1910). *The Association Method*. Lecture at Clark University, Massachusetts. Retrieved from: http://psychcentral.com/classics/Jung/Association/lecture1.htm.

Kaiser, H. (1956). *The Varimax Method of Factor Analysis* (doctoral thesis). University of California.

Kandinsky, W. (1911). *Über das Geistige in der Kunst (On the Spiritual in Art)*. (Trans. M. Sadler, *The Art of Spiritual Harmony*, 1914, 1959). Berne, Switzerland: Benteli Verlag. Retrieved from: http://www.mnstate.edu/gracyk/courses/phil%20of%20art/kandinskytext2.htm#1.

Kandinsky, W., Lindsey, K. & Vergo, P. (1997). *Kandinsky, Complete Writings on Art*. Cambridge, MA: Da Capo.

Karuna Center (2007). *Thinking about Reconciliation*. Centre Newsletter (Spring). Retrieved from: http://www.karunacenter.org/newsletters/newsletter2.html#SouthAfrica.

Kay, H., Dodd, B. & Sime, M. (1968). *Teaching Machines and Programmed Instruction*. London: Pelican Books.

Kear, K. (2011). *Online and Social Networking Communities: a best practice guide for educators*. New York: Routledge.

Kern, S. (1983). *The Culture of Time and Space: 1880–1918*. Cambridge, MA: Harvard University Press.

Klaas, J. (2003). Best practices in online polling. *International Review of Research in Open & Distance Learning 4*(2). Retrieved from: http://www.irrodl.org/index.php/irrodl/article/view/137/217.

Knight, J. (1997). Internationalization of Higher Education: a conceptual framework. In J. Knight & H. de Wit (eds.) *Internationalization of Higher Education in Asia Pacific Countries*. Amsterdam: European Association for International Education.

Knudsen, C. (2004) *Presence Production*. Stockholm: Royal Institute of Technology.

Kozma, R. (1994). Will media influence learning? Reframing the debate. *Educational Technology Research & Development 42*(2), pp. 7–19.

Krech, D., Crutchfield, R. & Ballachey, E. (1962). *Individual in Society*. New York: McGraw-Hill.

Krystek, L. (1998). *The Tower of Babel*. Retrieved from: http://www.unmuseum.org/babel.htm.

Kukulska-Hulme, A. (2005b). Mobile Usability and User Experience. In A. Kukulska-Hulme & J. Traxler (eds.) *Mobile Learning: a handbook for educators and trainers*. London: Routledge.

Kummer, M. (2008). *Session introduction: Dimensions of Cyber-security and Cyber-crime*. Retrieved from: http://www.elon.edu/docs/e-web/predictions/IGF%2008%20Cybersecurity%20and%20cybercrime.pdf.

Kurtz, E. (1959). *Pioneering in Educational Television 1932-1939*. Iowa: State University of Iowa.

La Rochelle, R. (1984). Committed Documentary in Quebec: a still birth? In T.Waugh (ed.) *Show Us Life: toward a history and aesthetics of the committed documentary*. London: Scarecrow.

Laaser, W. (2006). Virtual universities for African and Arab countries. *Turkish Online Journal of Distance Education* 7(4), Retrieved from: http://tojde.anadolu.edu.tr/tojde24/articles/article_13.htm.

Ladd-Franklin, C. (1929). *Colour and Colour Theories*. New York: Routledge.

Lasar, M. (2009). You know the name, but just who were the Luddites? *Ars Technica* (5 October). Retrieved from: http://arstechnica.com/tech-policy/news/2009/10/if-you-are-reading-this-post-you-are-not-a-luddite.ars.

Lashley, K. & Watson, J. (1921). A psychological study of motion pictures in relation to venereal disease. *Social Hygiene* 7, pp. 181–219.

Lasswell, H. (1948). The Structure and Function of Communication in Society. In L. Bryson (ed.) *The Communication of Ideas*. New York: Harper & Row.

Latchem, C. (2006). Editorial: a content analysis of the *British Journal of Educational Technology*. *British Journal of Educational Technology* 37(4), pp. 503–511.

Latchem, C., Abdullah, Z. & Ding, X. (1999). Open and dual-mode universities in East and South Asia. *Performance Improvement Quarterly* 12(2), pp. 3–28.

Latchem, C., Lockwood, F. & Baggaley, J. (2008). Leading Open and Distance Learning and ICT-based Development Projects in Low-Income Nations. In T. Evans, M. Haughey & D. Murphy (eds.) *International Handbook of Distance Education*. Bingley, UK: Emerald Group.

Lathrop, A. & Foss, K. (2000). *Student Cheating and Plagiarism in the Internet Era*. Englewood, CO: Greenwood.

Laurillard, D. (1987). *Interactive Media: working principles and practical applications*. New York: Wiley.

Laurillard, D. (2002). *Rethinking University Teaching: a conversational framework for the effective use of learning technologies* (2nd ed.). London: Routledge Falmer.

Laurillard, D. (2008). The teacher as action researcher: using technology to capture pedagogic form. *Studies in Higher Education, 33*(2), pp. 139–154.

Laurillard, D. (2009). The pedagogical challenges to collaborative technologies. *International Journal of Computer-Supported Collaborative Learning, 4*(1), pp. 5–20.

Lawrence, C. (2011). Personal communication, 19 March.

Lawrence, T.E. (1926). *Seven Pillars of Wisdom*. London: Doubleday.

Lees, J. (2006). *Virtual prostitutes make real cash*. Retrieved from: http://www.joystiq.com/2006/04/10/virtual-prostitutes-make-real-cash/

Lesser, G. (1974). *Children and Television: lessons from Sesame Street*. New York: Random House.

Lewin, K. (1946). Action research and minority problems. *Journal of Social Issues* 2(4), pp. 34–46.

Librero, F. (2010). Training Asian instructional designers. In J. Baggaley & T. Belawati (eds.) *Distance Education Technologies in Asia*. New Delhi: Sage India/Ottawa: International Development Research Centre.

Librero, F., Ramos, A., Ranga, A., Triñona, J. & Lambert, D. (2007). Uses of the cellphone for education in the Philippines and Mongolia. *Distance Education* 28(2), pp. 231–244.

Likert, R. (1932). A technique for the measurement of attitudes. *Archives of Psychology 140*, pp. 1–55.

Linton, K. (2009). Second Life to regulate virtual porn, prostitution and pedophilia. *Associated Content Technology* (29 July). Retrieved from: http://www.associatedcontent. com/article/1999500/second_life_to_regulate_virtual_porn.html.

Liu, L., Johnson, D., Maddux, C. & Henderson, M. (eds.) (2001). *Evaluation and Assessment in Educational Technology.* Philadelphia, PA: Haworth.

Loopt.com (2010). *Discover the world around you.* Retrieved from: http://www.loopt.com.

Luckin, R., Clark, W., Graber, R., Logan, K., Mee, A. & Oliver, O. (2009). Do Web 2.0 tools really open the door to learning? *Learning Media & Technology 34*(2), pp. 87–104 (special issue on Learning and Social Software).

Luddite Manifesto (1812). Declaration of the Framework Knitters. In A. Aspinall & E. Smith (eds.) (1996) *English Historical Documents XI,* Vol. 8, 1783–1832. New York: Routledge, p. 531.

Lumsdaine, A. & Glaser, R. (1962). *Teaching Machines and Programmed Learning: a source book.* New York: Wiley.

MacKay, C. (1852). *Memoirs of Extraordinary Popular Delusions and the Madness of Crowds.* London: Bentley.

MacKenzie, N. (2005). Genesis: the Brynmor Jones Report. *British Journal of Educational Technology 36*(5), pp. 711–723.

Mackworth, J. (1969). *Vigilance and Habituation.* Baltimore, MD: Penguin.

Malik, N. (2010). Virtual University of Pakistan. In T. Belawati & J. Baggaley (eds.) *Policy and Practice in Asian Distance Education.* New Delhi: Sage India / Ottawa: International Development Research Centre.

Martin, N. (2008). George Orwell diaries to be published as blog. *The Telegraph.* Retrieved from: http://www.telegraph.co.uk/news/uknews/2469672/George-Orwell-diaries-to-be-published-as-blog.html.

Maxwell, J. (1993). *Developing the Leader Within You.* Nashville, TN: Nelson.

McCarthy, K. (2006). How engineers tamed the Internet's Tower of Babel. *The Guardian* (23 November). Retrieved from: http://www.guardian.co.uk/technology/2006/nov/23/guardianweeklytechnologysection.insideit1.

McGuire, W. (1986). The Myth of Massive Media Impact: savagings and salvagings. In G. Comstock (ed.) *Public Communication and Behavior, vol. 1.* Orlando, FL: Academic Press.

McKee, T. (2010). Thirty Years of Distance Education: personal reflections. *International Review of Research in Open & Distance Learning 11*(2). Retrieved from: http://www.irrodl.org/index.php/irrodl/article/view/870/1576.

McKellar, P. (1968). *Experience and Behaviour.* Harmondsworth, UK: Penguin.

McKendrick, J. (2009). Enterprise mashup, defined. *ZDNet.com* (9 November). Retrieved from:http://www.zdnet.com/blog/service-oriented/enterprise-mashup-defined/3314? tag=rbxccnbzd1.

McLuhan, M. (1944). Poetic vs. rhetorical exegesis: the case for Leavis against Richards and Empson. *Sewanee Review 52*(2), pp. 266–276.

McLuhan, M. (1962). *The Gutenberg Galaxy: the making of typographic man.* Toronto: University of Toronto Press.

McLuhan, M. (1964). *Understanding Media: the extensions of man.* London: Routledge & Kegan Paul.

McLuhan, M. (1973). Empson, Frye and Wimsatt. *McLuhan Studies 1.* Retrieved from: http://projects.chass.utoronto.ca/mcluhan-studies/v1_iss1/1_1art2.htm.

McMichael, P. (2008). *Development and social change: a global perspective* (4th ed.). Thousand Oaks, CA: Pine Forge Press.

Mead, M. (1928). *Coming of Age in Samoa: a psychological study of primitive youth for western civilization*. New York: William Morrow.

Mead, M. (1937). *Cooperation and Competition Among Primitive Peoples*. New York: McGraw-Hill.

Mead, M. (1973). Preface to reprint edition: *Coming of Age in Samoa: a psychological study of primitive youth for western civilization*. New York: Quill.

Medvedkin, A. (1993). Interview comment. In C. Marker (dir.) *The Last Bolshevik* (film). Les Filmes d'Astrophore, Michael Kustow Productions, Epidem Oy.

Medvedkina, C. (1993). Interview comment. In C. Marker (dir.) *The Last Bolshevik* (film). Les Filmes d'Astrophore, Michael Kustow Productions, Epidem Oy.

Melton, R. (1977). Course evaluation at the Open University: a case study. *British Journal of Educational Technology 8*(2), pp. 97–103.

Merrill, M. (1980). Learner control in computer based learning. *Computers and Education 4*, pp. 77–95.

Merrill, M. (1983). Component Display Theory. In C. Reigeluth (ed.) *Instructional Design Theories and Models*. Hillsdale, NJ: Lawrence Erlbaum Associates.

Merrill, M. (1994). *Instructional Design Theory*. Englewood Cliffs, NJ: Educational Technology Publications.

Metallinos, N. (1996). *Television Aesthetics: perceptual, cognitive, and compositional bases*. Mahwah, NJ: Lawrence Erlbaum Associates.

Metallinos, N. & Tiemens, R. (1977). Asymmetry of the screen: the effects of left versus right placement of television images. *Journal of Broadcasting 21*, pp. 21–33.

Mezirow, J. (1991). *Transformative Dimensions of Adult Learning*. San Francisco: Jossey-Bass.

Mezirow, J. (2000). *Learning as Transformation: critical perspectives on a theory in progress*. San Francisco: Jossey Bass.

Mielke, K. (1968). Asking the right ETV research questions. *Educational Broadcasting Review 2*(6), pp. 54–61.

Milgram, S. (1963). Behavioral Study of Obedience. *Journal of Abnormal and Social Psychology 67*, pp. 371–378.

Millard, W. (1992). A history of handsets for direct measurement of audience response. *International Journal of Public Opinion Research 4*(1), pp. 1–17.

Miller, A. (2001). *Einstein, Picasso: space, time, and the beauty that causes havoc*. New York: Basic Books.

Miller, J. (1971). *McLuhan*. London: Fontana/Collins.

Millerson, G. (1972). *The Technique of Television Production*. London: Focal Press (14th edition, 2009).

Minderovic, Z. (2007). *Alexander Scriabin: Biography*. Retrieved from: http://www.allmusic.com/artist/q7982.

Mishra, S. (ed.) (2010). *STRIDE Handbook vol. 8: e-Learning*. New Delhi: Indira Gandhi National Open University.

MMU (2011). *Faculty of Creative Multimedia*. Malaysia Multimedia University. Retrieved from: http://creative.mmu.edu.my.

Mohan, G. (2008). Participatory Development. In V. Desai & R. Potter (eds.) *The Arnold Companion to Development Studies* (2nd ed.). London: Edward Arnold.

Monroe, P. (ed.) (1911). *Fatigue. A Cyclopedia of Education (vol. 2)*. New York: MacMillan.

Moor, P., Heuvelman, A. & Verleur, R. (2010). Flaming on YouTube. *Computers in Human Behavior 26*(6), pp. 1536–1546.

Moore, K. & Pflugfelder, E. (2010). On being bored and lost (in virtuality). *Learning Media & Technology 35*(2), pp. 249–253.

Moore, M. (1985). Some observations on current research in distance education. *Epistolodidaktika 1*, pp. 35–62.

Moreno, J. (1951). *Sociometry, Experimental Method and the Science of Society: an approach to a new political orientation.* New York: Beacon House.

Morgan, H. (2010). Miley Cyrus. *Travel 3 Sixty.* Kuala Lumpur: Air Asia.

Morningstar, B., Schubert, J. & Thibeault, K. (2004). WebCT: a major shift of emphasis. Instructional Review of Research in *Open & Distance Learning 5*(3). Retrieved from: http://www.irrodl.org/index.php/irrodl/article/view/194/276.

Morrow, R. (2006). *Sesame Street and the Reform of Children's Television.* Baltimore, MD: Johns Hopkins University Press.

MSCMalaysia.my (2011). *The Malaysia Super Corridor.* Retrieved from: http://www.mscmalaysia.my/.

Muhirwa, J-M. (2009). Teaching and learning against all odds: a video-based study of learner-to-instructor interaction in international distance education. *International Review of Research in Open & Distance Learning 10*(4). Retrieved from: http://www.irrodl.org/index.php/irrodl/article/view/628.

Murphy, F. (1993). *Pseudo-Philo: rewriting the Bible.* Oxford: Oxford University Press.

MuslimHeritage.com (2002–10). *The world-class University of Sankore, Timbuktu.* Retrieved from: http://www.muslimheritage.com/topics/default.cfm?ArticleID=371.

MuteMail.com (2010). *Secure and Anonymous Email Services.* Retrieved from: http://www.mutemail.com.

Naftulin, D., Ware, J. & Donnelly, F. (1973). The Doctor Fox lecture: a paradigm of educational seduction. *Journal of Medical Education 48* (July), pp. 630–635.

Newsom, C. (ed.) (1952). *A Television Policy for Education: proceedings of the Television Programs Institute held under the auspices of the American Council on Education at Pennsylvania State College.* Washington, DC: American Council on Education.

NIHCE (2011). *About the HDA.* National Institute for Health & Clinical Excellence. Retrieved from: http://www.nice.org.uk/aboutnice/whoweare/aboutthehda/about_the_hda.jsp.

NIOS (2010). *NIOS at a Glance.* National Institute of Open Schooling. Retrieved from: http://www.nios.ac.in/glance.htm.

Noble, D. (1993). *Progress Without People: in defence of Luddism.* Chicago: Charles H. Kerr.

Noble, D. (2002). *Digital Diploma Mills: the automation of higher education.* Toronto: Between the Lines.

Nostbakken, D. (1983). Personal communication by McLuhan's former teaching assistant at the University of Toronto.

O'Connell, S. (1975). Television and the Eskimo people of Frobisher Bay. *Arctic 28*(3), pp. 154–158.

Oliver, M. (2007). *Exclusion as an Aspect of Communities in Second Life.* London: Knowledge Lab, Institute of Education.

O'Loughlin, E. & Wegimont, L. (eds.) (2007). *Global Education, Public Awareness Raising, and Campaigning on Development Issues.* Conference on Development Communication, Advocacy, and Education. Bonn, Germany: OECD.

O'Neill, N. (2010). Report Ranks Facebook as Greatest Corporate Security Risk. *All Facebook* (1 February). Retrieved from http://www.allfacebook.com/2010/02/facebook-corporate-risk.

OPCC (2009). *Facebook agrees to address Privacy Commissioner's Concerns.* Office of the Privacy Commissioner of Canada. Retrieved from: http://www.priv.gc.ca/media/nr-c/2009/nr-c_090827_e.cfm.

O'Reilly, T. (2009). *What Is Web 2.0: design patterns and business models for the next generation of software.* Retrieved from: http://oreilly.com/web2/archive/what-is-web-20.html.

OUC (2010). *Statistical Bulletin 2010.* Open University of China. Retrieved from: http://en.crtvu.edu.cn/about/annual-report/2010.

OUUK (2010). *History of the OU.* Open University of UK. Retrieved from: http://www8.open.ac.uk/about/main/the-ou-explained/history-the-ou.

Oppenheim, A. (1977). *Ancient Mesopotamia.* Chicago: University of Chicago Press.

Orwell, G. (1945). *Animal Farm.* London: Secker & Warburg.

Orwell, G. (1949). *Nineteen Eighty-Four.* Harmondsworth, UK: Penguin Books.

Orwell, G. (2010). *The Orwell Diaries.* London: Penguin Modern Classics.

Osgood, C., Suci, G. & Tannenbaum, P. (1957). *The Measurement of Meaning.* Chicago: University of Illinois Press.

PANdora-Asia.org (2007). Distance education policy in China and Mongolia. Online panel discussions, *Global Knowledge Summit,* Kuala Lumpur. Retrieved from: http://video.yahoo.com/watch/5342955/14082274.

Pask, G. (1976). Conversational techniques in the study and practice of education. *British Journal of Educational Psychology 46*(1), pp. 12–25.

PBS-TV (2010). *College Inc.* (TV documentary, *Frontline* series). Retrieved from: http://www.pbs.org/wgbh/pages/frontline/collegeinc/view/.

Perraton, H. (2007). *Open and Distance Learning in the Developing World* (2nd ed.). New York: Routledge.

Peterman, J. (1940). The program analyzer: a new technique in studying liked and disliked items in radio programs. *Journal of Applied Psychology 23*(6), pp. 728–741.

Piaget, J. (1967). *Six Psychological Studies.* New York: Random House.

Picasso, P. (1910). *Girl with a Mandolin (Fanny Tellier).* Retrieved from: http://www.artchive.com/artchive/P/picasso/tellier.jpg.html.

Picasso, P. (1912). *Still Life with Chair Caning.* Retrieved from: http://www.arthistoryarchive.com/arthistory/cubism/.

Picasso, P. (1923). Interview with Mario De Zayas. Reprinted in Barr, A. (1946). *Picasso: fifty years of his art.* New York: Museum of Fine Art.

Pick, J. & Azari, R. (2008). Global digital divide: influence of socioeconomic, governmental, and accessibility factors on information technology. *Information Technology for Development 14*(2), pp. 91–115.

Pina, A. (2010). Online diploma mills: implications for legitimate distance education. *Distance Education 31*(1), pp. 121–126.

Plato (c. 400 BC). *The Republic (Book 3.10–3.12).* Retrieved from: http://www.euphoniousmonks.com/platomus.htm.

PleaseRobMe.com (2010). *Raising awareness about over-sharing.* Retrieved from: http://www.pleaserobme.com.

Popham, W. (1988). *Educational Evaluation* (2nd ed.). Englewood Cliffs, NJ: Prentice Hall.

Postman, N. (1986). *Amusing Ourselves to Death: public discourse in the age of show business.* New York: Viking Penguin.

Postman, N. (1993). Of Luddites, learning, and life. *Technos Quarterly 2*(4). Retrieved from: http://www.ait.net/technos/tq_02/4postman.php.

Postman, N. (1996). *The End of Education: redefining the value of school.* New York: Knopf.

Prochaska, J., Norcross, J. & DiClemente, C. (1994). *Changing for Good: the revolutionary program that explains the six stages of change and teaches you how to free yourself from bad habits*. New York: Morrow.

Psychology.com (2011). *Informed Consent*. Retrieved from: http://psychology.about.com/od/iindex/g/def_informedcon.htm.

Pudovkin, V. (1949). *Film Technique and Film Acting* (trans. I. Montagu). New York: Grove Press.

Pynchon, T. (1984). Is it OK to be a Luddite? *New York Times* Book Review (28 October). Retrieved from: http://www.themodernword.com/Pynchon/pynchon_essays_luddite.html.

Qian Long, Emperor of China (1793). Letter to George III. *Chinese Cultural Studies: Emperor Qian Long*. Retrieved from: http://academic.brooklyn.cuny.edu/core9/phalsall/texts/qianlong.html.

QuitFacebook.com (2010). *It's time to get out of Facebook*. Retrieved from: http://www.quitfacebook.com.

Raby, M. (2007). FBI probes Second Life for illegal gambling. *TG Daily* (4 April). Retrieved from: http://www.tgdaily.com/business-and-law-features/31475-fbi-probes-second-life-for-illegal-gambling.

Rahim, R. (2005). *Genghis Khan: a little PR problem?* Retrieved from: http://pakistanlink.org/Opinion/2005/Sep05/23/02.HTM.

Ramos, A. & Triñona, J. (2010). Mobile Technology in Non-formal Distance Education. In J. Baggaley & T. Belawati (eds.) *Distance Education Technologies in Asia*. New Delhi: Sage India/Ottawa: International Development Research Centre.

Raphael, J. (2009). Facebook Privacy Change Sparks Federal Complaint. *PCWorld* (17 February). Retrieved from: http://www.pcworld.com/article/159703/facebook_privacy_change_sparks_federal_complaint.html.

Recognizr.com (2010). *Your Professional Internet Video Business Card*. Retrieved from: http://www.recognizr.com.

Reed, H. (1942). Naming of Parts. *New Statesman and Nation* 24(598) (8 August), p. 92.

Reid, R. (1959). *American Degree Mills: a study of their operations and of existing and potential ways to control them*. Washington, DC: American Council on Education.

Reigeluth, C. (1999). The Elaboration Theory: guidance for scope and sequence decisions. In C. Reigeluth (ed.), *Instructional-Design Theories and Models: a new paradigm of instructional theory* (Vol. 2). Hillsdale, NJ: Lawrence Erlbaum Associates.

Reigeluth, C. & Carr-Chellman, A. (eds.) (2009). *Instructional-Design Theories and Models, III: Building a Common Knowledge Base*. New York: Routledge.

Reigeluth, C. & Stein, F. (1983). The Elaboration Theory of Instruction. In C. Reigeluth (ed.) *Instructional Design Theories and Models*. Hillsdale, NJ: Lawrence Erlbaum Associates.

Reuters India (2008). *Mobile Fair-Telstra sees 60-70 pct 3G penetration by 2010*. Retrieved from: http://in.reuters.com/article/asiaCompanyAndMarkets/idINL1170097420080211.

Rheingold, H. (2002). *Smart Mobs: the next social revolution*. New York: Perseus Books.

Rivera, E. (2011). Chile: nurse expedites organ transplants using Twitter. *Global Voices* (21 April). Retrieved from: http://globalvoicesonline.org/2011/04/21/chile-nurse-expedites-organ-transport-using-twitter/.

Robertson, H-J. (1998). *No More Teachers, No More Books: the commercialization of Canadian schools*. Toronto: McClelland & Stewart.

Rorschach, H. (1921). *Psychodiagnostik*. Bern, Switzerland: Bircher.

Rosen, C. (2008). The Myth of Multitasking. *The New Atlantis* 20 (Spring), pp. 105–110.

Rosenberg, S. (ed.) (1995). *The Bloomsbury Group: a collection of memoirs and commentary*. Toronto: University of Toronto Press.

Rouch, J. (1955). Positif. In M. Eaton (ed.) *Anthropology – Reality – Cinema: the films of Jean Rouch*. London: British Film Institute, 1979.

Rouch, J. (1979). Five Faces of Vertov. *Framework* (Autumn), pp. 28–29.

Rousseau, J-J. (1762). *Emile: or, On Education*. Translation by A. Bloom. New York: Basic Books.

Russell, T. (1999). *The No Significant Difference Phenomenon*. Chapel Hill, NC: Office of Instructional Telecommunications, North Carolina State University.

Salmon, G. (2004). *E-moderating: the key to teaching and learning online* (2nd ed.). London: Routledge Falmer.

Salmon, G., Nie, M. & Edirisingha, P. (2010). Developing a five-stage model of learning in Second Life. *Educational Research 52*(2), pp. 169–182.

Salomon, G. (1979). *Interaction of Media, Cognition, and Learning*. San Francisco: Jossey Bass.

Samaranayake, V., Jamtsho, S., Rinchen, S., Mishara, S., Khan, Z., Sangi, N., Ahmed, S., Wimalaratne, P., Hewagamage, K. & Attygalle, D. (2010). The Emergence of Distance Education in South Asia. In J. Baggaley & T. Belawati (eds.) *Distance Education Technologies in Asia*. New Delhi: Sage India/Ottawa: International Development Research Centre.

Sartre, J-P. (1972). *The Psychology of Imagination*. London: Hutchinson.

Schramm, W. (1972). What the Research Says. In W. Schramm (ed.) *Quality in Instructional Television*. Honolulu: University of Hawaii Press.

Schramm, W. (1977). *Big Media Little Media: tools and technologies for instruction*. Beverly Hills, CA: Sage.

Schramm, W., Coombs, P. Kahnert, F. & Lyle, J. (1967). *The New Media: memo to educational planners*. Paris: UNESCO.

Schumpeter, J. (1942). *Capitalism, Socialism and Democracy*. London: Unwin.

Schweizer, K. (2010). Facebook Near to Agreement About Location Service, Founder Zuckerberg says. *Bloomberg* (23 June). Retrieved from: http://www.bloomberg.com/news/2010-06-23/facebook-pretty-close-to-offering-location-service-ceo-zuckerberg-says.html.

Schwier. R. & Misanchuk, E. (1993). *Interactive Multimedia Instruction*. Englewood Cliffs, NJ: Educational Technology Publications.

Science Express (2011). *The Science Express*. Retrieved from: http://www.sciencexpress.in/.

Scott, S., McGuire, J. & Shaw, S. (2003). Universal design for instruction: a new paradigm for adult instruction in post-secondary education. *Remedial & Special Education 24*(6), pp. 369–379.

Scriven, M. (1967). The Methodology of Evaluation. In R. Tyler, R. Gagne & M. Scriven (eds.) *Perspectives of Curriculum Evaluation*. Chicago: Rand McNally.

Secondlife.com (2010a). *The Internet's Largest User-created, 3D Virtual World Community*. Retrieved from: http://www.secondlife.com.

Secondlife.com (2010b). *Second Life: community standards*. Retrieved from: http://secondlife.com/corporate/cs.php.

Seely, P. (2001). The Date of the Tower of Babel and Some Theological Implications. *Westminster Theological Journal 63*, pp. 15–38.

Selwyn, N. & Grant, L. (2009). Researching the realities of social software use—an introduction. *Learning Media & Technology 34*(2), pp. 79–86.

Setjorini, L. & Adnan, I. (2010). Universitas Terbuka (Indonesia Open University). In T. Belawati & J. Baggaley (eds.) *Policy and Practice in Asian Distance Education*. New Delhi: Sage/Ottawa: International Development Research Centre.

Shaffer, P. (1980). *Amadeus*. London & New York: Samuel French.

Shaw, G.B. (1916). *Androcles and the Lion; Overruled; Pygmalion*. New York: Brentano. Retrieved from: http://www.monologuearchive.com/s/shaw_006.html.

Shearer, R. (2007). Instructional Design and the Technologies: an overview. In M. Moore (ed.) *Handbook of Distance Education* (2nd ed.). Mahwah, NJ: Lawrence Erlbaum Associates.

Shearer, R. (2008). CNN's 'Thingamajig': 'live audience reaction' graphic flat-lined at the Presidential Debates. *StinkyJournalism.org* (1 October). Retrieved from: http://www.stinkyjournalism.org/latest-journalism-news-updates-132.php.

Shepherd, J. (1967). *A comparative analysis of production techniques found in randomly selected commercial and educational programs*. Washington DC: Office of Education (DHEW).

Siemens, G. (2005). Connectivism: learning as network creation. *e-Learning Space.org* (August 10). Retrieved from: http://www.elearnspace.org/Articles/networks.htm.

Siliconindia.com (2008). *3G users in India to reach 30 million by 2012*. Retrieved from: http://www.siliconindia.com/shownews/3G_users_in_India_to_reach_30_Million_by_2012-nid-49358.html.

Skinner, B. (1938). *The Behavior of Organisms*. New York: Appleton-Century-Crofts.

Skinner, B. (1958). Teaching machines. *Science 128*, pp. 969–977.

Smith, P. & Ragan, T. (2005). *Instructional Design* (3rd ed.). Hoboken, NJ: Wiley Jossey-Bass Education.

SocialMarketingForum.net (2010). *The Community for Social Media Marketing Ideas and Conversations*. Retrieved from: http://www.socialmarketingforum.net.

SocialMedia-Forum.com (2010). *Social Media World Forums*. Retrieved from: http://socialmedia-forum.com.

Stanton, F. (1935). *A Critique of Present Methods and a New Plan for Studying Radio Listening Behavior* (doctoral thesis). Columbus: Ohio State University.

Stevic, A. (2010). Mr. Bennett and Mrs. Brown. *The Modernism Lab*. Retrieved from: http://modernism.research.yale.edu/wiki/index.php/%22Mr._Bennett_and_Mrs._Brown%22.

Stoll, C. (1995). *Silicon Snake Oil: second thoughts on the Information Highway*. New York: Anchor Books.

Stufflebeam, D., Foley, W., Gephart, W., Guba, E., Hammond, R., Merriman, H. & Provus, M. (1971). *Educational Evaluation and Decision Making*. Itasca, IL: Peacock.

Surowiecki, J. (2004). *The Wisdom of Crowds: why the many are smarter than the few and how collective wisdom shapes business, economies, societies and nations*. New York: Anchor.

Swift, J. (1727). *Thoughts on Various Subjects*. Reprinted in *The Battle of the Books, and Other Short Pieces* (1886). London: Cassell.

Taylor, F. (1911). *The Principles of Scientific Management*. New York: Norton.

Taylor, J. (2001). *Fifth Generation Distance Education*. Report No. 40. Department of Education, Training and Youth Affairs: Higher Education Division. Retrieved from: http://www.dest.gov.au/archive/highered/hes/hes40/hes40.pdf.

Taylor, J. (2010). *Sustainable Higher Education Learning Futures*. Keynote address to AACE conference: Global Learn Asia Pacific, Penang.

Taylor, L. (2010). Rudd gives Abbott a lesson in wormology. *The Age* (24 March). Retrieved from: http://www.theage.com.au/opinion/politics/rudd-gives-abbott-a-lesson-in-wormology-20100323-qu4q.html.

Thelwall, M. & Stuart, D. (2010). Social Network Sites: an exploration of features and diversity. In P. Zaphiris & Chee Siang Ang (eds.) *Social Computing and Virtual Communities*. Boca Raton, FL: Chapman & Hall.

Thom, R. (1975). *Structual Stability and Morphogenesis: an outline of a general theory of models*. Reading, UK: Benjamin.

Thomas, J. (2009). 21st century governance? What would Ned Ludd do? *2020Science.org* (18 December). Retrieved from: http://2020science.org/2009/12/18/thomas/.

Thompson, E. (1963). *The Making of the English Working Class*. London: Victor Gollancz.

Thorndike, E. (1921). *The Teacher's Word Book*. New York: Teachers College.

Thorne, K. (2003). *Blended Learning: how to integrate online and traditional learning*. London: Kogan Page.

Thouless, R. (1953). *Straight and Crooked Thinking*. London: Pan.

TMCnet.com (2000). *Multitude Adds Voicemail To Firetalk, Continues To Build Voice Communication System Of The Future*. Retrieved from: http://www.tmcnet.com/tmcnet/newscti/cti1000699.htm.

Tomczak, M. (n.d.). *The Luddite movement: organisation of handicraftsmen in 19th century England*. Retrieved from: http://www.es.flinders.edu.au/~mattom/science+society/lectures/illustrations/lecture27/luddites.html.

TubeTape.net (2011). *PhotoKey 4 Pro* and *CompositeLab Pro* chroma-key software. El Dorado Hills, CA: TubeTape.net.

Turnitin.com (2010). *The Global Leader in Addressing Plagiarism*. Retrieved from http://www.turnitin.com.

UNICEF Canada (2011). *Global Classroom: an agent for change*. Retrieved from: http://globalclassroom.unicef.ca/.

USO (2011). *Explore Ohio's Higher Education System*. University System of Ohio. Retrieved from: http://www.uso.edu/network/usoSchools/index.php.

Urban Dictionary (2011). *Ismism*. Retrieved from: http://www.urbandictionary.com/define.php?term=ismism.

Vasconcellos-Silva, P., Castiel, L. & Rivera, F. (2003). Assessing an Internet health information site by using log analysis: the experience of the National Cancer Institute of Brazil. *Pan American Journal of Public Health 14*(2), pp. 134–137.

Vasudevan, L. (2010). Education remix: new media, literacies, and the emerging digital geographies. *Digital Culture & Education* (31 May). Retrieved from: http://www.digitalcultureandeducation.com/uncategorized/vasudevan_2010_html/.

Venezky, R. (2000). The digital divide within formal school education: causes and consequences. In OECD (ed.) *Learning to bridge the digital divide*. Paris: Organisation for Economic Co-operation & Development.

Verleur, R. (2008). *Affective Video on the Web: exploring presentation and task effects* (doctoral thesis). Twente, Netherlands: University of Twente.

Verleur, R., Heuvelman, A. & Verhagen, P. (2011). Trigger videos on the Web: impact of audiovisual design. *British Journal of Educational Technology 42*(4), pp. 573–582.

Verleur, R., Verhagen, P. & Arentsen, M. (2006). Video persona or avatar: who is more liked and who is more credible as coach within a multimedia programme? 6th International DIVERSE Conference, Glasgow.

Verleur, R., Verhagen, P. & Heuvelman, A. (2007). Can mood-inducing videos affect problem-solving activities in a web-based environment? *British Journal of Educational Technology 38*(6), pp. 1010–1019.

Vertov, D. (1984). Notebook and diary entries. In A. Michelson (ed.) *Kino-Eye: the writings of Dziga Vertov*. Berkeley: University of California Press.

Vigyan Prasar (2011). *Vigyan Rail*. Retrieved from: http://www.vigyanprasar.gov.in/vigyanrail.htm.

Vision.org (2001). Genesis 11: 5–9. Cited in *Scaling the Heights of Hubris*. Retrieved from: http://www.vision.org/visionmedia/article.aspx?id=1379.

Vivian, J. (2010). *The Media of Mass Communication* (10th ed.). Boston: Allyn & Bacon.

Voice&Data.com (2007). *3G: 3G of Communication*. Retrieved from: http://voicendata.ciol.com/content/service_provider/107020706.asp.

Vygotsky, L. (1962). *Thought and Language* (translation). Cambridge, MA: MIT Press.

Walt Disney Company (1940). *Fantasia*. Full-length film. Opening segment retrieved from: http://www.youtube.com/watch?v=a1z12_Ps-gk&feature=fvst.

Walt Disney Company (1954). *20,000 Leagues Under the Sea*. Organ segment retrieved from: http://www.youtube.com/watch?v=Zq8k8Rsd9oY.

Warman, M. (2010). Tim Berners-Lee defends net neutrality. *The Telegraph* (15 September). Retrieved from: http://www.telegraph.co.uk/technology/internet/8003908/Tim-Berners-Lee-defends-net-neutrality.html.

Wayback Machine (2010). *Internet Archive Wayback Machine*. Retrieved from http://www.archive.org/web/web.php.

Wayodd.com (2008). *The Philippines Reaffirms Status as Text-messaging Capital of the World*. Retrieved from: http://www.wayodd.com/the-philippines-reaffirms-status-as-text-messaging-capital-of-the-world/v/8783/.

Wesley Null, J. (2003). *A Disciplined Progressive Educator*. New York: Peter Lang.

Whewell, W. (1840). *The Philosophy of the Inductive Sciences* (2 vols.). London: Parker.

Wikipedia.org (2011a). *Ergograph*. Retrieved from: http://en.wikipedia.org/wiki/Ergograph (20 March).

Wikipedia.org (2011b). *List of Largest Universities by Enrolment*. Retrieved from: http://en.wikipedia.org/wiki/List_of_largest_universities_by_enrollment (21 April).

Wikipedia.org (2011c). *List of People with Synaesthesia*. Retrieved from: http://en.wikipedia.org/wiki/List_of_people_with_synesthesia (23 April).

Wikipedia.org (2011d). *Size of Wikipedia*. Retrieved from: http://en.wikipedia.org/wiki/Wikipedia:Size_of_Wikipedia.

Wikipedia.org (2011e). *Text Messaging*. Retrieved from: http://en.wikipedia.org/wiki/Text_messaging (20 April).

Wikipedia.org (2011f). *The Tower of Babel*. Retrieved from: http://en.wikipedia.org/wiki/Tower_of_Babel (25 April).

Wikipedia.org (2011g). *Wikipedia: the encyclopedia that anyone can edit*. Retrieved from: http://en.wikipedia.org/wiki/Main_Page.

Wikipedia Commons (2010a). *Travels of Marco Polo*. Retrieved from: http://commons.wikimedia.org/wiki/File:Travels_of_Marco_Polo.png.

Wikipedia Commons (2010b). *Tatlin's Tower*. Retrieved from: http://commons.wikimedia.org/wiki/File:Tatlin1.jpg.

Wikramanayake, G., Jamtsho, S., Rinchen, S., Sangi, N., Ahmed, S., Wimalaratne, P., Hewagamage, K. & Attygalle, D. (2010). Accessibility, Acceptance and Effects of Distance Education in South Asia. In J. Baggaley & T. Belawati (eds.) *Distance Education Technologies in Asia*. New Delhi: Sage India/Ottawa: International Development Research Centre.

Wilks, A. (2001). *A Tower of Babel on the Internet?* Retrieved from: http://www.brettonwoodsproject.org/art-16140.

Williams, R. (1974). *Television: technology and cultural form*. London: Collins.

Woodcock, A. & Davis, M. (1978). *Catastrophe Theory*. London: Penguin.

Woolf, V. (1924). *Mr. Bennett and Mrs. Brown*. London: Hogarth Press.

Woolf, V. (1966). *Collected Essays, Vol. 3*. London: Hogarth Press.

Wurtzel, A. & Dominick, J. (1971–72). Evaluation of television drama: interaction of acting styles and shot selection. *Journal of Broadcasting & Electronic Media 16*(1), pp. 103–110.

Wurtzel, A. & Rosenbaum, J. (1995). *Television Production* (4ᵗʰ ed.). New York: McGraw-Hill. (1ˢᵗ ed., 1979.)

Yamshon, L. (2010). Mobile apps can compromise your privacy. *PC World 28*(5), May, pp. 41–42.

Yeung, Sze Kiu (2010). *Designing E-presentation with Digital Media Contents: tools and techniques for building interactive and interoperable solutions.* ICT2010 Conference. Singapore (July).

Young, M. (1999). Network Patrol. *NetworkWorldFusion* (23 August). Retrieved from: http://www.networkworld.com/reviews/0823issues.html.

Yuen, W. & Chu, W. (2010). *Comparing the Effectiveness of Using YouTube, Blog and Wiki in teaching economics.* ICT2010 Conference. Singapore (July).

Zelevansky, L. (ed.) (1992). *Picasso and Braque: a symposium.* New York: Abrams.

Zerjal, T., Xue, Y., Bertorelle, G., Wells, R., Bao, W., Zhu, S., Qamar, R., Ayub, Q., Mohyuddin, A., Fu, S., Li, P., Yuldasheva, N., Ruzibakiev, R., Xu, J., Shu, Q., Du, R., Yang, H., Hurles, M., Robinson, E., Gerelsaikhan, T., Dashnyam, B., Mehdi, S. & Tyler-Smith, C. (2003). The genetic legacy of the Mongols. *American Journal of Human Genetics 72*(3), pp. 717–721.

Zettl, H. (1968). The study of television aesthetics. *Educational Broadcasting Review 2*, pp. 36–40.

Zettl, H. (2010). *Sight Sound Motion: applied media aesthetics* (6ᵗʰ ed.). Belmont, CA: Wadsworth. (1ˢᵗ ed., 1973.)

Zettl, H. (2011). *Television Production Handbook* (11ᵗʰ ed.). Belmont, CA: Wadsworth. (1ˢᵗ ed., 1961.)

Zillmann, D., Williams, B., Bryant, J. & Boynton, K. (1980). Acquisition of information from educational television programs as a function of differently paced humorous inserts. *Journal of Educational Psychology 72*(2), pp. 170–180.

Zimmermann, E. (1903). *Preis-Liste über psychologische und physiologische Apparate.* Leipzig, Germany: Eduard Zimmermann. Retrieved from: http://www.chss.montclair.edu/psychology/museum/x_393.htm.

Zuckerberg, M. (2009). An Open Letter from Facebook Founder Mark Zuckerberg. *Blog. Facebook* (1 December). Retrieved from: http://blog.facebook.com/blog.php?post=190423927130.

INDEX